BREAKING OPEN BARRIERS

IVORY BOOKS
UK | UAE | INDIA

Published by
Ivory Books Ltd.
9 Edinburg Drive Ickenham
Uxbridge, England, UB108QY

ISBN : 978-1-7391433-8-1

Printed and bound in india by
Vattoly Nirmala Hiprint Pvt. Ltd. Thrissur
www.ivorybooks.uk

BREAKING OPEN BARRIERS

YVETTE ELIZABETH STEVENS

IVORY BOOKS
UXBRIDGE, ENGLAND

"This book is dedicated to my late son Boris, who was more than a son to me, and to my other children, Rebecca, Yvette, Yvonne and Unblind."

Contents

PART THREE

Serving Humanity at the United Nations

FOREWORD

It is the evening of 24 August 2021 when an email appears from Imperial College London Alumni Relations Office: "Part of our programme is to share the exceptional achievements of alumni with the wider community. In October, we wish to spotlight Ambassador Yvette Stevens, our Distinguished Alumni Award winner. She studied for an MSc in Electrical Power Systems and Machines in the 70's and went on to become Sierra Leone's first female engineer followed by roles in the UN. She's undeniably inspiring, she studied as a single parent to five children and has a wonderful story to tell. October, as I'm sure you know, marks Black History Month and our wish is to run an event to share Yvette's story and her success as part of the College's programme of events to commemorate the month". The question to me was: "I'd like to ask if you would be interested in chairing the event". Even in this very brief description, something stood out inspiring me to find out more about this remarkable woman with so many firsts to her name. Naturally, I accepted the invitation to Chair the 'In conversation with Ambassador Yvette' session to celebrate Black History Month.

The session with Ambassador Yvette deepened my admiration for her, and the more we conversed the more I wanted to know about this accomplished African woman with a most illustrious career and a burning desire to create a better society for all. I recall that at the end of the session, I cheekily enquired if she would consider writing and publishing her memoirs. Her response, which I later discovered to be typical, was that I was too late, as she was already preparing them – as always ahead of the game. Unbeknown to me at the time was that by raising this issue, I had inadvertently applied for the honourable job of writing the Foreword to this wonderful and captivating work. When offered to me, I remember thinking that 'wild horses could not have stopped me from taking up the golden opportunity to celebrate the work of this wonderful African Queen'.

The memoirs are a must-read for all, especially women and girls everywhere – a story about values, principles, tenacity, perseverance, confidence, family support and a bit of luck, in the face of sustained trials and tribulations. Ambassador Stevens retraces her life and trajectory from growing up in colonial Sierra Leone, to making a significant impact in her own country, Sierra Leone, in Africa and beyond, in a world that is male dominated and filled with many other prejudices and obstacles, while raising a family singlehandedly. Ambassador Stevens' impact is varied, covering engineering, diplomacy, human rights and helping the destitute and harder-to-reach groups, including refugees.

They say never meet your heroes for fear of disappointment, but in the case of Ambassador Stevens, I beg to differ, and it is my great pleasure to have read her story and reflected upon it. I know that this work will live forever, inspiring future generations for years to come- please read, enjoy and may it help as a source of inspiration for you and others around you.

Professor Washington Yotto Ochieng, EBS, FREng
Head of the Department of Civil and
Environmental Engineering and Director
of the Institute for Security Science and
Technology, Imperial College London.

INTRODUCTION

In view of the diversity of my life experiences, and to cater for the different categories of readers, who may be interested in the various aspects of my life story, I decided to present it in four parts. Part One gives a short narrative of my early life, growing up in colonial Sierra Leone, highlighting the experiences that shaped me. This is followed by three parts that are linked to the themes of my childhood dreams.

Part Two which covers the periods 1963 to 1980 and 2009 to 2012 describes my pursuit of science and engineering, a field dominated by men, and how I overcame the challenges to succeed as an engineer. Part Three deals with my work at the United Nations, covering the periods 1980 to 2008 and 2012 to 2018. Finally, Part Four narrates my experience as a single mother raising five children while pursuing a successful career, as an engineer and working at the United Nations.

The presentation by themes means that the story, as a whole is not in chronological order, but chronology is maintained within each of the four parts.

PROLOGUE

The tarmac road was scorching, with stone pits and cart potholes, but, as a young girl growing up in British colonial Sierra Leone in the 1950s, each day before going to school, I went barefoot to the communal tap on our street to fetch water. Although we were not considered poor in comparison to the vast majority of Sierra Leonean families, we were far from wealthy and lived modestly in a wooden house with an outside kitchen and pit latrine but no running water.

Even then, I pictured a life full of abundance and opportunities, for myself, and for my future children. I envisaged a future where poverty's restraints would shatter like fragile glass, and where opportunities would grow like lovely gardens in full bloom. A future in which my children would be caressed by the gentle arms of education, knowledge and wisdom, helping them to discover their real identity. I wanted to give them the opportunity to achieve their best in life, and not be faced with the poverty that I encountered each day.

My "exposure" to the outside world started quite early in my life at around six years old. I would spend evenings, especially when it was raining, listening to the BBC Radio which was transmitted through a little box in our small living room. We called it the "magic box", because it opened a portal that took me to the wonders of the outside world beyond my own day-to-day reality.

As I sat there, often in the dark, taking in every word that was uttered, I tried to imagine this dream world outside my country, where so much was happening. My mind took flight like a group of colourful birds soaring beyond the bounds of my birthplace. A wonderful universe opened up before me, with tales from different cultures carrying accounts of both joy and tragedy.

A world in which, injustice, violence, and poverty were linked with delicate strings of hope, bravery, and compassion and where so many people were making great efforts to resolve these problems. I was entranced and fascinated with the intricate complexities of the situation. A special treat for me, was listening to the radio in the company of my Uncle Joseph, who was my hero in those days. He was a treasure trove of information and would patiently answer all my questions. He was my companion, storyteller, and confidante, always prepared to explain the world's riddles in a calm and collected manner. 'These things will happen', he would say to me. 'There is evil in the world, but luckily, there are some good people out there as well, and in the end good will prevail'. I had to believe him, even though, in my child's mind, the evildoers seemed to be winning most of the time. Uncle Joseph's words calmed the storm of questions and doubts in me and made me experience the world in a more realistic way, a place where both good and bad cohabited. The reassuring tone in Uncle Joseph's voice made me think of myself as a participant in the stories that surrounded me rather than as an observer. I was ready to contribute my part to this world in the battle for a better future.

I began to keep abreast of international affairs and when tragedies occurred around the world, I would offer prayers before going to bed and hope that the next day's news would be better. I hoped that my prayers might reach people in need, like milkweeds drifting on a soft breeze. I experienced a feeling of purpose and belonging to something bigger than myself at those times. Sometimes the prayers seemed to work, but most times they did not. Even when they did not, I believed that this was the only contribution I could make, so I took it seriously. If I forgot to pray, I felt guilty. 'Maybe when I grow up, I could do more', I used to tell myself. I resolved that I would make every effort in life to enter that world, but deep in my heart, I could not have known what that journey would hold. The little girl from colonial Africa was daring to dream and hoping for miracles. My nights were filled with dreams to reach for the unattainable stars which shined bright as if beckoning to me.

At school, my appetite for the world outside was sharpened by the geography and history taught at the time, which only covered the world outside Africa. The only science subject we were taught was General Science, which consisted merely of the basic concepts of science. I developed a love for the subject and would spend hours at the town library within walking distance from my house, during the long vacations to learn more about it. I devoured every science book I could get my hands on and decided then that I wanted to pursue a career in science when I grew up. Every science book I read opened yet another door to a world of discovery, and as I turned each page, my drive to become a scientist grew stronger. It was the time of the space race between the USA and the USSR and I followed it with interest. When Yuri Gagarin became the first human to go to space in 1962, a deep desire to become a space scientist, to seek for the stars, and to travel the vastness of space, where fantasies merged with reality, arose in me.

Three significant dreams that would influence the direction of my life were fostered in the depths of my heart. The first was breaking down barriers as a scientist and entering a field that had to this point been controlled by men. The second was to influence the world outside Sierra Leone and go beyond its borders. The third dream was to start a family and provide my kids the opportunities I had not had as a child.

This book is a testament to the transformational power of dreams and to the courage and relentless drive it takes to make them come true. It details the challenges I overcame, the defeats I endured, and the victories I attained during my career as an engineer, diplomat, and—most importantly—as a single mother to my five children. Like in the words of Maya Angelou in her renowned poem,

Still I Rise

Out of the huts of history's shame
I rise
Up from a past that's rooted in pain
I rise
I'm a black ocean, leaping and wide,
Welling and swelling I bear in the tide.

Leaving behind nights of terror and fear
I rise
Into a daybreak that's wondrously clear
I rise
Bringing the gifts that my ancestors gave,
I am the dream and the hope of the slave.
I rise
I rise
I rise.

Writing this book was a challenge for me, as it evoked the whole spectrum of emotions, from the highs of great pride and immense joy to deep sadness and pain. Yet, I am so thankful for the journey it has taken me on and the opportunity to see my life through a different lens. That young girl who walked barefoot to school brimming with curiosity and yearning for the world is still very much a part of me. There is still so much life to live and so much knowledge to be gained. Thank you for reading my story.

PART ONE

Early Experiences That Moulded Me

"No matter how far a stream flows, it never forgets its source".
– African Proverb

Chapter 1
Growing up in Colonial Sierra Leone

Freetown

Freetown is a location of timeless tales and fascinating legends, nestled between the majestic, lion-like mountains and the enormous embrace of the Atlantic Ocean. During the rainy season, the heavens open up and the mountains come to life, resounding with a symphony of thunder that reflects the soul of the region itself. Centuries ago, in the wake of exploration, the intrepid Portuguese explorer Pedro da Cintra named this land "Serra de Leão", a tribute to the mountain's resemblance to a prostrating lion.

The nation bore witness to a transformation of its name, each iteration interwoven with the threads of its rich history. As the seventeenth century dawned, the name bloomed into the melodious "Sierra Leone", reminiscent of a verse from an ageless sonnet. It was the British who, following the abolition of slavery in 1787, bestowed upon it an identity that would endure through the ages. They brought 400 Africans liberated from British slavery to Sierra Leone—a land brimming with potential—and laid the foundation for what they termed the "Province of Freedom". These early settlers were joined by groups of freed enslaved

Africans from the USA and Nova Scotia, and captive Africans freed from boats intercepted by the British, after the abolition of the slave trade in England. The settlement soon became fittingly known as Freetown, a place where those once enslaved were now free. These groups, their hearts ignited with expectation and yearning for a future filled with promise, knitted the fabric of a flourishing community—a shining beacon of hope and resilience.

The region presents a tapestry of perseverance and victory, serving as a testament to the indomitable spirit of humanity. The reverberations of liberation echo through the annals of time, with tales of freedom etched into every wave that caresses the sandy coastline. Freetown, with its rich history and boundless potential, beckons like a siren's song, drawing in adventurers and truth-seekers alike. Its name, now etched onto the world map, stands as a beacon of hope. It serves as a constant reminder to all who gaze upon it of the enduring power of emancipation and the strength required in carving out a fresh start.

A significant turning point in the history of Freetown occurred in 1792 when it elegantly took its place as one of Britain's most ancient colonies in West Africa. The next century was a time of awakening, a phase of profound metamorphosis that would shape the course of the nation for all time. It was during this time that the institutions that would play an integral part in my life were established and emerged as beacons of contemporary education in tropical Africa. The Fourah Bay College (1827), the Church Missionary Society (later known as Sierra Leone) Grammar School (1843), and the Annie Walsh Memorial School (1849) were all founded on the principle of illuminating minds and nurturing spirits. As Freetown grew, it blossomed into a beautiful mosaic of cultural influences, reflecting the diverse heritages of its immigrants who hailed from every corner of Africa. Among them, we were affectionately known as "Krios", a tribute to our unique roots and the ties that bound us together. Many of the Krios were of Nigerian Yoruba origin.

Freetown gained the distinction of being known as "The Athens of West Africa", a haven where ideas flew, minds soared, and the seeds of wisdom were sown.

My birth

I was born as the sixth child in the family on May 11th 1946. As a Krio, my heritage was a monument to the rich diversity of Sierra Leone's history. For Krios, per the Yoruba naming convention, names were given to children, based on the circumstances tied to their birth instead of a choice by their parents. For example, "Abiodun" meant "born on a festival". So, if you happened to be born on a festival that would be your name, as well as anyone else's born on a festival day. Names were believed to become our soul, our identity, and the permanent record of our history in the world. Every name carried a heritage, a story created into the threads of time.

I was a breech birth; born feet first, thus, per the naming convention, my name would be "Igeh" literally meaning, "I walked into the world". People carrying this name were respected, as it implied that you were a level-headed, down-to-earth person, but there was one problem – the mad man who roamed the town in filth and tatters was called Igeh and my mother, for good reason, was conflicted and did not want to name her child after him.

Aware of the situation, a nurse at the hospital approached my mother on the third day after my birth with the suggestion that she consider a name, which bore some similarity to Igeh such as to maintain the convention, but would also be different enough to avoid the association with the mad man. The nurse had been reading a novel, translated from French and liked the name of the main character "Yvette" which she had learnt to pronounce, thanks to the translator's notes. She presented this name to my mother as an alternative, a name that echoed "Igeh" but carried a gentler charm. The name flowed like a melody from her lips. My mother loved the idea and instantly felt an inexplicable connection to the name. It seemed as if fate herself had whispered this name into her heart, intertwining it with my life's narrative. However, the nurse who went to register my birth spelt my name as E-V-E-T, which is the name on my birth certificate. This was corrected by the time of my baptism three months later.

No. 13 Regent Street

Life took an unexpected turn when, at the age of three, my father passed away. His death created a vacuum in my heart and a blow to my childhood perception of the world. For the first time, I was faced with grief and loss and their sting. My mother, a rock of strength, was suddenly given the challenging task of parenting six children by herself. She was resolved to make it through this challenging task with elegance and courage while providing for herself and her children. In her steadfast determination to support her family, my mother made the decision to go back to work, using her training as an elementary school teacher. She was offered a position at St. Anne's Roman Catholic school and thus, a new chapter in our lives began.

Returning to the workforce after over a decade of dedicating solely to raising her family was a formidable task and her first few months were very challenging. Each stride she took felt weighed down by unseen shackles, yet her unyielding spirit fuelled her progress. Embodying the tenacity of a warrior refusing to accept defeat, she persevered, balancing her duties as an educator with the colossal demands of motherhood. As a child, I was in awe of her fortitude and the audacious way she navigated her dual roles. Her resolve stood unflinching in the face of trials, akin to a beacon piercing through the darkest nights. Unbeknownst to me then, her stoicism harboured a profound lesson and a kernel of resilience that would germinate within me, influencing my personal journey. Her perseverance served as an inspiration for me to strive, endure, and confront life's hurdles with determination. Later in life, as I navigated through the many challenges that came my way, I would reflect on and be inspired by my mother's resilience.

An experience that is etched in my memory was when as a three-year-old, I accompanied my mother to school. I was wide-eyed and very curious about the mysteries concealed behind those hallowed walls where my mother spent her days. As I stepped into the classroom, a realm of wonder unfolded before my innocent gaze. I was captivated by the enchanting worlds depicted on the classroom walls and was spellbound by the sight of young children immersed in the magical tasks of reading, writing, and solving math problems. My heart swelled with longing as I realized that those letters and numbers held the key to unlocking a treasure trove of knowledge and narratives.

My desire to study and learn the stories, and the mysteries of the world for myself was born that day. The mere thought of immersing myself in the realm of words sparked my imagination, fuelling my determination to pursue education. When it was time for my sister to take me home that day, I could not bear to leave. I hid in a cabinet, not wanting to leave the school I had grown fond of so quickly. A search was initiated to locate the audacious young dreamer on the premises. To my dismay, I was found but proceeded to plead with all the earnestness of a child's heart to be allowed to stay in the school. The Mother Superior, moved by the genuine passion burning within me, granted me permission to join the older children, thus bestowing upon me my place in the kingdom of knowledge. I was beyond delighted. Donning my pride and a beautiful blue and pink uniform, I began my first day at St. Anne's Roman Catholic School. I felt akin to a peacock displaying its majestic plumage. It was a transformative day, a day of growth and finding my place in the ever-evolving narrative of life.

My mother, fondly referred to as Mama, emerged as an indomitable figure who showered us with limitless love but also a firm hand. Despite the rigours of her bustling days, Mama would initiate the evening ritual of crafting our meals, a culinary dance that she would let me help with. With the precision of a heart surgeon planning a complex procedure, Mama choreographed each phase of the meal preparation, infusing it with meticulous care and attention. One dish stood out as my favoured treat: an exquisite sauce crafted from rice and cassava leaves that tantalized my taste buds, a medley of flavours that encapsulated the quintessence of home.

The preparation required thoughtful planning, and at times, the pantry did not have all the necessary ingredients. In those moments, Mama's creativity shone through. She sought cheaper alternatives for expensive items, such as manually grinding peanuts for hours instead of buying the ready-made store version.

Mama instilled in me, the importance of making do with what you have available rather than bemoaning what you lack. Her words remain with me to this day, 'Yvette', she would say, her eyes radiating with maternal affection, 'it's not so much about what you have, but how you use it'. Those simple words encapsulated a profound lesson and a life philosophy that would guide me through life's peaks and valleys. My mother's resilience and ingenuity taught me to view challenges as stepping stones and that imagination could unlock infinite possibilities.

Her fierce protectiveness, driven by a profound concern that we might face hardships, was shaped by a blend of love and discipline. With an unwavering resolve, she exercised her authority, steadfast in her mission to steer us towards righteousness. When we misbehaved, she would invoke the adage 'spare the rod and spoil the child', and her stern hand would administer spankings on our bottoms. Each dawn brought with it a sense of renewal, as if our slate of transgressions had been wiped clean, with a hug from Mama, offering us a fresh start. Mama meticulously crafted the lessons that would shape our characters and weave the very fabric of our existence, striking a delicate balance between love and firmness.

Being the youngest of my siblings, I relished the special sense of luxury of being the family's baby, with my sisters Hannah and Yamide serving as guardians of my development. Hannah, who was 13 years my senior, gave me a monthly stipend of sixpence with advice on how to manage it, and Yamide, who was just nine years older than me, always kept an eye out for me.

My bond with Yamide was so deep that she "adopted" me as her own, and even asked my mother to give me to her as a present. She took care of me from the day I was born, growing to be both my buddy and my guardian. Yamide was tasked by Mama to sleep next to me each night on my bed, in case I rolled off, as we did not have a crib. She tells the story of how she would pinch me, so I could wake up and she could then go outside to play with her friends. Her kind actions helped me to define what it meant to be valued. Not only did I find a sister in her, but also a confidante and a guardian angel who gave me the gift of unfailing love.

Amid the cherished recollections of my childhood, are the memories of my brothers. William, the eldest among us, left this world prematurely, his life extinguished after a brief flicker of fourteen candles. I was merely a two-year-old toddler then, yet the void left by his absence would forever resonate as a poignant pang in my heart. Ade, my brother, was an introvert—a soul that found comfort in the divine whispers of the church. A paragon of devotion, as a child, he yearned to embrace the priesthood, his life rhythmically intertwined with prayers and the solemn duties of an altar boy. Within the sanctified confines of faith, he voiced his dreams, reserving a special place in his heart for me. He emerged as my advocate, proudly sharing my accomplishments with his peers, a gesture that fuelled my ambition to excel and reach the pinnacle of his faith in my abilities. Jide, my other brother, carried a formidable burden—sickle cell anaemia, a relentless adversary that transformed his childhood into a battlefield of recurring pains. In his eyes, I witnessed resilience—a spirit that defied surrender to the ailment that threatened to overshadow his existence.

A cousin who joined our household in the late 1950s was Fumi, the daughter of my mother's cousin, Uncle Herbert, who had lost his wife and was struggling to bring up three children. Fumi was his only daughter, so when she reached the critical age of about 12, he solicited the support of his cousin, Mama. For me, this was good news during my teenage years, as my own sisters were much older and were leaving home. We bonded so well together and became inseparable "partners in crime". We would dress alike, attend social functions together and advise each other on the choice of boyfriends. Together, we dreamt about our future and those of our children. Unfortunately, she lost her life after a road accident in New York in 1971.

Our family lived at 13 Regent Street in a two-storeyed wooden structure built in the style of housing from Louisiana. Our kitchen, pit latrine, and "bathroom" were all housed in separate corrugated iron sheet structures in the yard. My mother's brother, Uncle Joseph resided in the top storey, with his family, while my mother's unmarried sister Modu took a room on the ground level. The "cellar", a basement room was available to renters as a source of supplementary income. Education was the unseen architect behind our walls, changing our home into a place of learning each day after the final school bell. Mama, Uncle Joseph, and Auntie Modu would each undertake private coaching sessions for young children, their voices creating a symphony of knowledge that echoed through our home's halls. Uncle Joseph was the headmaster at the Ebenezer School and Auntie Modu was headmistress at the Holy Trinity Girls' School. I was drawn to the haven of Uncle Joseph's instruction, a choice rooted not only in my thirst for knowledge but also in his nurturing approach. Unlike the strict hand of discipline that occasionally marked my learning journey, his lessons flowed with a gentleness that sought to kindle the spark of understanding without the sting of a cane.

My mother's aunt, endearingly referred to as "Granaunty", was a virtuoso storyteller who breathed life into African traditional tales during the rainy season. As the heavens unleashed a deluge upon the earth, accompanied by the thunder's roar and lightning's brilliant flashes, the aroma of roasted cashew nuts wafted through the air. The family's children would huddle around Granaunty, our eager faces illuminated by both the lightning and the allure of her narratives. We became captives in her realm of storytelling, as if the rain had summoned the spirits of ancient legends. The tales unfolded like ancestral secrets which had been passed down from generation to generation.

Our home did not have running water, so each morning the siblings set off on our daily trek to the public standpipe which served as a water source for the homes in our neighbourhood. Our morning mission involved going back and forth from the standpipe until we had filled a colossal 200-litre barrel in the yard. This endeavour was necessary as the water was used for bathing, cooking, and cleaning, but it also provided an opportunity to unite us in a common goal. As the neighbourhood kids met at the standpipe, friendships were forged, disputes were resolved and the juiciest neighbourhood gossips were shared.

A notable memory from that time was one day, at the standpipe, when I had a dispute with one of the girls over my place in the queue waiting to fill our buckets. I was taunted and laughed at by a group of her friends, calling me "burka", a derogatory term used for girls who were "uncircumcised". As Krios, we did not belong to the indigenous powerful female secret societies and were thus not subjected to the initiation practices. Not being "circumcised" was looked upon negatively as I found out that day. I rushed back home with tears streaming down my face and falteringly asked my mother, 'Why am I not circumcised?' I was upset and felt that I had been deprived of this "privilege" that the girls at the standpipe had all received.

'You do not want to be circumcised', my mother responded.

It was clear from her tone, that I was not going to get an explanation, and that the conversation was over. I would have to accept that as my elder, she knew what was best for me and that I should not question it. My task was to silently accept to her acquired knowledge by absorbing her wisdom without inquiry. However, my curiosity tethered to the acceptance of the unknown. Years later, as life unfolded and understanding grew; I came to realize the weight and meaning of that exchange.

In the panorama of our family, my youthful existence mirrored that of my siblings, with one distinct detail shared among us—a single pair of shoes each, reserved for our Sunday visits to the church. Walking barefooted provided an array of challenges as the sun's fury scorched the asphalt roads, turning them into blazing coals beneath our tender soles. On the hottest days, the route home from school resembled the quick flight of impalas followed by the insatiable hunger of lions, our pace fuelled by a collective desire to avoid the searing contact of the ground.

Our faith, which was rooted in the Roman Catholic tradition, provided us with a thorough religious education. We would go to the church for confessions as the sun's rays gave way to the dusk of Saturdays, a rite that prepared us for Sunday's solemn mass. At the confession box, my memory appeared to waver in recalling my faults in those hallowed times, pushing me to manufacture offences and enrich them with a handful of extras, to ensure that all my sins were catered for, before the consecrated sacrament of communion on Sundays.

Yamide always enjoyed dressing me up nicely, seizing the opportunity to practice the latest hairstyles on a very willing customer. I also served the purpose of being her alibi when she wanted to spend time with her boyfriend. In those moments, there would suddenly be an instance when Mama would be informed that I needed to go to the library or needed help with an errand, and off we would go. I was a precocious reader, and by the age of four would read anything that I set my eyes on. I remember a humorous incident in which my voracious reading appetite almost landed Yamide and me in some trouble. On one of our frequent outings, we sat on the double-decker bus, and as we drove past a huge billboard, I read out loudly "A shop at Kingsway, it pays". As I was under five, I had been admitted onto the bus for free, but my clear and accurate reading of the billboard definitely piqued the bus conductor's interest and the look he gave us as he slowly turned around, suggested that he was not at all convinced that I was indeed four. In spite of this, he let us continue our trip and I learnt a valuable lesson that not everything had to be read out loud.

During our school holidays, we would go to Hastings, a tranquil village hidden behind the majestic "Lion Mountains" just outside Freetown. A natural elegance emerged in this rural refuge. The green woodlands that surrounded the village rang with the bright sounds of many bird species and the joyful antics of primates. The ritual of streamside laundry, where our hands patiently washed the clothes before letting them bask in the sun to dry, was one of my favourite activities. Once laundry was done, we would throw off our clothes and plunge into the cool waters of the stream, a moment of pure unbridled enthusiasm. Fruit-filled trees in the forest's canopy, their branches sagging under the weight of their riches, called to us, encouraging us to indulge in their offerings. We ate mangoes and guavas until our tummies were full. We felt a sense of oneness with the natural world as we basked in the cool shade they offered, an indelible connection that has coloured the course of my life ever since.

As darkness fell, our world was only lighted by the flickering glow of candles or the open flame of kerosene lamps. A deep darkness surrounded our nights as a result of these inadequate sources of illumination. In this darkness, my young mind imagined a future in which individuals living beyond the capital's borders might likewise bask in the splendour of electricity's shine after sunset. Even as a young child, access to this "contemporary marvel" felt like an intrinsic right for every human being, independent of location, social or economic standing.

When I turned six, I transitioned from St. Anne's School to Holy Trinity Girls' School, under the watchful guidance of my Auntie Modu. This shift was motivated by my mother's aspiration for me to commence my secondary education at the esteemed Anne Walsh Memorial School—a school that prioritized girls from Anglican backgrounds. She believed that Holy Trinity would provide me with a solid foundation to achieve this goal. Life at Holy Trinity was in stark contrast to the comforts of St. Anne's. Auntie Modu's pedagogical approach emphasized the use of the cane as a tool to engrave the intricacies of Mathematics and English grammar into our young minds. The vivid memory of reciting grammatical rules while she clutched a cane nearby, waiting for a misstep, still lingers in my mind. I vividly recall reciting the rules of Grammar as I was being caned:

"i" before "e" except after "c".

She was left-handed and the absence of her watch on that hand served as the indicator that someone was soon to be caned or had recently been caned.

Driven by an intense passion for learning and a strong aversion to the cane's sting, I immersed myself in my studies with unwavering focus. This endeavour culminated in an extraordinary outcome: I was awarded a "double promotion" after my first year, enabling me to skip from Standard 2 to Standard 4, having completed the workload of Standard 3 at home. As a result of this, at the age of nine in 1955, I was ready to take the Common Entrance Examination for Secondary School, two years ahead of the typical schedule.

That day, when I got home after my exam, my brother Ade grilled me on my answers to the test questions. He was quick to share that my answers to his questions were incorrect, eliciting some concern as to how well I had done. He spoke with confidence about my failure, his doubt stemming from my alleged ignorance of the Grammar School Principal's name. As I cried, convinced I had failed, Granaunty, a source of comfort in times of trouble, hugged me and led me to her sanctuary. We started a ritual of comfort and prayer together to ask God for help in my time of need.

A storm of controversy arose as people awaited results, with reports of exam papers being leaked raising concerns about the integrity of the selection process. Needless to say, I was very unhappy to take the exam again; anyway, I felt that this would give me the chance to correct the mistakes I had made the first time around. Was this a response to our prayers? With this opportunity of a second chance, I finished the exams considerably more confident of my performance this time around. The final results were released a fortnight before the start of a new academic year, on Christmas Eve. The postman's arrival interrupted the chaos of last-minute holiday preparations taking place in Auntie Modu's cosy kitchen. We all held our breath as she opened the envelope, then collectively breathed a sigh of relief when she exclaimed in a joyous voice, 'Alleluia! Yvette made it!'

I entered the revered halls of the Annie Walsh School in the early morning hours of 9 January 1956, along with the other new initiates. In spite of passing the Common Entrance Examination with flying colours, due to my young age and perceived immaturity,

I was required to begin my academic adventure in the Prep form. I received a year of special attention as the school's youngest pupil, which was characterised by invitations to events, such as puppet shows and children's films held by the venerable British Council. At the school's annual prize-giving ceremony, I was even given the privilege of offering a bouquet to the governor's wife and was very honoured.

'Lady Dorman, on behalf of the girls of the Annie Walsh Memorial School, I present you with this bouquet'.

I still distinctly remember those words.

As a young child, I was aware of the enormous transition that the African continent was experiencing between the 1950s and 1960s. The Gold Coast was the first country to gain independence from the British in 1957 and changed its name to Ghana. As the news spread across the continent, the air vibrated with the joy of the people and the hope that independence was now a tangible goal. I recorded these key events in the sanctuary of my young heart, preserving to memory the stirring songs that were composed in their honour. My favourite song contained the lyrics:

Ghana. Ghana is the name Ghana. We wish to proclaim.

I started making a scrapbook when I was around 10 years old, a crucial time in my development. I painstakingly pasted photographs that I had selected from the pages of the *Daily Mail* our town's daily newspaper. My interest was sparked by the blossoming independence movements in several African countries and beyond. As a result, the likenesses of Sukarno of Indonesia, Patrice Lumumba of the Congo, Fidel Castro of Cuba, and Kwame Nkrumah of Ghana all found a permanent home within the pages of my scrapbook.

My memories included the Bandung Conference in 1955, when Sukarno, the acclaimed leader of Indonesia, organized a meeting with the aim of uniting developing Asian and African countries into a potent non-aligned force. This convergence, created in the polarity of the Cold War, aimed to establish a path free from the gravitational pull of the dominant superpowers. In 2004, as I worked on the Bandung Conference's commemoration planning in my role as Director for Africa at the United Nations Office of the Special Adviser for Africa, I was reminded of these events, when I attended the ministerial conference to plan the commemoration in Bandung. The commemoration celebration took place in the same chamber where the confluence was held in 1955. The halls were decorated with wax statues of the founding Heads of State. I became deeply aware that the once-imaginary world of my youth was now a reality and that gave me a feeling of purpose.

On April 27, 1961, Sierra Leone reached a historic juncture in its narrative as it unfurled its long-awaited banner of independence. To a young girl keenly attuned to the evolving political tableau across the continent, this occasion was a pinnacle of pride. Our national anthem, a triumphant symphony unfolded in three verses that I committed to memory with unbridled fervour. The poignant line of the second stanza left an indelible imprint on my young heart and resonated within me.

Ours is the labour, thine, the fame.

On that Independence Day, I committed myself, to work tirelessly, to promote the image of Sierra Leone and make her proud of me.

During the years I spent in school, the curriculum's reach went well beyond the limits of our country. I pictured in my mind trips across the expansive Prairies and the territories of Lapland, explorations of the regal fabric of England's history and the epic odyssey of the Hundred Years' War.

My life's calling was discovered within the confines of the Literary and Debating Society, a dynamic arena where intellectual duels were fought with unrestrained fervour amidst the revered corridors of the secondary schools. As a student at the Girls' School, I actively engaged in these debates, undeterred by the male-dominated landscape. Each competitive event served not only as a platform to showcase the collective prowess of the female cohort but also as a personal challenge, in which failure was not an accepted outcome. Concurrently, my association with the Daily Mail Teenage Club opened up a new avenue for discourse. While nestled within the classrooms, we engaged in discussions that mirrored global dialogues within the United Nations. This engagement kindled a passionate interest in international diplomacy within me, setting the course for my future pursuits.

After school, there were not many options to keep us occupied. We could not afford the available attractions, such as the amusement parks at Victoria Park or Queen Elizabeth the Second Playing Field. An affordable alternative for me was the local library. It became my sanctuary once household chores like fetching water and preparing dinner were completed. Boredom found no foothold amidst the towering shelves brimming with bound knowledge. It was here that I embarked on my journey into the realm of science, a field that both fascinated and baffled me. Within these sacred walls, I unravelled the often-enigmatic world of science. As I grappled with complex concepts, I sought books that offered simpler explanations, driven by my determination to decipher these riddles. I found comfort in the pages of books that portrayed other worlds. A.E. Van Vogt's *The Voyage of the Space Beagle* chronicled humanity's audacious journey to distant galaxies, while Ray Bradbury's *The Martian Chronicles* transported me to Mars fuelling my imagination with tales of encounters with enigmatic inhabitants. These books opened portals to alternate universes where dreams were boundless, in an era before small screens existed.

The dawn of Sierra Leone's Independence and the inaugural session of Parliament in 1961 unveiled new avenues for exploration. My sojourns to the Parliament building on Tower Hill were a cherished pastime. I would secure a spot in the gallery to watch the debates and allow myself to think of a time when I too could lend my voice to these deliberations. Little did I know then, that my voice would eventually be heard on the largest global platform, the *United Nations*.

PART TWO
Making it in a Man's World

*"Knowledge is like a garden. If it is not cultivated, it cannot be harvested". - African proverb

Chapter 2
High School Education

During the 1960s, the educational environment inside girls' schools appeared to revolve around deeply rooted preconceptions, relegating scientific fields to the "stronger" sex. Science disciplines were deemed to be too tough for girls, who were apparently thought to be less intelligent than boys. At Annie Walsh Memorial School, I was taught Domestic Science, which included embroidery and cooking. I did not like Domestic Science and fared poorly in it. I tried my best to master the new abilities, but I was never successful. Despite my best attempts, the elegance of embroidery evaded me, and my ventures into crocheting, knitting, and other creative forms produced outcomes that were far from satisfactory. The displays of our work were moments of excruciating self-consciousness, with my flaws on full show. My poor performance in the subject gave a clear image of my mismatch with this area of study.

The completion of the third form marked a watershed moment in my academic experience, as the split of classes into two different streams—Domestic Science and Arts—brought much-needed relief. I was classified in the latter category, a seismic step that cemented my path towards scholarly pursuits. The load of inadequacy I had carried in the world of Domestic Science gradually dissipated, replaced by the promise of unfurling potential in the intellectual currents that lay ahead. This experience taught me that I should not be deterred from following my interests, even if they were not typically seen as "feminine" topics. I am thankful that I had the opportunity to study science in high school, and I believe that it has helped me to become a well-rounded individual.

My academic career in the Arts stream included disciplines such as History, Geography, Bible Knowledge, English Language, English Literature, and Latin. Surprisingly, the History and Geography we studied had little relation to our own country. Even in the post-independence age, the requirement of assimilating this foreign material looked confusing to young brains evolving in the African milieu. After all, our final exams were based on the prestigious British "O" Levels. Within the world of History, our courses brought us to the courts and corridors of power in England, unravelling the stories of kings and the complicated constitutional evolution of the United Kingdom. The treasured tome that guided us through this voyage was appropriately named *How the People of Britain are Governed*. Surprisingly, this moment of reflection coincided with our country's newfound independence and the establishment of our own Parliament. My interest in the Parliamentary procedure was sparked at these points. My vacations took on a new meaning in the hallowed halls of Tower Hill, where our embryonic Parliament met. I spent hours in the gallery, immersing myself in the discussions and debates that resonated throughout the rooms. Interventions in discussions, particularly those masterfully wielded by Cyril Rogers-Wright, left a lasting impact on my awareness. These were the moments that planted the germ of a desire to engage in political debate, a desire that would influence my career in the years to come.

This viewpoint seemed to have some validity in my opinion. We were raised with the idea that in order to advance in the world arena, we needed to go beyond the borders of our ostensibly inconsequential home countries. Even in the very foundation of my lineage—I am a direct descendant of enslaved Africans—this mindset was deeply ingrained.

In fourth form, we were introduced to the venerable subject of Latin, considered a badge of honour for those deemed "learned". I can vividly recall our dedicated teacher, Mrs. Greene, her eyes lit with pride as she presented the mysteries of Latin to us. "Salve discipulae", she would warmly address us at the outset of each lesson, to which we would respond in unison, "Salve magistra".

Mrs. Greene was a woman of medium height, with a hint of sturdiness, and she emanated achievement. She had made history by becoming one of the first women from Sierra Leone to get a bachelor's degree in the challenging subjects of Latin and Mathematics. She was aware that her audience was made up of students who were struggling with the intricacies of the Latin language, though. Despite this, she delighted in reading extended passages from the famous Latin author Virgil, holding us spellbound with her dulcet tones. She periodically strayed into regions beyond our linguistic reach in her quest to preserve and transmit the gems of the classics.

My early enthusiasm with Latin, which is sometimes referred to as the divine "language of the Gods", quickly waned. The language's intimidating nature quickly became apparent through the elaborate dance of verb conjugations and noun declensions. I began to wonder why I had to spend so much time and energy learning a language that was no longer spoken. My Latin performance eventually suffered, as evidence to my difficulties. Nonetheless, amidst my challenges, a sliver of appreciation emerged. It was the wisdom encapsulated in the aphorisms, the pearls of ancient sagacity that graced our lessons. The motto I adopted for the rest of my life was:

"Aut optimum, aut nihil", which translates as "either the best or nothing".

By way of chance, General Science, a combination of the fundamental concepts of Biology, Chemistry, and Physics, appeared on our curriculum. This topic rapidly made a home in my heart and rose to the top of my list of favourites. Miss Buchan, an Englishwoman with a round face and short brown hair, led us through the intricate procedures. Although she rarely smiled, her grasp of the topic was indisputable. The accuracy with which Miss Buchan carried out her laboratory experiments made a lasting impact. She treated every experiment with painstaking care, and she did not hesitate to chastise any student who dared to deviate from the rules of the lab. In the midst of this severe temperament, I came across a ray of hope. She gave me constant praise for my accomplishments, which fed a reservoir of inspiration inside of me. I found a mentor in her, whose impact would be very helpful. I started a passionate search for knowledge as the wonders of science unfolded. The complexity that science presented in its attempt to unlock the secrets of life enthralled me. I spent hours reading textbooks, and the local library turned into a haven where I ravenously devoured all the scientific material, I could get my hands on. My scores, which were a reflection of the hours I spent studying diligently, reflected my commitment. From third to fifth form, I won the annual class prize for General Science.

After finishing fifth form, I emerged triumphant as a GCE "O" Levels graduate, as I earned a first division. The subjects I took were Bible Knowledge, English Language, English Literature, French, History, Geography, and General Science. I had a strong ambition to make my mark in the field of science, and it had been ingrained in me. An additional year of study at a boys' school, before beginning the two-year journey of sixth form education, was the requirement for pursuing further studies in the sciences.

Girls from Annie Walsh School, who wanted to study science after taking the "O" levels, were sent to the Prince of Wales School, where they spent Form 5 Special, a pivotal year that prepared them for their eventual sixth form undertakings. A dramatic turn occurred as the possibility of this changeover grew closer; a letter sent to my mother, during the final week of the term revealed an unexpected development. Annie Walsh Memorial School was to provide us the additional year to study Physics, Chemistry and Biology, so there was no need for a transfer. I felt a sense of regret since I had been looking forward to moving to a boys' school that had top-notch facilities and a wide range of knowledgeable scientific teachers. I found it difficult to explain the risks of this change to my mother, but it was difficult to persuade her otherwise.

'You only want to be among the boys', she accused me.

While it was true that boys' schools had their own fascination, since they seemed more unrestricted than the strict institutions for girls, my predisposition was driven by a more subdued mood. My encounters with the boys during our joint interschool activities revealed an underlying truth: I felt more comfortable among them. Being among the male companionship brought about an inexplicable sense of ease, which I could identify with. My mother's answer to my hopes, however, brought on a flood of disappointment. Our parents held fast to the idea that keeping a certain distance from people of the other sex could protect us from the dangers of unintended pregnancy, a fate that may overshadow a girl's educational path. I made an effort to argue my case and made serious pleadings, but sadly, they were ineffective. The parents' point of view persisted in those times: they took a protective position to shield our education from any roadblocks. It later became clear that Annie Walsh Memorial School had launched the alternative because of their desire to keep the best students in the school.

Thus, it was that, Joan Asgill, with whom I had been together in class since my preparatory year, Christiana, Cole, who had joined us in first form and I had to continue our education in science at the Annie Walsh School for an extra year, starting in September 1962. We were joined by Cecilia Henry who came to us from the Methodist Girls' High School.

Unfortunately, despite the passing of months, no new lab doors opened, no consignment of scientific equipment appeared, and no specialized science teachers were recruited. Our chances were severely hampered by the absence of these essential elements, which became clearly evident in our "O" level results in Chemistry, Biology and Physics at the end of the year- a disappointment that greatly affected us. But the School Principal's daring stood out as being the most amazing. After a year of inaction, she suddenly issued a decree ordering our complete abandonment of science and a shift toward the arts. This announcement was difficult to take, especially in the light of how far behind of our classmates we had fallen—peers whom we had surpassed in the "O" level exams a year earlier. My dreams were crushed against the rough beaches of reality by the weight of her words, which left me broken.

A choice was made more clear-cut when with Joan, a steadfast companion; we refused to let the environment control our path any longer. We decided to start a new chapter by removing the mask of inaction, taking charge of our fate. We chose the Sierra Leone Grammar School as our final destination because it was a centre of learning with a science program that offered us the possibility to rekindle our interest in science. So, we embarked on a new journey, carried along by the winds of our own tenacity.

It was thus that we headed to the school on the day for the sixth form admissions, with optimistic uncertainty. Given our mediocre results in the science subjects, we were well aware that the deck was loaded against us. However, a glimmer of resolve inspired us to attempt the unlikely. We prepared our application forms and, armed with them, we handed them over to fate, waiting with expectation. A stroke of luck brought Mr. Jacobs, a British math instructor, into the picture as the minutes passed and our pulses beat frantically. Our paths had previously crossed while participating in the Youth for Christ organization, a place where I could express my young missionary enthusiasm and work toward "spreading the Gospel" throughout our nation. Mr. Jacobs came from the conference room with a strong presence and stood upright, his familiarity a pleasant sight. He struck me as a straightforward individual who was led by a strong, steadfast faith. I had no idea that he would eventually turn out to be a kind of guardian angel, a lighthouse of hope illuminating the path to unexpected chances in the field of science. He started our conversation by really asking a question, which gave me the opportunity to describe our situation. His sympathetic ear allowed the story to develop, and empathy wrapped itself about him like a garment.

'You know the competition is quite steep, and space is limited. I will see what I can do', he said.

We waited outside all day, and around 4 p.m. Mr. Jacobs emerged from the meeting room.

'I have good news and bad news for you two', he started. 'First the good news – after I explained your dilemma, the committee decided to accept you in sixth-form science. However, the bad news is that this is provisional and your performance will be assessed after the first term, to determine whether you can continue'.

Before leaving for our homes, we gave Mr. Jacobs our sincere thanks. I am struck by a profound sense of appreciation when I go back to those times and realize how much I owe him. It is an obligation that goes far beyond words because, without his help, I would never have been able to enter the world of science. A change in the tides was predicted for the next week. We were prepared to take on the task that lay before us as we stood there in our brand-new school uniforms of purple skirts and spotless white blouses. We were equipped to navigate the intricate changes to the scenery.

A universe of rivalry waited in the revered halls of Sierra Leone Grammar School—a challenge that profoundly spoke to me. The male companions we travelled with exhibited a range of emotions. While some offered their friendship, others were unconvinced that a woman could compete with them in the field of science. Our conditional admission to the institution served as a continual reminder that our position in the scientific community was not guaranteed. The aim was crystal clear: to throw down the gauntlet, outperform expectations, and etch our names in the annals of science. We were engaged in a conflict over where we should belong. The challenge made us work harder. We had to succeed.

My memory of the exams at the end of the probationary first term is still clear. It was an exciting period filled with optimism as we eagerly anticipated learning our exam results. The scenario of the Physics class's grade announcement sticks out as a significant recollection inside this tapestry. A British instructor named Mr. Welford was in charge, and he left an enduring impression. He had a strong body that was complemented by a preference for informal clothing, a quick wit, and a sharp sense of humour. He took enjoyment in the contrast between his mood and the youngsters' macho bluster. His amazement at my success in the Physics class, where I was the only female student, had an effect on me. Mr. Welford entered the classroom with a knowing smile on his lips and an alluringly enigmatic appearance. I had a mix of trepidation and optimism as his words started to float through the air. His opening remarks appeared to go on for an eternity while my heart raced. I prayed fervently, calling out to God in the stillness of my thoughts, 'O God, grant me this moment. Let my efforts be seen, for the scientific road calls to me. Being rejected right now would be a grave betrayal, a dream dashed for no other reason than my gender'. That crucial moment carried the weight of my ambitions, hanging over it was the future of my scientific career.

I could not hear anything he was saying, as I had my eyes fixed on the ceiling. Suddenly I heard my name and I emerged from my dream world – it was pleasant news – I was top of the class for Physics and by such a wide margin- I had obtained 83%, while the second person had 68%. All attention turned on me, and I did not know if it was in admiration or in envy. But I was proud. I actually beat some eighteen men in science – whoever said women could not do well in science? Similar pictures emerged from my other two subjects, Mathematics and Chemistry, with my friend Joan doing better than me in Chemistry. A male classmate was so shocked at the result that he dropped Mathematics and vowed, rather unexpectedly, that he would never accept being outperformed by a woman in the subject.

I pursued the remainder of my two years at Sierra Leone Grammar School with an unrelenting ardour, armed with the new-found conviction that I could compete favourably with my male peers in the field of science. Within me, a dazzling blaze of enthusiasm was burning.

The second year of sixth form presented unexpected difficulties even while it was developing. Mr. Welford, the Physics master, and Mr. Pullin, the maestro of Chemistry, were two of my three instructors, but owing to health issues, they had to depart for England. This interruption made my objectives seem unclear. It occurred to me that this would perhaps prevent me from achieving my desired aim of majoring in science at the university. It seemed as though the powers of the cosmos were working together to obstruct my progress to the place I so ardently sought, erecting barriers at every turn.

"Either the best or nothing".

So, with unwavering resolution, I took control of my fate. Our library's textbooks became my friends as their pages revealed secrets that had before seemed impenetrable. I negotiated the maze-like complexities with tenacious resolve and many hours— nights blending into days—eventually turning the seemingly incomprehensible into the understandable. The fog gradually began to clear, and my confidence began to grow.

I frequently discovered myself studying while sprawled across the foot of my mother's bed in the silence of the night. Even while she was asleep, her very closeness served as a source of inspiration. A fleeting glance at her figure, still and at rest, served as a moving reminder of my goals and a tangible example of what I was working for. However, on the night before the Physics exam, I started to feel uneasy. The topic circular and simple harmonic motion eluded my understanding. What if, in a tragic turn of events, this subject came up in the exam? I decided to retire early to bed as a result of my weariness. I made an often-repeated plea to my mother to wake me up at the stroke of midnight. It was my last-ditch attempt to fill the gap in my knowledge before taking on the forthcoming exam. When I opened my eyes, it was 7 a.m. and I had to leave for the exam at 8a.m. I was livid.

I was worried about the exams on that day. I had studied hard, but I was still nervous, so I reprimanded my mother.

'Why did you not wake me up?' I exclaimed.

'I knew that you were tired and felt a good night's sleep was what you needed to adequately prepare for the exams, based on what you already studied', she said. 'But let us kneel and pray for God's guidance for you'.

Mama's belief in prayer was unparalleled. She always said that prayer could console her, whatever the circumstances. I felt my own anxiety start to melt away as we prayed together.

I went to the exam feeling confident. I knew that I had done my best, and I trusted that God would help me through it. Sure enough, the questions on the exam did not include *circular and simple harmonic motion,* which were two topics that I had been struggling with. I am grateful for my mother's faith in prayer. It helped me to calm down and focus on the exam. I believe that God answered our prayers that day, and I am so thankful for His help.

The wait for the results of my "A" level exams was long. I knew that I had done well, but I was still nervous. I had no fairy godfather like Mr. Jacobs to help me get into university this time around. Finally, in mid-August, the results came. I had passed all three subjects: Chemistry, Mathematics, and Physics. I was eligible for a government scholarship and could basically choose where I wanted to study. I was excited to attend Fourah Bay College, but then the Ministry of Education announced that, following the then-recent establishment of diplomatic ties between Sierra Leone and the USSR, the USSR was offering scholarships to Sierra Leonean students. I was torn. I had always dreamed of attending Fourah Bay College, but the USSR scholarship was a once-in-a-lifetime opportunity to travel abroad, to the country that had made such remarkable advances in science, and benefit from a world-class education, as well as to experience a new culture and meet new people.

The announcement of the USSR scholarship was timely, as I had had the opportunity to read a great deal about advances in science in the USSR during my many library visits. My admiration for the USSR's space program peaked when Yuri Gagarin became the first human to travel into space in 1961. I believed that this was my opportunity to study space science, and I could think of no better place to do so than the USSR. I therefore applied for the scholarship. I must admit that although the thrill of studying abroad and the possibility of entering a world outside of Sierra Leone, which I had dreamed of since early childhood, was a contributory factor in my decision, it could be argued that, with my good A-level results, I could have also pursued opportunities to study in America, Canada, or the United Kingdom.

My decision to study in the USSR was met with some raised eyebrows. For one, the reputation of the USSR for higher education had been tarnished by the number of scholarships that had been offered for political reasons, to students without the necessary qualifications, to study at the Patrice Lumumba University. However, this offer by the government of the USSR was for placement in established Soviet academic institutions. Additionally, I would be parting ways with my childhood friends, especially Joan, with whom I had been in class for nine years. We had faced many obstacles together in our quest to study science, and I was sad to leave her behind. I would also be leaving behind my childhood boyfriend, Flavius. Finally, I would be entering the unknown, without the support of my immediate family. My sister Yamide was living in London, and she had offered to help me find a university there. However, I was determined to go to the USSR.

After learning that I had been awarded the scholarship, I started getting ready for the trip. I once more took refuge in the library's treasure troves of information, immersing myself in the complexities of the next task. The USSR's bitter winters loomed, requiring careful planning to provide enough warmth. My starting location of Freetown provided me with two options for getting the required apparel. The "Colisee" Boutique, located in the heart of Freetown, displayed clothes that were clearly out of my price range. In contrast, a more accessible option was offered by the humming street stalls that were overflowing with used clothing. It was in these shabby nooks that I discovered a solution, gaining warm clothes, thanks to Hannah's kindness. Our first days in Moscow coincided with the start of a significant blizzard that covered the countryside in a blanket of white. This serendipity proved to be quite helpful.

I was so buoyant with joy that certain realities went unnoticed. In the midst of my excitement, the idea of carrying money seemed unimportant. Hannah, though, had legitimate reservations. Using the information that had been communicated to us, when she suggested that I should take some money with me, I responded by extending my assurance and reassuring her that the Soviet government would take care of any financial issues once we were in Moscow.

'Just take this money with you. You might need it', she insisted.

Chapter 3

Engineering Education at Moscow Energy and Power Institute

On the 1st of October 1965, I arrived in Moscow, becoming part of the inaugural cohort of government-sponsored students benefitting from the USSR scholarship program. My journey had included transit in London, where Yamide, a cherished presence in my life, bestowed upon me essential items such as underwear and additional warm clothing. Having established herself in London since 1958, Yamide's yearning for my proximity, possibly in London, was undeniable. However, she gracefully accepted my choice to study within the broader European continent, enabling the possibility of visits during breaks.

Settling into Moscow was yet another transforming task, one that would profoundly shape my future. As I faced the difficulties of life in the USSR, the magnitude of the undertaking became clear. The awareness that had escaped me emerged—a clear knowledge of the difficulties that would accompany my schooling there. An initial test came in the form of learning the Russian language. Unlike my assumptions, the education process used an immersive approach, similar to how youngsters naturally learn languages. Our lecturer attended my first Russian lesson, held a two-hour session exclusively in Russian, and then left. Our tiny group's diverse language origins emphasized the complexities. Osama was from Sudan and spoke Arabic; Pablo was from Chile and spoke Spanish; Dinka was from Cameroon and spoke French; and Maria was from Brazil and spoke Portuguese. The lack of a common language between us—English—compounded the difficulty, leaving me with a combination of scepticism and irritation. In the midst of this situation, a single thought reverberated in my mind: 'This is a whirlwind. Perhaps I should go back home and seek some alternative place of study?'

After only a week of sessions, a critical crossroads appeared in my quest. I considered paying a visit to the Sierra Leone Embassy in Moscow, motivated by a desire to politely beg a return home. My outstanding achievement in the GCE "A" level tests had clearly qualified me for scholarships to a variety of locations. Nonetheless, an internal conversation reverberated within me among the seas of doubt and fear. 'Have I given this my best? Should I not try harder to master the language?'

Either the best or nothing.

In the months that followed, I went on an arduous journey into the domain of language learning. My comprehension of the Russian language evolved gradually, like the daybreak after a long night. The process was neither quick nor easy, but with perseverance, I began to understand the language intricacies. After nine months of persistence and concentration, I had arrived at a critical juncture: I could think, speak and write in Russian. Literature was one of the aspects of Russian culture that captivated me the most. A specific affinity for Russian literature arose, enveloping me in its embrace. This passion resulted in a once-in-a-lifetime opportunity: I was chosen to recite Pushkin poetry at university functions and even on national television.

After a year of studying Russian, it was time to select our areas of study. For me, there was only one option: space science. This was the reason I had chosen to study in the USSR in the first place. I took the university entrance exams in mathematics and the sciences, and I passed each subject with distinction. I was excited to begin my career in space science, and I dreamed of becoming the first African woman-astronaut.

'Now, my career in space science would begin'.

The night before we were to appear at the Ministry of Foreign Affairs to learn about our placement in university, I barely slept. I had vivid recollections of the materials I had enthusiastically devoured in the library back in Freetown. When I did sleep, I dreamt of myself on the launch pad, heading for space.

I woke up early the next morning, filled with excitement and trepidation. I had to appear at the Ministry of Foreign Affairs, to learn about our placement in university. I proudly clutched a duplicate of my exam results, just in case. I caught the first train from Sokolov Station to Smolenskaya Station. The Ministry of Foreign Affairs was housed in a stately structure near the Afro-Asian Solidarity Centre. I had seen it from afar, but this was my first time inside.

The morning of my trip to the Ministry of Foreign Affairs was a welcome one. The metro station at Smolenskaya was a museum in its own right, with square, white marble columns with fluted corners and decorative ornamental moulding around the wall below the ceiling. At the end of the platform was a sculpture by G.I. Motovilov entitled *The Defenders of Russia,* which depicted soldiers of the Red Army in battle. Outside, the majestic building of the Ministry of Foreign Affairs was a sight to behold. The coat of arms of the Soviet Union, with its traditional Soviet emblems of the hammer and sickle and the Red Star over a globe, and two wreaths of wheat, was engraved in concrete on the building façade. The charismatic building rose from the ground to an impressive steeple as it reached the skies. I felt a sense of awe and excitement as I approached the building. I was eager to start my studies in space science.

Yes, one day I would reach for those skies, I thought to myself.

The interior of the building was even more impressive than the exterior. The marble pillars and the hanging chandeliers created a sense of grandeur and importance. The security checks were thorough, but they were conducted in a professional manner. We were ushered into a waiting room, where we met with a number of other foreign students who had been summoned to the Ministry on that day. We were given forms to fill in to indicate the courses of studies we wished to pursue. I wrote "Космическаянаука" (Space Science) on my form, as I was interested in learning more about the Soviet space program. After waiting for over an hour, I was called into the office of the official in charge of foreign students. He was a short, overweight man with a gruff exterior. He asked me to sit down and pulled out my form from the stack he had on his desk. Letting his round-rimmed glasses drop from his forehead, he studied the contents briefly, smiled, and blurted out:

'The purpose of our scholarships to your country is to train the beneficiaries to go back and contribute to the development of your country. Space science does not feature on our list of options for students from developing countries'.

This was quite a shock to me. I was dumbfounded.

'But', I started, but he shut me off before I could even speak.

'This is the list of courses you can pursue in science', he said, as he handed me a piece of paper with a long list. 'You can take it home and reflect on it, and let me know within a week, what your choice is'. With that, I was politely dismissed from his office.

I was heartbroken. I had defied my teachers and family to pursue my education in the USSR with the sole goal of becoming an astronaut. The Soviet Union was at the forefront of space research at the time, and I had fantasized about it since I was a child. I even specified this choice on the scholarship application form, and I was not informed at the time that this was not feasible. I returned to my hostel, locked the door to my room, and sobbed. I felt deceived. I had sacrificed so much in order to travel to the USSR, and now my ambition had been crushed. However, there was no turning back. It seemed improbable that I would be able to secure a scholarship to attend school somewhere else since I had already been in the USSR for a year. I eventually started to consider alternative fields of study. Even if I could not become an astronaut, I understood that there were other ways I might make a contribution to the area of space research. I made the decision to put my education first and to enjoy my time in the USSR. Though I was aware that I would always remember my disappointment, I also understood that I could not let it define who I was. I had to keep going forward and figure out how to effect change in the world.

It took a few days after I got back to the hostel for me to come to the understanding that the only way to move forward was to accept the situation, I was in. I looked through the list of choices with a sense of reluctant resignation. Any residual misgivings or hesitations were overwhelmed by the urge to move forward. I was drawn to the subject electrical engineering among the options presented since it had resonated with me during my academic career. I remembered when, as a child, I visited Granaunty in the village Hastings and how, in the dark nights, in the light of a kerosene lamp, I wished that every household in the world would have access to electricity. I started down this new path after being inspired by this memory and a resolve to make the best of the circumstances. It was thus, after giving it some thought that I decided to pursue my studies in Electrical Engineering.

The Moscow Energy and Power Institute, a venerable institution that had attained respect and distinction, and had been awarded the prestigious Order of Lenin, was where I was headed. The institute's motto, *Energia omnium fundamentum* ("Energy is the basis of everything"), aptly summed up its spirit.

Lenin stated in 1920 that 'Communism was Soviet Power plus the electrification of the entire country', underscoring the importance of energy in the national context. This inspirational message reverberated across time, highlighting the crucial role energy had in determining the course of the country. In 2011, the Moscow Energy and Power Institute obtained the status of National Research University and its official name now is National Research University, Moscow Power Engineering Institute.

The institute was established in the year 1930, but it did not open its doors to foreign students until the year 1946, which also happened to be the year I was born. A pillar of our academic path was the existence of the Faculty for Foreign Students inside the Institute's structure. This faculty provided all-encompassing support, attending to a wide range of aspects of our needs. The Faculty for Foreign Students embodied the embrace of a home away from home, from the facilitation of mentorship and tutoring across a variety of subjects being taught, to the provision of guidance including personal welfare, including addressing health and childcare problems. Within the cocoon of this faculty, foreign students like myself found our needs attentively tended to. Our monthly stipends amounted to 70 roubles, a contrast to the 45 roubles allocated to our Soviet counterparts.

I was in the faculty of Electrical Engineering, where I chose to specialize in electrical machines and apparatus. There were 20 students in my university class M-4-65, of which four of us were girls. Luba, Katya, and Natasha were students who came from outside Moscow, and were strangers to Moscow, just like me. I came to love them because they were very friendly and accommodating to me. Also, as the only girls in the class, we developed certain solidarity to study together, to compete favourably with the boys. We shared a room at the hostel, and we would often study together late into the night. We would help each other with our homework, and we would discuss the latest developments in electrical engineering. We were all passionate about our studies, and we were determined to succeed.

I also had the opportunity to go to many USSR regions with my girlfriends. Foreigners going more than 50 kilometres from Moscow had to apply for a travel permit. But one needed to show this permit only when purchasing tickets. I avoided asking for a permit by having my girlfriends buy my tickets. I must admit that I was constantly concerned that if I was discovered, it might be concluded that I was a spy, nevertheless, it added to the excitement.

The Master of Science course that I was enrolled in was a five-and-a-half-year course. The road seemed long, but my motivation was unparalleled. Now that I realized that I could best help the people in my country with access to electricity, I put all my efforts into achieving this. In the first two years, we did subjects across the engineering disciplines, such as Engineering Drawings and Strengths of Materials. I felt exactly as I did at school about Domestic Science and Latin. I wondered what these subjects have got to do with Electrical Engineering. It was no surprise that I did not do as well in these subjects, although later in life, whatever I retained from these courses became useful in the context of practising engineering in Sierra Leone, where all-round knowledge was required.

The exams were all oral, and the choice of question paper was by ballot. This meant that everything in the syllabus was in one or more question papers, and you had to pray that the question paper you chose had the subjects that you had studied. You were allowed time to work out the answers and present them to a panel of Professors. After your presentation, you waited outside the examination room while the professors deliberated and gave a grade, which was entered in your exam book, and handed back to you before you went home. The grades ranged from excellent (5) and fail (2 or below). While in the earlier years of the course, I managed to slip through with a "3" in the nonelectrical subjects, in the final three years when we specialized in electrical engineering subjects, I gained a "5" in virtually all subjects, including my dissertation which was on automatic control of signalling systems for the railway, using analogue electromagnetic relays. I finished my degree of Master of Science in Electrical Machines and Apparatus, with distinction, in February of 1972.

It was during the second year of my studies in Moscow that I got married to Alex Hindolo Stevens, whom I had met on my arrival in Moscow. By the time I finished my studies, I had given birth to two children and was in the initial stage of my third pregnancy. I joined Alex, who was pursuing a law degree in London in March 1972.

Chapter 4
Education at Imperial College, London

In the summer of 1971, when I visited Alex in London, I met with Dr Davidson Nicol, the Sierra Leone High Commissioner based in London. Dr Davidson Nicol was a distinguished scientist, who had excelled in research on insulin, and was Vice Chancellor of the University of Sierra Leone before he became High Commissioner. I discussed my academic interests with him, and as a result, our meeting was characterized by a reciprocal exchange of views. When he discovered that I was studying engineering, a sector that greatly appealed to him, his interest was sparked. His attention was piqued even more by the topic of my dissertation, which acted as an incentive for a stimulating discussion that went beyond the scope of ordinary talk. Dr Davidson Nicol portrayed a sincere interest in the topic I was pursuing in his role as a scientist.

'Did your studies involve digital computers?' he inquired with a discerning curiosity.

'Indeed', I responded. 'During our final year, we undertook a course introducing us to the realm of digital computers'.

'In fact', he continued, 'Imperial College is currently spearheading remarkable advancements in the utilization of computers online. It might be worthwhile for you to contemplate enrolling in a course there, specifically geared towards augmenting your comprehension of control systems'. With these words, he summarized his advice, leaving a profound suggestion that stayed with me.

After finishing my course at the Moscow Energy and Power Institute, a fresh chapter and a significant advancement awaited. At that point, I started the application procedure for the esteemed Master's program in Electrical Power Systems and Machines at Imperial College, which was planned to begin in the academic year 1972–1973, at Imperial College. As soon as I learned that I had been accepted into this highly sought-after program, the doors of possibility opened wide. This chapter, full with possibility and promise, signalled the start of my journey to a wider horizon of understanding and achievement. Just before my course started, I gave birth to twins.

My class at Imperial College had six of us from different parts of the world who came together to pursue a common goal. We made up a microcosm of civilizations, a dynamic assembly of cultural variety, hailing from India, Hong Kong, Greece, Cyprus, Iran, and Sierra Leone, my own country. My eyes were awakened to the beauty of appreciating and comprehending various cultures and countries by this international tapestry, which echoed the variety I had previously seen in Moscow. I had no idea that these encounters were building the groundwork for a future with global vistas, though. Two of us were women—Poly from Greece and I. Under the guidance of Professor Laithwaite, "the Father of the Linear Motor", Poly, a shining example of academic prowess and consistent work, had decided to dive into the intricacies of the linear motor. My recall of her persistent commitment and the sight of her caring for her linear motor model will always be likened to a mother caring for her child.

The age of the application of digital computers was just beginning, and Imperial College was at the forefront of it. My most treasured memories revolve around my successful interactions with these devices. The CDP mainframe computer, which covered a whole level of the City and Guilds building, served as our canvas. As students waiting in line to enter their programs into the computer's grasp, we created programs using intricate engineering formulae and encoded them onto painstakingly punched cards. Our hopes and prayers rose as the sun fell below the horizon in the expectation that our programs would run without a hitch and that we could respect the due dates for assignment submissions. This regular dance of invention, expectation, and dread broke the endless restless nights. But the mornings at the computer centre frequently had a mysterious air. We were greeted by printouts that served as silent messengers and provided a peek into our programming activities. Some mornings, the printouts produced only a few pages, indicating a program that did not work well. In these situations, it was necessary to go through the cards, identify the faulty ones, make changes to some of them, rearrange them like the pieces of a disassembled jigsaw, and re-start the procedure. This required both patience and resilience and woe betide you if you dropped the cards, because they had to be in a specific order when introduced into the computer. I still remember how delighted I was the first time I got a program working. As I observed the perfect graphs on the printout, I felt as happy as a child in a sweet shop. This experience left me with a deep respect for the interplay between human intellect and technology, as well as the calm determination needed to overcome the challenges that they posed.

For my dissertation, I worked on computer programs for the on-line tap-changing of transformers and the check-synchronising of electric generators, both important components of the control and protection of electrical power systems, as any mistiming of these functions would create malfunctioning or even breakdown of the power system. My supervisor Brian Cory, a pathfinder leading ground-breaking investigation in digital power system control and safety, the then unexplored subject of high voltage direct current transmission, and the complex field of power system economics, guided my steps along this adventure.

The Computer Department served as my venue for my attempts, to draw up a program, as I carved out my place among the buzz of innovation. The PDP8 computer served as my exploring partner, turning my thoughts into workable programs with its buzzing circuits. The *Basic* programming language was used for this purpose, and punched cassettes were chosen as the delivery system for my work. The programs I drew up were punched into paper tapes that were fed into the computer. Compared to their card equivalents used in the mainframe computer, these tapes were more difficult since exactitude was required to prevent meters and meters of tape from being ruined by a single mistake.

A pillar of support was an expert from the computer department, Mr Rafiq, a small Bangladeshi, who was pleased with his mastery of this state-of-the-art technology. He offered me a helping hand, leading me through the many subtleties of these demanding procedures, with his knowledge and experience. I will not forget my elation at the first instance when my programs worked. This pivotal moment, marked by a triumphant harmony of technology and human endeavour, remains etched in the corridors of my memory.

The constraints of my family obligations and the demanding burden of my classes placed limits on my ability to participate in the dynamic social fabric of the institution. My limited involvement in the university social scene was evident by the small number of cheese and wine parties that I could attend. Although these soirées provided brief moments of relaxation, my main attention was on maintaining a careful balance between my family's obligations and the demanding academic path. Yet, amidst the academic rigours, there existed a confluence of learning, camaraderie, and merriment. Our educational study tours extended beyond the confines of the lecture hall as we embarked on field trips to power supply installations scattered across the United Kingdom. These journeys fused learning with bonding and joy, forging memories etched in camaraderie and shared experience.

As I traversed the corridors of Imperial College, my heart resided in a realm distant yet intertwined—the land I called home. Throughout my academic odyssey, the dream of returning to my homeland brimmed with purpose. A singular vision illuminated my path—a vision where I could play a pivotal role in extending the embrace of electricity to the marginalized, transforming their lives through access to this essential resource. In my mind, I recalled the belief that I had held, that access to electricity was synonymous with development, a key to unlocking progress. The development of my country yearned for growth, and electricity held the key to this transformation. The culmination of my endeavours arrived in December of 1973, with the completion of my Master's course in Electrical Power Systems and Machines. In the crisp embrace of February 1974, my homecoming bore the anticipation of further academic pursuits—a realm where a PhD. course beckoned, bolstered by a secured scholarship. The horizon seemed promising, charged with the allure of continued studies. Yet, as the fabric of fate unfurled, the threads of my destiny wove a different narrative.

Chapter 5
The Return Home
An unexpected request

On my return to Freetown, I was resolved to catch my breath after a hectic period of studies, spend some quality time with my children and then see if I could get someone to accompany me back to London and help with the children while my husband and I pursue our studies. A call disrupted the cadence of my plans—a familiar voice that resonated from the corridors of my past. 'This is Jestina', she proclaimed, an old companion from my childhood neighbourhood, a face etched in memories of yesteryears. In her role as the secretary within the Department of Engineering at the Fourah Bay College, she had been instructed to extend an invitation to me. This invitation to visit the department was extended by none other than the Head of Department himself, Professor Koso Thomas.

This invitation struck a mellow chord inside of me since it seemed fated. The aftershocks of my return to Freetown appeared to be an intellectual counterpart to the crescendo of my nearly ten years of devoted study. I welcomed the chance with a ready heart, prepared to explore the possibilities that lay ahead. Professor Koso Thomas was there to greet me when I entered the department; he was a distinguished and charismatic figure. His manner was tinged with real respect as he expressed his satisfaction at seeing a Sierra Leonean woman succeed as a trained electrical engineer. He took me on a tour of the electrical engineering laboratory, which highlighted the gap between the facilities at Imperial College and those at the department. Despite being less sophisticated in contrast, these laboratories served as a blank canvas for Professor Thomas to rapidly paint his grandiose vision. We eventually made it to his office, a sanctuary of tranquillity, amid the buzz of machinery in the laboratories. As the meeting continued, Professor Thomas revealed his plans for the department, bringing a clear sense of direction to the room. He asked the crucial question that would determine my course in a time filled with anticipation.

'Would you be interested in teaching here?' he began. 'We have a position for a temporary lecturer in electrical machines and power systems, and I was wondering whether you would like to apply for it'.

I was taken aback by the question. I had always wanted to be a hands-on practising engineer.

'Well,' I said, 'I'm not sure. I've never really thought about teaching before. I want to practise engineering.'

'You can still practise engineering while working here', he said. 'There are possibilities to be engaged in research, as well as to do consultancy work'.

This sounded more appealing. I could still use my engineering skills, but I would also have the opportunity to share my knowledge with others, including budding engineers.

'I'll think about it,' I said. 'Can I get back to you?'

As I stepped away from the department, the contours of Professor Thomas's offer began to shape themselves within my thoughts. A newfound curiosity stirred, mirroring the yearning within me to play a role in propelling my country's development forward. The path of teaching, while not initially within my sights, gradually assumed a compelling hue.

An innate need to be engaged, coupled with an ardent desire to contribute to my nation's progress, cast a transformative light on the prospect before me. The notion of instilling knowledge, of fostering growth through the empowerment of others, took root as a noble endeavour. This realization resonated deeply, finding harmony with my upbringing—a family tapestry woven with threads of teaching. In the backdrop of my life, my mother, aunt, and uncle—educators by vocation—had nurtured my formative years, sowing the seeds of learning that would flourish within me.

Fourah Bay College

On the outskirts of Freetown, Fourah Bay College, established in February 1827, became a guiding light for learning. This centre of learning, founded by the Church Missionary Society as an Anglican missionary institution, signalled the beginning of education in West Africa along Western lines. The creation of an intellectual heritage was witnessed in Freetown, which became a haven for learning during colonial times and which earned the honorary moniker of "Athens of West Africa".

Fourah Bay College found its home on Mount Aureol, inside the embrace of the mountain range that bound Freetown. An awe-inspiring perspective of Freetown was provided by the vista from this vantage point, which unfurled like a panoramic masterpiece. I experienced a tremendous sense of pride in being a part of an institution that had left its stamp on history, as the first modern education institution in tropical Africa, with notable graduates from all over British colonial Africa.

The first year as a new lecturer was filled with difficulties, which were emphasized by the complex demands of parenthood. By the time I took up my appointment, I had five children, including the four I brought with me from London, and a baby born just before I started. In order to weave the fabric of my days with commitment, I had to juggle the duties of caring for my children and preparing lectures. This balancing act frequently left me with sleepless nights. Happily, my mother came to live with us and was a great help to us.

With my pupils, a symbiotic connection developed that was based not only on a shared intellectual environment but also on a feeling of kinship. Despite the age difference between us, I felt a maternal drive to mentor and mould them because of my position as their teacher. I was just 28 years old, and the majority of the student body was between the ages of 19 and 24.

I served as both a teacher and a disciplinary figure in the classroom, hammering home the value of responsibility and focus. I pleaded with them in an unrelenting voice to comprehend the fundamentals of electrical engineering. I implored them to memorize Faraday's electromagnetic formula to the point that they could recall it even if awakened in the middle of the night. Nevertheless, a light-hearted break stuck in my recollection despite the serious discussions and determination. At the end of a lesson, an apparently bored student delivered an impromptu declaration: "I believe it's time to call it a day". This voice was in opposition to the energy that buzzed throughout the classroom. A playful reminder that even in the world of academics, young vitality might puncture the air with genuine candour.

I was infuriated. "You start with calling it a day, and you would later call it a week, then a month, then a year and very soon you will be calling it a life". That kept him quiet, and I could continue my teaching.

The students exuded an infectious enthusiasm and a genuine hunger for knowledge. Their eagerness to grasp the intricacies of engineering was palpable, and the fact that they were being guided by a woman in the field ignited a special spark. This shared sentiment translated into a deep-seated respect they accorded me. They affectionately bestowed upon me the moniker of "mummy", a testament to the nurturing approach I embraced, treating them as I would my own children.

Reflecting on those years, I am heartened by the achievements of many of my students during my tenure of six years at the Fourah Bay College. They forged their paths in engineering, both within Sierra Leone and on the global stage. The legacy I helped shape resonates in their responsible roles, with one of my early students, Jonas Redwood-Sawyer, ascending to the esteemed position of Principal of the college- an accomplishment that fills me with pride.

Amidst the realm of academia, my pursuits extended beyond teaching. Together with my colleagues, I got involved in research endeavours aimed at advancing alternative, cost-effective technologies for food processing in the rural areas. An era marked by the burgeoning concept of appropriate technology; our pursuits aligned with the goal of enhancing the living standards in rural areas. Characterized by labour-intensive methods and resource-conscious approaches, this brand of technology harnessed readily available, low-cost materials while being attuned to the socio-cultural and ethical dimensions of the communities it served.

Work on appropriate technology in the engineering department was of an inter-disciplinary nature and that allowed me, to rub shoulders and learn a lot from my mechanical and civil engineering colleagues. I particularly gained a lot from Michael Bassey, a colleague from the mechanical engineering department, who was passionate in his research on palm oil presses, among other areas. He was a committed colleague and would spend countless hours making do with the rudimentary components that he could access. Research funds at the university were limited and called for ingenuity in the development of technologies.

I also worked on project contracts given to the engineering department. The first such task was using the computer to calculate cut and fill in road construction for a major civil engineering consultancy firm, TECHSULT. At the time, I was the only member of staff at the department who had acquired skills in computer applications, and this came in handy.

Another task that I was involved with, was working with a colleague in the electrical engineering section, John Sesay, on the first-ever installation of traffic lights in Freetown. John was an energetic and self-confident colleague and had a keen sense of humour, which turned out to be useful in our assigned task. The truth was that traffic lights were unknown to the majority of drivers in Freetown and we faced mounting opposition from them. They did not like the "delays" that these lights seemed to cause. In a city where a tenacious driving ethos prevailed, characterized by a brazen recklessness, only those who dared to assert their vehicular prowess claimed the right of passage. This spirited approach to driving was a badge of honour, a testament to their ability to outmanoeuvre and outpace any traffic obstruction. But now they were being expected to stop in places where they were used to just "wriggle" their way through. Our collective determination to enhance road safety often clashed with the impatience of the drivers. During the testing of the installations, as the sun bore down upon us, the cacophony of dissenting voices rang out—indignant, frustrated, and impatient.

'Why don't you go and install them in your living room?' they would shout back at us as they sped through, once the light turned green. Others would insult us personally.

'As long as a woman is involved in anything, they would seek to make life complicated for everyone'.

I got on very well, with my colleagues at the department, with one exception- my immediate boss, the head of electrical engineering, Mr Abdul Khanu, who taught electronics. Mr. Khanu was a pompous, misogynist. He behaved as if, as a male head, a female should be subservient to him. He contradicted everything I said, as he strove to assert, what he perceived as his authority.

Things came to a head, when one day, I arrived at the scheduled classroom for my lecture, only to find it occupied by him, whose class was supposed to have ended. I waited patiently outside the door, with my students and when he showed no sign of leaving, I entered the classroom and gently reminded him that it was my turn to use the classroom. He was furious.

'You have no right to interrupt my class', he screamed at me, in front of the students.

I found that humiliating, but I kept my cool. I quietly left and found another classroom for my class. Later in the day, I went to see him in his office to protest his treatment of me. I expected an apology, but he was unyielding. 'I am the head here, and you just have to accept what I do', he said.

I went to see the Head of Department, Professor Koso Thomas, but he only asked me to be patient. After that event, the battle lines were drawn. He became increasingly petty. One day, he blocked my car by parking behind me so I could not drive out. He accused me of parking in his spot, even though there were no officially designated parking spaces. He refused to move his car, but it happened to be on a hill. Some of my colleagues pushed his car away so I could leave. He was enraged when he came out and saw that I had successfully removed my car. I got a good laugh out of it, but the feud continued throughout my time at the university.

My mother told me that a co-worshipper at the Bethel Temple Church, the wife of Mr. Khanu, had said that I was giving her husband a hard time because I was in love with him. I was surprised by this because I had never been attracted to him. In fact, I found him to be arrogant and overbearing. A few years after I left the college, I ran into him at a conference in Geneva. He invited me to dinner, and I accepted out of politeness. However, I was shocked when he started making romantic advances towards me.

'I always loved you', he said, 'but you are such a resolute person'.

'You did?' I said, Well, that was an odd way to manifest love. Thanks though for letting me know'.

As a renowned single woman paving her way in a society made by and for men, navigating the maze-like realm of a predominately male domain became a characteristic of my journey. Men occasionally saw me as easy prey, while spouses saw me as a possible competition. The complexity of this environment revealed itself in a myriad of ways. I learned how to thread my way through this complex dance of prejudice and perception, which needed a deft choreography.

While the disagreement with Mr Khanu served as a clear reminder of these difficulties, friendship and unity also recurred throughout my story. A pattern of friendships that would last a lifetime was woven by the diverse mix of co-workers in the civil engineering, mechanical engineering, and electrical engineering sections.

The perks I had as the only female faculty member served as a counterweight to the difficulties I encountered. I was appointed to represent the newly established Faculty of Engineering at the University Senate as the department changed into a faculty in 1978. In addition, I was chosen to serve on the Sierra Leone National Committee for Science and Technology, which had the responsibility of defining the nation's position for the UN Conference on Science and Technology for Development, which took place in Vienna in 1979. These responsibilities also included representing the department at both domestic and foreign conferences, where I took the chance to promote our academic goals.

Gaining practical experience as an engineer

Working for consultancy companies offered opportunities for my area of expertise. I stepped into consulting businesses alongside my male co-workers so that I could use my skills in real-world settings. Zac Richards, a mechanical engineer and head engineer of the Palm Kernel Oil Mill in Freetown, started one such project. We co-founded Mechanical, Electrical and Management Consultants (MEMCON) with my colleague, Michael Bassey. One noteworthy work was the comprehensive inspection of electrical equipment in the recently built residence of the Nigerian High Commissioner at Hill Station, and the installation of a stand-by generator to ensure uninterrupted electricity supply during the frequent power cuts. This project served as my first dive into really using the knowledge I had gained at university. I negotiated the complex web of technicalities armed with a copy of the Institution of Electrical Engineers (IEE) regulations on electrical installations, a prized keepsake from my time living in London. In many respects, this book served as my main source of reference, showing me the route and launching me into a brand-new area of practical competence.

The new residence of the Nigerian High Commissioner was a fairy-tale castle, which stood out like a sore thumb in the area. It was bigger than the biggest hotel in Freetown, with air-conditioning in each room. The design specifications were challenging, as the Ambassador wanted us to assume that all the power outlets would need to provide full power simultaneously and I had the difficult task of explaining to him that this would not be the case and that, in fact, installation systems were designed on the basis of the assumption that only a percentage of the total power would need to be catered for, at any point in time.

'I want these electrical facilities in this building to be fully functional', he kept insisting. 'This is why I need a dedicated electricity generating system to provide for the needs in each room'.

In the end, I thought that the only way to convince him was to do the calculations and let him know the implications of designing to his request. We came out with a figure of over one Megawatt, the size of one of the four generators in the Freetown power station. It was then that he understood. We ended up installing a 75KW generator.

This situation was typical of the sort of problem that working as an engineer in places where people in positions of power were ill-informed. A lot of patience was required in asserting oneself as the expert.

I also worked with another company, the Electrical Consultants and Associates, together with two engineers, Kobi Hunter and Fennel Greene. Kobi was a very ambitious and forceful young man, who had vast plans for us to expand. In contrast to him, Fennel, who was the chief engineer at the Sierra Leone Broadcasting Services, was cool and calculated. We did get a challenging job to design the electrical system for the new broadcasting house in New England. For obvious reasons, Fennel had to take a back seat. Under normal circumstances, conflict of interest would have excluded ECA from this job, but there was no option within the country to carry it out.

The complexity of highly specialized and complex electrical installation technologies proved to be a difficult problem. The demands of sophisticated technological equipment required solutions to be designed on many weekends. This project required tenacity and a large time commitment. Even though I was unable to see the project through to completion, as I had to leave to take up an appointment in Geneva, the experience itself was priceless in terms of improving my skillset and broadening my knowledge of real-world applications.

In 1975, I joined the Sierra Leone Institution of Engineers, becoming the organization's lone female member, and was immediately elected as Deputy Secretary. I realized at the time that my pick could have been influenced by gender stereotyping, but I found comfort in fitting in with this largely masculine environment. I started serving as Secretary in 1978, a post I proudly carried out and thoroughly loved. The interplay with my male co-workers' spouses during this voyage exposed a new side of social interactions. My friendship with their spouses caused some of the women to have a chilly attitude towards me. Events like the institution's annual dinner dance were characterized by sly looks full of hostility, and unpleasant behaviour. One distinct recollection recalls a wife yanking her husband away in the middle of a conversation during a dance I was having with him.

I started a new journey in 1980 when I moved from Freetown to take up an appointment at the International Labour Office as a village technology expert. With the help of this position, I was able to enter the world of the United Nations, where I worked until I reached the statutory retirement age of 60 in 2006, after which I served as a consultant for a number of organizations. During this period, I continued to focus on energy, particularly solar energy, be it in the capacity as a technology expert, when I introduced solar equipment in refugee camps and settlements, or as the officer in charge of refugee operations. Also, I succeeded in highlighting the importance of access to energy, including electricity for the development of African countries. I wanted to go back and serve my country, but an opportunity did not present itself until 2009.

Chapter 6
The Second Return Home

The phone rang. The caller ID said "Freetown". I did not recognize the number, but I was curious to know who it was.

'Hello, Yvette', the voice said. 'This is Ogunlade. As you may have heard, I've just been appointed Minister of Energy and Power'.

'Yes, I know. Congratulations'.

'I just learned that you recently retired from the United Nations, and I thought you might be interested in giving back to Sierra Leone in a meaningful way'.

Since my retirement from the United Nations, I had been looking for the appropriate chance to give back to my country of birth by returning and making a significant contribution. However, this goal was hampered by circumstances such as my gender, ethnicity, and even assumed political connections. As a member of Sierra Leone's Krio ethnic group, I am descended from emancipated slaves who were relocated or liberated in the country's western region. The colonial era conferred significant benefits on the Krio, causing discontent among indigenous people. This historical backdrop resulted in both overt and covert estrangement of the Krio after independence, a situation that still exists today.

When I married someone from a non-Krio background, I believed that I had demonstrated my willingness to transcend ethnic boundaries. My husband's ancestors came from four indigenous ethnic groups: Mende and Limba from his father's side, and Temne and Madingo from his mother's. One might expect such a diverse combination to transcend ethnic boundaries, would be recognized, and yet cultural beliefs were more robust. He was fundamentally identified as a member of the Northern Province's Limba ethnic group, demonstrating how deeply embedded ethnic identities may remain despite diverse origins.

To make matters worse, my father-in-law was the founder of the All-People's Congress (APC) party, which played a key role in the political scene. During the period of self-rule, he rose through the ranks of the Sierra Leone People's Party. When he was part of the Sierra Leone delegation to negotiate the country's independence in London, his path took an unexpected turn. He declined to sign the independence agreements since he considered the terms unjust and the time limits for studying the documents were ridiculously short. For instance, one condition required the United Kingdom and Sierra Leone to have unrestricted skies within each other's country for military usage, forcing him to question the need for Sierra Leone's armed troops to fly over Britain.

'Why would our military forces need to fly over Britain?' he had questioned.

He spent our Independence Day in prison, but later formed the All People's Congress and served the country as prime minister and president for over 17 years before his retirement in 1985.

When I retired from the UN in 2006, the ruling party was the SLPP, so every attempt I made, as a Krio woman with APC affiliation did not bode well for me to be given any important position within the country. For instance, I was informed by the then Minister of Energy and Power, Lloyd During, the only Krio Minister in the government in 2006, of the possibility of me being appointed to fill a World Bank sponsored post as adviser to his Ministry, as the incumbent had just passed away. I was excited about this prospect and already started providing background papers for him to present to Cabinet and at international fora. This went on for about six months but suddenly all correspondence ceased. I was later to learn that the then Vice President had sanctioned the appointment of a perceived APC supporter to such a high-profile internationally sponsored job. It was now 2009 and the APC had won the elections and appointed a Krio as the Minister of Energy and Water Resources. This was my chance.

Ogunlade Davidson, a thickset man with a grey beard, reflected the stereotypical image of a seasoned professor. Our paths crossed in the late 1970s when we were both colleagues in the Faculty of Engineering at Fourah College. He rose through the ranks to the prestigious post of Professor of Mechanical Engineering. Our collaboration went beyond the academic setting, with Ogunlade serving as co-chair of a working group inside the Intergovernmental Panel on Climate Change, while I worked at the UN. Our friendship became stronger as we participated in international events together, especially during my time as the Director for Africa at the United Nations Secretariat in New York.

He was now on the other end of the phone line. He had gone to my sister's house to get my phone number and was calling to give an invitation that immediately struck a chord with me. Ogunlade's suggestion was simple: he wanted me to return to our country and work alongside him. I quickly accepted his proposal without hesitation.

'This is the time for us to put into action all these theories we advanced at the international fora', he continued.

'Yes', I said, 'We should start with drawing up an energy policy and strategy'. He agreed.

The first-ever Sierra Leone Energy Policy and Strategy

So, in August 2009, I set off for Freetown. The reality that awaited me upon my return was shocking. Despite the fact that the country now had a significant number of female engineering graduates, the discipline held tenaciously to its male-dominated character. The echoes of it being primarily a man's world lingered on.

My first steps entailed leading a group of determined and highly motivated individuals, including Sidi Bakarr, a civil engineer, who had experience working for a mining company and with a consultancy group, Patrick Tarawally, an ex-employee of the National Power Authority and Michael Conteh, a young graduate from Fourah Bay College. The working atmosphere was conducive, with each of us realizing that the task ahead of us was crucial, as a first step to address the formidable problem of energy supply in the country. We started out to create a comprehensive plan and policy, armed with resolve and propelled by our shared commitment. It is worth mentioning that there were no contracts or promises of remuneration offered to us, but we plodded forward.

'I will endeavour to secure funds to provide you with an honorarium', Ogunlade pledged.

Yet, to us, the prospect of compensation was secondary to our burning desire to achieve our goals. Fuelled by determination, we embarked on the task.

Our efforts resulted in the production of the first-ever Sierra Leone Policy and Strategy document after extensive consultations and heated discussions. I had the honour of presenting this revolutionary work to the Cabinet at State House, and it was welcomed with real enthusiasm and attention. The Ministers were unfamiliar with the topic, and my presentation ignited a lively debate. Following that, the Cabinet officially adopted the policy and plan in September 2009. As I left for Geneva, I felt satisfied, knowing that our high officials realized the need to tackle energy challenges.

My excitement, though, was tempered with cynicism about the actual implementation of the action plan we had painstakingly drawn up. The lack of a designated technical section within the Ministry of Energy and Water Resources was the stumbling issue. Unlike other technical ministries such as health, this ministry was governed primarily by civil servants who lacked experience in the complexities of the subject. I expressed my concerns to the Minister, who agreed and pledged to establish an Energy Department inside the Ministry. Nonetheless, I recognized that such a substantial organizational shift would need time and careful planning to ensure its success.

Energy Policy Adviser

Ogunlade's perseverance paid off in November 2009, with the approval under a UNDP-sponsored "Return of Talent" project, which, among other specializations, included the provision of an energy policy adviser to the Ministry of Energy and Power. Fortunately, I was picked to fill this position for two years. As I began this new chapter, I was ecstatic at the idea of being able to make a significant contribution to the advancement in my home country.

When I returned to Sierra Leone for this appointment, it became clear that the work facing me was significant and varied. Due to its lack of a dedicated technical department, and because of its proximity to the National Power Authority, the Ministry's focus was mostly on problematic electricity supply issues. The President's Agenda for Change, on the other hand, emphasized the importance of energy as a critical development pillar. As a result, the need for concentrated attention to the provision of energy became clear. The National Energy Policy and Strategy provided a guiding framework, but there was a need for a responsible body to monitor its implementation. This need was met with widespread approval, including from important players and large donors.

The proposal for the setting up of an Energy Division was approved by the Cabinet and the Public Sector Review Commission in 2009, following the Functional Review of the Ministry of Energy and Water Resources. However, progress in taking action on this was stalled, until January 2010, when the Minister requested me to act as interim Director of the Energy Division, and in that capacity, to assist in putting in place a well-functioning Energy Division.

What I did not expect was the lack of support I would receive from within the Ministry. During my almost three years working at the ministry, there was a turnover of three permanent secretaries, each of which did not provide the required support. The source of this resistance became clear over time. My foreign position came with a salary in dollars that was approximately five times that of the Permanent Secretary, which irritated several senior staff members. Furthermore, some saw the move to form a technical section as weakening their authority within the ministry. One Permanent Secretary's statement during a meeting, in reference to the nation's turbulent 11-year war that ended in 2002, epitomized the issues I faced.

'We have stayed on during the war and the difficult period, and now, you people who left are coming back and getting the most lucrative positions'.

In my efforts to advance the implementation of the energy policy, I came across various potential chances and worked hard to capitalize on them. However, various hurdles impeded my efforts, making my job far more difficult. First and foremost, I struggled with the absence of any allocated support workers assigned to me, throughout my time at the ministry. This circumstance required me to act as my own secretary, messenger, and, at times, office cleaner. As a result, I found myself spending a lot of time on trivial activities that could have been spent on strategic objectives.

Second, unlike my colleagues at the ministry, I lacked access to official cars and modes of communication. This lack of critical resources was a severe impediment, especially when it came to managing projects like the street lighting installation. Despite the fact that large sums had been amassed from bid sales, my efforts to get basic means to carry out preparatory activities for the installation of the streetlights were not approved. When I asked for help, the Permanent Secretary pointed to my comparably substantial salary and said that it should be enough to cover such expenditures. Despite these obstacles, I stayed committed and achieved a number of notable triumphs.

Progress in setting up the energy division

Following the functional review of the Ministry of Energy and Water Resources, the proposal to form an Energy Division was approved by both the Cabinet and the Public Sector Review Commission in 2009. Nonetheless, work towards implementation stalled until January 2010, when the Minister asked me to temporarily assume the job of temporary Director for the Energy Division in order to construct an effective and well-organized body.

Taking on this responsibility, I formulated a comprehensive organizational structure for the newly envisioned division. I meticulously crafted job descriptions for various positions, which were then submitted to the Director General of Human Resources Management. The Public Service Commission proceeded to advertise the positions, and I participated in the short-listing process, forwarding the chosen candidates' names to the Public Service Commission in February 2011. Regrettably, until my departure from Freetown in early 2012, the interviewing process had yet to commence.

Anticipating the imminent recruitment for the Energy Division, a budget for its establishment and operational activities for the year 2011 was thoughtfully devised and submitted during the annual budget discussions. However, during these discussions with the Ministry of Finance, the then Permanent Secretary omitted to extend an invitation for me to defend the Energy Division's budget, a process that other high-ranking professionals in the Ministry underwent for their respective submissions. Astonishingly, as reported by the Permanent Secretary, the Ministry of Finance decided to exclude the budget allocation for the Energy Division from the final approved budget, in stark contrast to the budgetary approval received by the Water Division.

Despite my tireless efforts, the inability to establish an Energy Division presented a troubling scenario. It meant that when I left, the Ministry was still lacking in the essential human resources to prepare applications for available funds from sources such as climate change grants, which were critical for promoting the sector's success. I am pleased to note, however, that there is currently a functioning professional energy department within the Ministry of Energy.

Addressing the problems of electricity supply

The country's electrical supply was in a state of disarray. The government found itself dedicating a considerable percentage of its budget to acquiring fuel supplies, which were required to keep generators running. Despite these significant efforts, periodic power interruptions continued. This terrible reality was linked to a number of issues, including fuel theft, old infrastructure, non-standardized components, and a lack of dependable protective mechanisms to ensure continuous power delivery.

My engagement in the power production sector took numerous shapes during my tenure. I participated in ad hoc meetings held throughout the development stages of thermal plants for the district capitals. I was tasked with chairing a Task Force formed by the Minister to make suggestions on the organizational structure of the fossil fuel power stations, as well as advice on the most ideal workforce composition for electricity generating stations and sub-stations. In addition, my position included evaluating and advising on proposals for electricity generation brought to the Ministry from a variety of sources, including private sector and non-governmental groups. I also worked on a study of the possibilities for renewable energy-based electricity generation.

Upon the request of Dr Kelfalla Marah, Chief of Staff of the Office of the President, I embarked on an exhaustive assessment of the transmission and distribution system serving the Western Area, in September 2010. My investigations revealed that the system was in a desperate state of disrepair. Notably, the medium voltage, 11 KV network exhibited signs of age and vulnerability, with approximately 60 per cent of the network deemed unreliable. The existing aged switchgear and protection equipment were rendered obsolete by the passage of time. Further scrutiny unveiled undersized conductors and substation capacities, while distribution transformers grappled with overloading issues. Additionally, the scarcity of maintenance materials emerged as a pressing concern.

The consequential effect of these deficiencies was starkly evident on May 15, 2010. A fault materialized within one of the two interconnectors connecting the two diesel-generating stations at Kingtom and Brookfields, each boasting a transmission capacity of 10MW. Tragically, during the process of isolating and repairing the fault, the second interconnector succumbed to problems and consequently tripped out of service. The dual interconnectors were thereby rendered inoperative, collectively reducing the network's transmission capacity to 10MW. The subsequent process of re-commissioning these interconnectors extended over a two-month period, hampered as the sole available fault-locating instrument had been damaged during the rebel conflict.

The low voltage distribution system was characterized by inappropriate conductor sizing, the use of sub-standard conductors, unacceptable lengths of distribution lines, disorderly and dangerous installations, non-existence of design standards, illegal connections and power theft. All these had resulted in huge losses and low voltage problems.

Protection systems were faulty and led to faults in a single location spreading to the rest of the system, without being isolated. Faults at the two diesel generating stations resulted in complete system breakdowns. There was a need to improve the power systems planning capacity within the National Power Authority, to ensure that proper power planning, which is essential for the smooth running of power systems operations, was done.

After the review, I recommended a two-pronged approach. First, the upgrading of the system to allow for the reliable transfer of the current generating capacity, considering spare capacity, to the consumers. This would involve the drawing up of a detailed project proposal, and resourcing the funds required. The low-voltage networks would need to be thoroughly addressed at this stage, to ensure that the problems at this level do not compromise the gains made in the improvement of the medium-voltage transmission/distribution system. Requirements to improve these networks would also need to be financed.

Second, a comprehensive planning of the Western Area Power system needed to be done, in light of longer-term needs and the anticipated increase in electricity generating capacity.

In addition, the Ministry should continue to work closely with National Power Authority (NPA), to draw up a loss reduction plan, to address the huge losses in the system.

Electricity tariffs in the country were among the highest in the world. One of my first assignments at the Ministry was the drawing up of a methodology for determining tariffs for the purchase of electricity from independent power producers. To do this, I considered the cost of electricity from existing thermal plants in Sierra Leone, the tariffs for the purchase of electricity from fossil fuels and the feed-in tariffs for electricity from renewable energy sources, in the form of micro-hydro generation, wind power generation, solar photovoltaic power generation and biomass energy resources. I also drew up procedures for the purchase of electricity from prospective independent power producers.

In addition to my responsibilities, I evaluated the current tariff structure provided by the NPA for consumers. This was in reaction to the widely held view that the advent of hydropower would automatically result in lower tariffs. My preliminary investigation, on the other hand, showed a more complex reality. While hydropower normally has lower production costs than thermal electricity, the coming to existence of the Bumbuna hydropower facility did not result in tariff reduction.

The construction of the Bumbuna hydro-plant started in 1975, but it was only commissioned in 2009, due to lack of adequate funding and the civil war. The lengthy duration of the construction and recurring adjustments to the structural plan of the Bumbuna project increased the overall construction cost, which amounted to be about US$327 million. This meant an installation cost of around US$7 million per MW installed capacity, much more than the average construction cost for hydropower plants, which was typically between US$1 to 1.5 million per MW. The significant cost disparity was reflected in the pricing of power generated by the Bumbuna hydroelectric station. A detailed assessment resulted in a cost of about US$0.18 per kWh, compared to the rate of US$0.15 per kWh, being charged. In addition, the distribution system serving the Western Area faced substantial losses, estimated to be within the range of 50% to 55%. This implied that over half of the electricity generated was essentially unaccounted for, highlighting significant inefficiencies within the system. This meant that the Bumbuna hydroelectric facility was operated at a loss and the cost of electricity production needed to be heavily subsidized by the government.

The need for reforming the power sector

One of the overarching goals outlined in the Energy Policy and Strategic Plan was the enhancement of governance within the energy sector. This objective aimed to holistically address the crucial elements that would facilitate the effective execution of the energy policy. The strategies designed to realize this goal encompassed a range of initiatives, with a significant focus on power sector reform. This reform was regarded as pivotal, not only for enhancing sector performance but also for extending electricity accessibility throughout the nation. The significance of power sector reform was underscored by its classification as a prerequisite for receiving donor budgetary support, underlining its paramount importance in Sierra Leone's development agenda.

Given the government's high priority on electricity supply to spur socio-economic advancement, the availability of reliable and affordable electricity played a fundamental role in attracting foreign investment for the optimal exploitation of the country's abundant natural resources. This, in turn, held the potential to stimulate economic growth and provide employment opportunities, particularly for the youth.

The establishment of the National Power Authority (NPA) in accordance with the NPA Act of 1982, which underwent amendments in 1993 and 2006, bestowed upon it the sole authority for electricity generation, transmission, and distribution within Sierra Leone. The subsequent revision in 2006 opened up power generation to private sector involvement, enabling initiatives such as the emergency power facility at the Kingdom and the operationalization of the Bumbuna Hydroelectric Plant.

To realize the sanctioned policy and governmental objectives, a comprehensive restructuring of the power sector was imperative. This restructuring sought to dismantle institutional hindrances obstructing electricity provision, intensify private sector engagement in power service development and delivery, and institute an integrated framework for governing the power sector. Addressing the challenge of elevated costs associated with scaling electricity generation to meet burgeoning demand, compounded by latent demand underscored the necessity for substantial capital investment. To this end, incentivizing private sector participation emerged as a pivotal strategy to alleviate the financial burden on the government.

This approach necessitated transitioning from the NPA's monopoly over the power sector to the inclusion of independent power producers (IPPs). Moreover, facilitating concessions for operators to engage in the distribution and marketing of electricity services while safeguarding government-owned assets were also identified as a significant avenue for reform. The overarching objective remained to be the promotion of private sector involvement as a means to foster economic development, alleviate financial pressures, and enhance overall power sector performance.

Within this revised framework, the power sector's administration and governance would undergo a marked enhancement. The Ministry of Energy and Water Resources would strategically focus on pivotal aspects like policy formulation, coordination, and the critical roles of monitoring and evaluation. Concurrently, the operational responsibilities would be entrusted to the pertinent agencies, each diligently executing their designated tasks.

This paradigm shift required the establishment of a robust regulatory structure, which would be instrumental in ensuring equitable and transparent operations across the multifaceted spectrum of both public and private entities engaged in power generation and distribution. Its overarching aim would encompass not only upholding fairness but also fostering an environment conducive to prudent financial practices and maintaining stringent technical standards. In essence, the regulatory mechanism would be a cornerstone to sustainably steer the sector toward comprehensive efficiency and stability.

A critical component of this transition was spreading the benefits of modern energy services, particularly electricity, to Sierra Leone's neglected rural communities. These areas had long been neglected in terms of service delivery. A specific arrangement geared to the unique constraints of rural regions was required to overcome this gap. Such a focused strategy will ensure that the transformational potential of readily available and high-quality energy resources is used to boost rural communities and move them toward sustainable development.

In tandem with the broader sector reforms, this rural-focused initiative stood to alleviate long-standing energy disparities and empower communities that had hitherto been on the fringes of progress. Through these multifaceted changes, Sierra Leone's power sector aspired to emerge as a dynamic and inclusive force, fostering growth, and resilience across the nation.

The restructuring plan for the electricity sector

Following a thorough examination of many models in various countries, I adopted a strategy that cleared the way for a full change. This called for the formation of separate entities, each fitted to a certain purpose within the energy environment. This complex structure included an Energy Asset Company, an Electricity Generation and Transmission Company, a redesigned National Power Authority, to be known as the Electricity Distribution and Supply Authority, a Regulatory Commission, and a Rural Energy Agency. This precisely developed arrangement was designed to enable a wide range of participation options, including Independent Power Producers specialized in solar energy, biomass energy, thermal energy, and hydropower.

I diligently drafted two crucial draft Bills in close collaboration with Ms. Sonia Frazer, a very competent and reliable lawyer from the Law Officers' Department - the Electricity and Water Regulatory Commission Bill and the National Electricity Bill. These drafts were rigorously designed based on the Cabinet-approved framework and were strengthened by incisive inputs from the prestigious World Bank. This close coordination guaranteed that the legal framework behind the energy sector's transformation was firmly based on both local policy agendas and international best practices.

The Electricity and Water Regulatory Commission Act

Unlike most countries in the world, electricity and water supply in Sierra Leone still remained unregulated. Such a situation was undesirable, as it did not ensure the optimum quality of services to consumers. Quality of supply issues, both technical and commercial, were areas which were often neglected but which have significant impacts on economic and social development.

The need for a regulatory framework was also seen in the context of the long-awaited reforms in the electricity and water sectors, in which the sectors would become open to the private sector. The increasing involvement of the private sector would reinforce the need for autonomous regulation, which would entail balancing the needs of both consumers and utilities.

Thus, through regulation, utilities would be able to operate in an environment where they can get a reasonable rate of return on their investment while providing a quality service to consumers. The Electricity and Water Regulatory Commission Act would result in the assignment of distinct and clear roles for different players in the sector: Government would formulate policy; utilities would provide the services while the EWRC would regulate the electricity and water sectors. This would help to boost investor confidence in the energy and water sectors as it would provide a higher likelihood of a level playing field. It should also be noted that in recognition of the urgent need to reform the power sector, power sector reform has been included as one of the triggers for donor support to the country.

The National Electricity Act

I proposed the formation of three independent institutions, each with its own set of functions and responsibilities, inside the framework of the National Electricity Bill. The government-owned Energy Asset Company was established to monitor and manage all government energy facilities, both current and prospective, for efficient development and operation.

The power Generation and Distribution Company emerged as a key player, entrusted with generating power from government-owned facilities and selling it to the reorganized National Power Authority under a regulated Power Purchase Agreement (PPA). Its domain included the administration of high voltage transmission lines across the country, as well as the operation of critical thermal power plants such as those at Kingtom, Blackhall Road, and several provincial districts, including the Bo/Kenema Power producing facilities.

The revamped National Power Authority, as the Energy Distribution and Supply Authority, would have control over distribution lines; primary and secondary substations, as well as manage the financial and technical elements of energy operations. The company's responsibilities included demand forecasting, power supply planning in partnership with power generating entities, and coordination of generation plans and system operations, encouraging collaboration among all parties involved.

In my attempts to address chronic energy theft, intentional asset damage, and cable theft, I made an important step forward by including a crucial provision in the draft Bill: the introduction of sanctions. I observed that illegal actions were substantially interfering with the energy supply, resulting in higher expenses for law-abiding users. I recommended strong fines as deterrence to such acts, drawing inspiration from punishment regimes in many countries. The decision of punishments, however, eventually came under the authority of the Law Officers Department, which specified the following penalties in the Bill:

For electricity theft, imprisonment for a term of not less than one year but which may extend to five years or a fine of not less than ten million leones.

The theft of electric cables, equipment or materials, was to be considered as an offence, liable upon conviction to imprisonment for a term which may extend to five years or with a fine of not less than six times the financial gain on account of such theft of electricity, or with both.

In preparation for the parliamentary hearing for the Electricity and Water Supply Regulatory Commission Bill and the National Electricity Bill, I diligently produced thorough briefing notes, including explanatory information that were intended to assist in a seamless comprehension of the proposed law. These illuminating materials were sent to the parliamentary committee ahead of time. With unshakeable trust in the soundness of my briefing, I held out hope that the measures would pass the traditional three statutory readings and be welcomed without incident. Unfortunately, my optimism proved to be unfounded, as events took an unexpected turn.

The first reading of the legislation went over without a hitch, giving rise to immediate confidence. However, when the legislative process progressed to the second reading, both sides of the parliamentary chamber raised a red flag. This unanticipated development revealed a looming difficulty that required cautious management at a critical point in the legislative process.

'We need closer examination of these bills', the Member of Parliament from the government side of the house started. 'I would request that these Bills are referred to the Legal Committee'.

The Member of Parliament from the opposition also endorsed this statement. In the end, the Speaker of the House ruled.

'These Bills are now referred to the Legal Committee. I declare this session adjourned'. And with that, he hit the gavel and it was the end of the session.

I was disappointed because my initial trust in the clear character of the draft legislations and their ability to solve an urgent and recognized need was greeted with unanticipated pushback. I thought it would have been preferable if the concerns expressed at the second reading had been properly outlined, allowing for targeted talks to resolve those concerns. However, because this clarity was absent, I switched my attention to the upcoming Legal Committee hearings.

At the committee meeting, I went through each of the clauses meticulously. Following the debate that ensued, I had a feeling of success, knowing that I had efficiently performed my obligations. I anticipated the next phases of the legislative procedure, picturing the appointment for the third reading and the final passage of the two bills into laws.

This landmark was finally attained in November of 2011.

Surprisingly, this achievement coincided with my appointment as Ambassador to Geneva. Despite the fact that this new responsibility prevented me from developing the original implementation plan, I was able to construct a complete matrix outlining the essential follow-up tasks. Furthermore, I was fortunate in obtaining the World Bank's approval to financially assist several of these critical programmes.

Rural energy/electrification

Rural energy and electricity are critical components of Sierra Leone's overall rural development and poverty reduction plan. Energy service supply has far-reaching ramifications for a variety of rural economic activities, including agriculture, entrepreneurship, social services, gender equality, and poverty reduction. Surprisingly, a fewer than 1% of Sierra Leone's rural population had access to electricity, emphasizing the urgent need for coordinated action.

I advocated for the creation of a Rural Electricity Agency to address the critical issue of rural electricity accessibility. This envisioned organization, backed by a separate Act, would be created to address the special issues that rural communities face. Its primary missions would include enabling access to power, stimulating energy infrastructure development, and promoting productive energy consumption.

I was able to secure funding for rural energy programs totalling US$3.4 million from both the World Bank and the Department for International Development (DFID). These funds were to go towards the development of a policy framework and regulatory strategy for rural electrification. It would also help to establish the Rural Energy Agency and conduct a comprehensive Rural Energy Program. Furthermore, this funding stream would enable a pilot project, including the installation of solar photovoltaic systems in selected communities around the country.

Sierra Leone was divided into 149 Chiefdoms, each with its own Chiefdom Headquarters. Working with the World Bank, we selected 14 of these Chiefdoms for the pilot initiative I negotiated, with the goal of eventually supporting all 149 Chiefdom Headquarters. Our systematic approach included the development of a selection committee comprised of officials from the Ministries of Energy and Water Resources, as well as Local Government and Rural Development. The committee's selection criteria considered factors such as equitable district representation, gender ratios within villages, Chiefdom size, availability of communal amenities (e.g., schools, clinics, community centres, judicial facilities, and water pumps), efficient Chiefdom administration including the Village Council, villages' willingness to train volunteers for solar system maintenance, and villages' commitment to securing funds for system upkeep. Before I left, I produced a detailed preliminary list of possible communities for this revolutionary endeavour.

The Konta Line Solar System Management Committee was formed in 2004 by the non-governmental group Safer Future Youth Development Project. The group inspired this idea after solar-electrifying ten residences. The project's major goal was to improve rural communities by providing them with relevant technical skills, thus increasing their income and contributing to environmental preservation. Two outstanding women, Nancy Kanu and Fatu Koroma, were taught as Solar "Engineers" at India's Barefoot College in 2007, thanks to considerable sponsorship from the Government of India. Upon their return, these empowered women provided solar lighting for 41 dwellings in the Kontaline and Moyebana Villages on the borders of the Western Area. This program received a lot of attention since it included illiterate women, trained in India, who were successfully building systems to power solar lamps for use in rural communities. Recognizing the potential for improvement in their efforts, I felt compelled to contribute; however, a peculiar circumstance arose: the project was overseen by the Ministry of Finance and Economic Development, a body lacking the technical expertise required to maximize the project's impact.

I strongly advocated for a transfer of responsibilities, thinking that the Ministry of Energy and Water Resources would be better qualified to handle this initiative. After careful study, the Cabinet approved this request, directing that control be transferred to the Ministry of Energy and Water Resources. Other major ministries, such as Internal Affairs, Local Government and Rural Development, Education, Youth and Sports, Lands, Country Planning, and the Environment were expected to play critical roles in boosting grassroots participation and delivering necessary training for the targeted youth groups.

Despite the Cabinet decision and repeated requests from the Ministry of Energy and Water Resources, the transfer was not implemented. I later learnt that the Ministry of Finance and Economic Development had, contrary to the ruling by Cabinet, decided to transfer the project to the Ministry of Education, Science, and Technology, though this had not occurred by the time I left.

The Solar Streetlight Project

During a visit to Guinea, President Koroma was impressed with the solar street lighting that adorned the city. When a group from the Economic Commission of West African States (ECOWAS) Bank for Investment and Development (EBID) visited Sierra Leone to examine prospective projects, the installation of solar streetlights came on top of the list.

In terms of infrastructure, it was clear that, with the exception of Freetown and parts of Bo and Kenema, streetlights were absent from other district headquarters throughout Sierra Leone. The provision of street lighting was critical, with the goal of improving traffic safety, reviving nocturnal urban activity, and reviving economic possibilities after sunset. Choosing solar technology was a sensible option, avoiding the load on an overburdened electrical infrastructure and investing in a long-term, sustainable, cost-effective solution for urban illumination.

As the foundation of the project, I painstakingly prepared a detailed technical specifications in partnership with EBID. Following that, a draft tender document was rigorously created during an enlightening expedition to EBID's headquarters in Togo headed by the Minister. The initiative expanded beyond district capitals, including Lungi, and culminated in an agreement to install a total of 10,000 lamps.

The tendering process began in April 2010, with a skilled technical team leading the rigorous evaluation procedure. The team comprised of experts such as Professor Jonas Redwood Sawyerr of Fourah Bay College, Ing. Mr Philip Mongorquee - NPA's Provincial Services Manager, Ing. Dr Kelleh Gbawuru Mansaray- a distinguished Renewable Energy Specialist and then Senior Lecturer at the University of Sierra Leone, Mr Christian Tonkoro-an EBID representative, and myself, ensured a thorough evaluation. Their scrutiny extended from the technical to the financial components of the proposals, finally leading to the selection of Angelique International, an accomplished Indian firm.

I travelled to India for a hands-on examination of the streetlight components and prototype with a small team of three: Dr Mansaray, Mr Mongorquee, and myself. Our voyage took us to significant manufacturing firms such as Tata BP Solar, a skilled maker of solar photovoltaic panels; HBL Power Systems Ltd, known for their gel batteries; and Goldwyn Ltd, a skilled manufacturer of light emitting diode (LED) lighting. We also inspected and assessed a complete prototype system built up at Tata BP Solar Limited's facilities.

Our inspection tour unfolded as a learning experience, providing us with first-hand knowledge of the various manufacturing processes. We extensively examined the painstaking fabrication of components at the HBL and Goldwyn plants, while also observing the professionalism of the manufacturing staff. Tata BP Solar showed us through their production line, where stringent testing protocols were carried out, including a simulated assessment of the durability of solar panels. Their dedication to quality and accuracy was felt throughout our visits to all three manufacturing sites.

The prototype evaluation at Tata BP Solar enabled us to identify areas that needed to be refined, which we swiftly discussed with both manufacturers and Angelique International. We worked together to make the required changes to improve the unit design of the solar streetlights.

Our combined evaluation led us to a definite conclusion: the solar streetlight system, when fitted with these high-quality components, would be robust and would meet our standards and aspirations. The critical component, however, was the precise assembling of these pieces, meticulously matching them with the technical drawings and electrical circuits we had diligently developed. Unfortunately, my departure from Sierra Leone came before the project's launch, but I hoped for a smooth start and successful completion.

The Fiftieth Anniversary of Sierra Leone Independence

It was the beginning of April in 2011 and plans were underway for the celebration of the fiftieth anniversary of Sierra Leone's Independence. The media was buzzing with information about the dignitaries who were planning to attend the event. Amid the excitement, a nagging fear settled in my mind, knowing all too well the status of the country's electricity supply system. The all-too-common power outages that ruined major gatherings lingered in my thoughts, and I spent sleepless nights worrying about the possible embarrassment of a blackout during the joyful festivities. I realized the need to take preventive precautions since I was painfully aware of the ramifications such an occurrence may have on our ministry's image. Recognizing that our reputation was at stake, I contacted the Minister with a sense of urgency, hoping to find a solution that would guarantee the celebrations went off without a hitch.

'Mr Minister', I said, 'I'm concerned about the power supply during the independence celebrations. How can we guarantee that there will be no outages?'

His eyes lit up for a moment. It was clear that he had not given much thought to this.

'Yes, that's a problem', he said. 'What do you suggest we do?'

'I think we need to sit down with the National Power Authority and see what needs to be done to avoid power outages', I replied. 'We should also reach out to the event organizers and make sure they are aware of the potential for power supply problems'.

The minister seemed relieved. 'Can I put you in charge of managing this?' he asked.

It was a difficult undertaking, but the risks of national embarrassment dictated that we moved quickly. I took on the job with zeal. To properly address this situation, my first step was to set up a task force under my chairmanship and I created a detailed set of task force terms of reference. These directives outlined our primary goals: to identify the critical venues requiring power supply during the Independence Day celebrations, calculate total electricity demands for the duration of the event, and establish a reliable mechanism for monitoring these requirements throughout the festivities. We also had to consider fuel requirements and develop contingency plans for conceivable scenarios such as thermal plant breakdowns or the entire shutdown of the Bumbuna Hydropower Station.

I prepared letters for him to send to the President's office and the National Power Authority announcing the creation of a Task Force and naming me as chairperson for it. I had to act fast as we had no more than three weeks before the start of the celebrations. Members of the Task Force were Dr Abdul Jalloh, the head of the Bumbuna Hydroelectric Plant that was the main supplier of electricity, Mustapha Kargbo, the Presidential adviser on energy, and Denis Garvie and Mahmood Timbo from the National Power Authority.

Although the discussion of the Task Force was centred on providing electricity for the entire City of Freetown which then had a restricted demand of 35MW, I insisted on calling the Chairman of the 50th Anniversary Celebrations Committee for a copy of the programme. This was for purposes of identifying the priority areas, where the main events were being planned. These were the State House, Brookfield Stadium, Parliament area, Lumley Beach Road, the city perimeter for the lantern parade, the presidential and vice-presidential lodges, hospitals, the military barracks and the police headquarters.

At the first meeting, the representatives from the National Power Authority were quite defensive. 'But all these venues have spare generators', they informed me.

'But are they functional?' I asked. 'We need to ensure that they are'.

To ensure the security of supply for the whole period, we developed a three-phased plan. First, we needed to ensure that the existing installed generation capacity of 42 megawatts from the thermal and hydropower stations could be deployed to cover the calculated power of 34 megawatts for Freetown. Next, we had to ensure that all the stand-by generators in the different venues, where the events were planned, were functional and lastly, we needed to secure the services of a mobile generator of 140 kilowatts that could be deployed in the venues should there be a power outage and a breakdown of the stand-by generators. By then, we had less than a fortnight before the operations. We had to act fast. Failure was not an option.

To keep the thermal generators, with a total capacity of 17 megawatts running, we needed to provide enough fuel, as the lack of fuel was one of the reasons why they were not always put in service. For 24-hour operations during the eight days of the celebrations, we needed some 32,000 gallons of fuel, at a cost of about 1.6 billion Leones. We needed to identify the most vulnerable sections of the distribution system and replace all the faulty cables, fuses, switchgear and other power system equipment around Freetown. These required a further 1.5 billion Leones. These could be purchased from Guinea and we needed to arrange for a road trip to Guinea to make these purchases.

On investigation, we found that most of the stand-by generators in the venues were non-functional and had to be repaired. NPA was assigned that responsibility. But the biggest problem we anticipated was for the street carnival, which the Vice President, who was in charge of the programme was keen on having. According to him, this would be the highlight of the celebrations as it would allow all citizens to participate. This was all well and good, but the problem was that he wanted that to take place along the over seven miles of Lumley Beach Road. This road had no street lights.

'But why don't we have the carnival in the centre of town?' I dared ask, at a meeting with the celebrations committee chaired by the Vice President.

He was adamant. 'No', he said, 'Absolutely no. The beach road provides best venue for a carnival without disrupting traffic in the centre of town'.

I would have agreed with him, except that I knew that we would need to find a solution within two weeks. But now, we had to find a solution. We first thought that the hotels along the road, which had individual generators, would be requested to provide the electricity along the road, which some agreed to do.

A visit to the road revealed that long sections of the road were not close to the hotels. We thus had to install streetlights along the 7.6-kilometre road in time for the carnival. To do this, we needed lights, poles, cables and generators, which all had to be installed within two weeks. NPA had some poles in their store but we had to buy the rest of the equipment required also from Guinea, at an additional cost of about one billion leones. The total amount required to put a system in place to guarantee electricity supply was calculated at about six billion leones.

We needed the money urgently, so we presented the case to the chair of the celebrations committee Dr Magbailey Fyle. He had been recently selected to replace the original chairperson, who had been sacked due to some alleged irregularities. He was very cautious and queried why we needed so much money. I decided to draft a letter for the Minister to send to him, as there was no time to waste. No one wanted to be blamed for embarrassing power cuts during the independence celebrations, so the funds were made available.

The equipment from Guinea arrived one week before the celebrations. The NPA technicians occupied themselves with the repairs to the distribution system. I had to keep an eye on the works along the beach road. I realized that I needed to supervise the works myself, so I convinced the General Manager of the NPA, Mr Kaloko, to go along with me for the week in which the installations were being made. One of our tasks was to motivate the workers to complete the work before the start of the carnival. It was quite an experience. It was the hottest time of the year and there we were, pacing along the long road under the sweltering heat, and making sure that everything was being done well. I found that these workers, if not closely supervised, were making dubious connections with the potential of failing. Each connection thus needed to be verified.

On the eve of the celebrations, everything was ready. But I was still nervous. 'What if we missed something?' I thought.

'Will you be coming tomorrow for the opening of the carnival?' asked Mr Kaloko.

'Definitely not', I said categorically. 'I will watch it on TV'.

Besides the fact that I was exhausted, I could not imagine what I would do if the electricity failed in the middle of the celebrations. I went to bed and spent a sleepless night. But it all went well and there was no power outage during the entire eight days of the independence celebrations. I was grateful for the maximum cooperation, which I received from the members of the Task Force. This showed that it was possible to work together to ensure the security of the electricity supply in the country.

Other activities at the Ministry

During my time at the Ministry, I worked on a number of other projects that helped to advance Sierra Leone's energy landscape. Among these was the staging of a major Solar Energy seminar and exhibition, which featured the distinguished participation of Dr Kandeh Yumkella, the then-Director General of the United Nations Industrial Development Organization (UNIDO). The event highlighted the outstanding efforts of small enterprises and non-governmental groups who were actively promoting solar energy applications around the country. In addition to these efforts, I gave a public talk at the Sierra Leone Institution of Engineers titled *Leveraging Solar Energy to Meet Sierra Leone's Energy Needs*.

Diverse bioenergy initiatives in Sierra Leone were in various phases of execution, drawing a large number of potential investors. The lack of a unified strategy and operating procedures aroused worries about the possible negative consequences of such investments. The Sierra Leone Investment and Export Agency (SLIEPA) drew our ministry's attention to this.

I was aware of the role that bioenergy production could play in the achievement of "The Agenda for Changes Priorities", by creating a new market for producers as well as offering new forms of employment that would positively impact agricultural and rural incomes, poverty reduction and economic growth. In addition, bioenergy developments offered the opportunity for enhanced energy security by reducing the dependence on fossil fuels.

However, there was a need to have a proper understanding of the "full" costs and benefits of bioenergy in the country and to develop guidelines for prospective investors. In this context, the Ministry of Energy and Water Resources (MEWR) formally requested on 14th of February 2011 the technical support of FAO to assess the potential for sustainable bioenergy development in the country through the implementation of the FAO Bioenergy and Food Security (BEFS) approach.

I then established and chaired a working group called the Bioenergy and Food Security Working Group (BEFSWG), comprising representatives from the relevant line Ministries and together with the FAO, we prepared draft guidelines which were circulated widely but which were not finalized before I left.

To focus on institutionalizing multi-sector consultation on energy access MEWR established a National Multi-Sectoral Group on Energy Access, comprising representatives from the Ministry of Energy and Water Resources; Ministry of Agriculture, Food Security & Forestry, Ministry of Employment and Social Security; Ministry of Internal Affairs, Local Government and Rural

Development, Ministry of Works, Housing and Infrastructural Development, Ministry of Social Welfare, Gender and Children Affairs, Ministry of Finance and Economic Development, Ministry of Education, Youths and Sports, Ministry of Information and Communications, Ministry of Foreign Affairs and International Cooperation, the Environmental Protection Agency, the University of Sierra Leone, Njala University, DFID, JICA, UNDP, UNIDO, World Bank, FAO, NGO and Private Sector representatives.

The Sierra Leone Multi-stakeholders' Group on Energy Access was created in February 2011, when it held an inaugural meeting, with the sponsorship of UNDP. The main outcome of the meeting was the three-year workplan of the Group.

End of my UNDP-funded contract – unfinished business

The UNDP contract under which I worked was initially set for two-year duration, with the agreement made with the government that it would absorb the experts, after this initial period. Among experts assigned under this project, there were several experts working in various ministries, and within the Ministry of Energy and Power, Joe Ben Davies was the policy adviser on Water, while I held the role of adviser on Energy.

The process for absorption into the government was contingent upon a formal request from the Permanent Secretary of the ministry to the Public Service Commission. In my case, unlike for the other experts, no action was taken. The Permanent Secretary seemed to feign misunderstanding of the process. Despite others being successfully absorbed into the government, the request for my absorption never materialised. I later understood the reasons for this. First and foremost, setting up an energy division, with a professional head, which I was advocating for, was deemed to limit the power and control that the Permanent Secretary had had. But what I only discovered at that point was that I was expected to donate a percentage of my salary to the poorly-paid Permanent Secretary, known as "facilitation", which I was not aware of and had failed to do. All the reasons for the hostility towards me became clear.

I spent six months without receiving a salary, but I was determined to move on, as there was so much to accomplish. The streetlight project had to start and I was rather concerned that without the technical expertise within the ministry, things could get out of hand. Many of the reforms I recommended had still not been made. The streetlights project was of particular concern. This was a major project and the necessary preparatory activities for it had not been done. The money we raised through the payments for bids was intended to be used to support the preparatory activities for the project, including visits to the district capitals to select the sites and make arrangements for security, care and maintenance of the lights. I was instructed that the payments for the bids were to be channelled to the government's consolidated budget, which I did. However, all my requests for funds to prepare the project were not provided. For me, the consolidated fund was a black hole into which monies paid could not be recuperated for the services for which they were meant.

In addition, I believed that the high cost of the project justified the setting up of a dedicated unit to monitor its implementation. I was shocked when I visited Freetown later that this had not been done and that decisions on technical matters were being made for political reasons. I was travelling along the main Wilkinson Road and noticed that the streetlight poles were being put too close to each other. I was told that the decision to do so was made by the senior officials of the ministry, who thought that the lights were too dull and that to increase their luminosity they had to be placed closer together, against the physics behind luminance. There were upcoming elections and it was politically correct to speed up the project.

Looking back, even though I could not finish all the work I had started, I had set the process of implementing the much-needed changes in progress. I thus found my return to Sierra Leone most rewarding. I had spear-headed the drawing up of the energy policy and strategy, created a technical department for energy within the Ministry of Energy and Water Resources, reformed the power sector, drew up the twin Electricity legislations and set in progress projects and mechanisms for the use of renewable energy technologies in the country.

Appreciation of my accomplishments was reflected in my elevation to become a Fellow of the Sierra Leone Institution of Engineers and my receipt of a *Woman of Excellence Award* for "Excellence in Engineering, Science and Technology" on the occasion of the 50th anniversary of Sierra Leone Independence.

PART THREE
SERVING HUMANITY AT THE UNITED NATIONS

"He who does not seize opportunity today will be unable to take tomorrow's opportunities".-African Proverb

Chapter 7
Entry to the United Nations

A Surprise Visit

It was the year 1980. I left home on a bright June morning for another day of work as a lecturer at the Fourah Bay College. The sun's soft beams hinted at a promising day, and I had carefully planned my schedule. After dropping off my five children at school on the college campus, I will go to my office and spend the morning carefully preparing my lectures for the impending afternoon classes.

'There is an Indian wearing a turban waiting for you in the waiting room', announced the messenger, as I arrived at the office.

'What? An Indian in turban? I don't know any'. I thought to myself, *'There goes the time I need to prepare my lecture for the afternoon'.*

'Good morning, Mrs Stevens,' the visitor greeted me warmly as we strolled towards my office. He was a middle-aged man with a good build who projected the assurance of an economist. He gave a polite grin and apologised for his sudden appearance, saying the phone lines were then down.

'I am Agit Bhalla, the Director of the Technology and Employment Branch at the International Labour Organization', he introduced himself. 'I'm currently on a recruitment mission in West Africa. Yesterday, I happened to come across your curriculum vitae, and it struck me that your profile aligns perfectly with the kind of talent we're seeking. We're embarking on a two-year project funded by the Norwegian Government, which aims to introduce technologies that can alleviate the burdens faced by rural women across Africa. I'm here to gauge your interest in this project'.

His words carried an air of earnestness, making it clear that he saw potential in my skills and experience. I pondered his proposal, realizing that this opportunity could be the next significant step in my career journey.

His expression, lit with the glow of enthusiasm, as he handed me two pages, outlining the project idea a blueprint for a dream project. As I perused the contents, it became clear that the initiative was both commendable and closely aligned with the work I had been deeply engaged in. With growing interest, I posed a question that was paramount to me: 'Could this project potentially be based here in Sierra Leone?'

His response was swift but carried a certain weight, like a hammer driving a nail. 'Oh, no', he replied. 'It will be based in Geneva, Switzerland. The project requires my direct supervision'.

The project glimmered with promise, a beacon of light in the darkness, addressing critical issues and challenges I had faced first-hand. Yet the thought of returning to Europe, even for a worthy cause, was a weight upon my heart, a burden I could hardly bear.

Six years past, I had made the difficult decision to leave behind my studies, my husband, and my home in London, all in the pursuit of a better life and a stable and supportive environment for my children. I believed that it was a place where they could thrive.

Upon discovering my fifth pregnancy, I knew that returning to any Western country was not an option. Financially, I simply could not afford the kind of support necessary to raise five children in Geneva. Sierra Leone, on the other hand, offered me the sweet embrace of family assistance: nannies, cooks, cleaners, and gardeners were all readily available. With my mother's presence and an extended network of relatives, I felt embraced by a supportive community. It was nothing short of a paradise, a stark contrast to my previous life in London.

Glancing again at the job description, I noted the phrase "frequent travel to the field". The realization struck me like a chord. The commitment would take me away from the sanctuary I had painstakingly built. I was content in my beautifully subsidized housing on the campus, my children attending the campus school. My salary, though modest, allowed me to save a substantial portion each month. What more could I possibly need or desire?

'No', I said decisively, 'I am afraid that I cannot take up such an appointment. Thank you for considering me'.

He looked down, his eyes like a pair of lead weights. He found it hard to imagine that an African woman would turn down the chance to work for the UN. But he could tell I was determined by the expression on my face, a mask of steel.

'Well, why don't you think about it?' He said as he got up to leave.

'Yes, I will', I responded with no other purpose than to get him out of my office so I could start preparing my lecture.

Mr Bhalla's resolve remained unwavering. A telex message was waiting for me at the post office a few days later. It said simply, 'Interested in your candidacy, awaiting your positive reply'.

I stood in the post office and thought about the message. I knew I had to make a decision at that very moment. I quickly completed a telex form with the straightforward message, 'Sorry, I cannot accept your offer'. I handed it in and experienced a wave of relief.

But it appeared that fate had different ideas. A month or so later, Enyina, a young Nigerian ILO officer, who was in Sierra Leone on a mission got in touch with me to arrange a meeting. 'Not again', I thought.

Enyina, a sturdy and earnest individual arrived at my office. After our greetings, he got straight to the point. 'Please tell me', he inquired, 'Why are you declining such an intriguing opportunity? My boss, Mr Bhalla is greatly disheartened and has tasked me with finding out if there was any way to persuade you'.

Recognising the importance of honesty, I decided to be candid. 'The simple truth is that I cannot accept a job in Geneva, especially one with frequent field travel. I'm a single parent raising five children, all under the age of eleven'.

Curious, Enyina continued, 'How do you manage your responsibilities currently?'

'Well, my mother helps take care of my children', I replied.

'So, why don't you tell him that?'

'And then, there is my job', I added. 'This project lasts for two years only. I do not want to lose my job'.

'Why don't you ask for a leave of absence from the university?'

As I lay in bed that night, the calming sound of raindrops tapping on the rooftop transported me back to my early years. I could see myself sitting in the living room under the shelf where the radio receiver was placed, with my uncle, listening to the BBC on gloomy nights. On rainy days, this had been my haven, giving me the chance to indulge in this cherished activity when I could not play outside. Those experiences had inspired hopes that as I grew older, I would play a role in addressing global challenges.

And now, looking up at the black velvet sky, imagining the sparkling lights of Geneva, I had reached a crossroads in my life. Unexpectedly, a job offer to work for the United Nations, an organization that embodied my childhood dreams, had been bestowed upon me like a golden chalice.

'Where had the years gone?' I mused; my mind awash with memories of youthful aspirations.

'Could this be my chance to turn those dreams into reality, to learn more about the UN from the inside and perhaps have an impact on the lives of the less fortunate?'

Though my engineering background craved practical experience, I knew that spending two years in the captivating world of the UN would sharpen my skills for future endeavours. The allure of learning French, a language I cherished, while in Geneva, also signalled like a siren song.

As these thoughts swirled through my mind, a resolve crystallised within me. I would accept the UN offer, but only for a limited two-year span. However, my commitment hinged on a critical condition; I needed assurance of assistance to care for my five children. Buoyed by Enyina's wise counsel, I penned a message to Mr Bhalla, my words conveying my enthusiasm tempered by the challenge: *'Interested but unable to accept due to single-handed responsibility for five children, all under eleven years old, in Geneva.'*

I sent it before leaving the campus post office. The following day, there was an exchange of telex messages. The first was from Mr Bhalla, who wanted to know who was now assisting me with the children.

'My mother', I affirmed.

The UN official's words were a lifeline, offering a glimmer of hope in a sea of uncertainty. With my husband out of the picture, he indicated that I could classify my mother as a primary dependent and bring her with me to Geneva, with UN support. This was good news, and with that problem solved, I knew that I had to seize this opportunity. I later learnt that this offer was exceptional within the framework of the United Nations.

Little convincing was needed to get my Mum to come with us. She was a kind woman who had successfully raised five kids on her own as a single mum while working nonstop to make sure we were all taken care of. My academic successes were made possible by her unwavering encouragement, which helped me overcome many challenges. With a heart full of gratitude, I approached my mother with the proposal. Her eyes lit up with excitement, and she immediately agreed to join me on this journey. I knew that with her by my side, I could face any challenge that came my way.

With my mother's support secured, I felt a surge of confidence. I finalized my request for a two-year leave of absence to work for the UN and submitted it to the university's principal. To my surprise, the approval from the University Senate came through within days, as if the puzzle pieces were falling into place by some divine design.

Chapter 8
Employment at the International Labour Office

August 1980

I boarded a plane bound for Geneva, the city of my dreams. My heart was brimming with excitement and anticipation. I had been offered a position as an International Labour Organization Village Technology Expert, and I was eager to embark on this new chapter in my life.

Ifthikar, a slender Bangladeshi man who was the ILO official in charge of the project, greeted me at the airport. As we drove to the hotel, I could not help but be captivated by the city's serene ambience. Everything appeared to be straight out of a fairy tale: spotlessly clean, meticulously organized, and breathtakingly beautiful. I was particularly fascinated by a truck trailer washing the streets with soapy water. It was a sight I had never imagined before. As we continued through the city, I was drawn to the Jet d'Eau, a magnificent fountain with a 140-metre-high water jet that gracefully rose from the shores of Lake Geneva. It was a symbol of the city's grandeur and sophistication.

Geneva immediately impressed me. Nestled between the

majestic Alps and the rolling Jura Mountains, the city adorned the banks of Lake Léman, also known as Lake Geneva. The terrain of the area, which gradually ascends to the mountains from the lakeside, was evocative of Freetown. The surroundings' stunning natural beauty was incredibly inspiring and motivating. It was no wonder that so many renowned authors and intellectuals, including Mozart, Tchaikovsky, Wagner, Lord George Byron, Victor Hugo, Alexandre Dumas, Dostoevsky, Leo Tolstoy, Mark Twain, and Mary Shelley, had spent some of their most prolific years in and around Geneva.

Geneva, housing the headquarters of the Red Cross and many other humanitarian organizations, has acquired the moniker "Capital of Peace". Geneva is also known as the "Kitchen of the United Nations" because, unlike New York, the majority of operations in critical sectors such as health, trade, refugees, telecommunications, and intellectual property are carried out in different countries by organizations with headquarters in Geneva or branches of organizations whose headquarters were based elsewhere. The "Rive Gauche" in Geneva is home to the headquarters of several bodies of United Nations.

My cab ride to the ILO the next day was a whirlwind tour of the United Nations campus, passing by the World Health Organization, the World Intellectual Property Organization, the International Telecommunications Union, and the United Nations Geneva Office. But one structure stood out from the rest: an impressive grey colossus with granite walls that loomed majestically in the distance. As we drove up to it, I saw the sign: *International Labour Organization.*

I alighted from the taxi, my heart pounding with anticipation. Here I was, a modest girl from one of the world's most remote corners, about to commence work in this iconic institution—a cornerstone of global social justice that predated even the establishment of the United Nations. Founded in 1919 in the wake of the First World War, the ILO carried a formidable mission: to champion the rights of workers and promote social and economic justice. Its remarkable legacy was recognized in 1969 with the awarding of the Nobel Peace Prize, honouring its contributions to fostering international cooperation and peace, advocating for decent work and fair labour practices, and providing technical assistance to developing nations. Nestled within the ILO World Employment Programme, the Technology and Employment Branch was to be my new realm of endeavour.

The ILO Office

Upon arriving at the Technology and Employment Branch, I was greeted by Michelle, the branch's efficient yet somewhat condescending British secretary. She led me through the premises, explaining the various departments and their functions. When I entered "YES" under "Initials" on one of the forms I was asked to fill, an amusing thing occurred. Michelle tried to educate this woman from Africa, by telling me, with an air of authority, that initials referred to the first letters of my name. 'But these are my initials: Yvette Elizabeth Stevens', I said with a good-natured grin. My response caught her off guard and possibly embarrassed her.

The project team was made up of three people: Vivian, a motivated economist from Brazil, Eugenia, a compassionate sociologist from Ghana, and myself, an engineer. Our first goal throughout the first nine months was to create the groundwork for the project—a conceptual framework aimed at studying the daily routines of African rural women and identifying technology that could alleviate their responsibilities.

I met with a number of colleagues and was able to participate in meetings of the Office. I felt like a fish out of water in the Employment Department, surrounded by renowned colleagues, the majority of whom were economists. My engineering background set me apart, and this was my first experience working with social scientists. I noticed a big language barrier early on—our terms and viewpoints were significantly different. As an engineer, my thought process was simple: identify the jobs performed by women, obtain the required devices, and distribute them properly. That was the solution in my thoughts.

The village technology expert

Our primary goal during those early months was to develop the intricate conceptual framework that would pave the way for the integration of technologies into the lives of rural women across Africa. However, our team dynamics were anything but harmonious. Eugenia and Vivian, each with their own unique perspectives and passions, frequently found themselves embroiled in heated debates. Vivian was obsessed with economic feasibility, always looking for methods to ensure the programmes made money for the women engaged. Eugenia's sympathetic heart, on the other hand, tended toward tackling bigger socioeconomic- and cultural concerns. As an engineer observing the situation, I often felt like a bystander, quietly yearning for consensus so that we could direct our combined efforts towards concrete implementation.

We ultimately arrived at a point where our conceptual framework resonated with the director's vision, gratifying everyone involved, after what felt like a drawn-out dance of perspectives. This was a big milestone—the go-ahead to move our efforts beyond the planning stage. Our gaze was drawn to the field, specifically to villages in Ghana, Kenya, and my own country of Sierra Leone. These locations were to serve as our living laboratories, where we would conduct surveys and collect data directly from the rural women whose lives we hoped to improve.

During my first year at the ILO, a poignant experience left an indelible mark on my perspective. With the conceptual framework approved, I undertook a mission to Sierra Leone, to gather insights from rural villages for a comprehensive technology survey. In the company of officials from the Ministry of Social Welfare, we embarked on a journey that took me through familiar landscapes, yet brought forth a renewed sense of awareness of life in the rural areas.

As we approached the seaside settlements, the clean, unspoilt beaches stretched out like pearls down the shore. The raw beauty was evident, and it hit me once more—Sierra Leone was a place of enormous potential, rich in natural resources and promising wealth. Nonetheless, the sad reality remained that our country was still struggling with poverty.

The inconsistency between the country's abundant resources and its ongoing challenges drove me to consider beyond the current project I was working on. Something had to change, and it had to be bigger than the survey we were conducting. This journey strengthened my determination to contribute to long-term change that will improve the lives of Sierra Leoneans.

When we arrived at the village of Fallu in northern Sierra Leone, a greeting ceremony was already underway to welcome the "expert" who had arrived from Geneva, as was the custom. As I got closer to the village, I could not help but be mesmerized by the colourful tableau that had been painstakingly set up. The women dressed to the nines in their festive and brightest garb, truly donning their "Sunday Best." The undulating swing of their hips appeared to connect with the very heartbeat of the earth as the drummers' repetitive beat set the tone for their dance.

The celebrations extended beyond the dance, with masked "devils" making an appearance as well, a beloved component of Sierra Leone's rich cultural legacy. These complex masks, worn for important occasions, were decorated with beautiful patterns and held special significance in the community's customs.

A hint of disappointment was evident on the Village Chief's

face as the lively dance gradually transitioned into a seated gathering at the village community centre. An unexpected turn of events had occurred. The villagers had been anticipating the arrival of an "expert", often stereotyped as a white male who did not speak their language. The Chief's spokesperson voiced their bewilderment and questioned why the expected expert had not shown up.

In a flash of insight, we understood the source of the malaise. I did not fit the description of the expert they had in mind. My presence as a local woman seemed to challenge their basic notion of what an expert looked like. The Social Welfare Department representative struggled to explain to the villagers that I was the "expert" whom they had been waiting for, the communication gap compounded by their preconceived notions.

The Village Chief, a shrewd politician, navigated this tricky situation with finesse. He seized the opportunity to deliver a powerful message, confidently addressing the gathered people, telling them that the "expert" was not only a woman but also someone from their own country, who had broken down the barriers that had traditionally restricted such roles to men from the "First World". He then addressed the parents, utilising this incident as an advocacy opportunity.

'Now you have seen how a female compatriot has made it to the United Nations, you should realize that educating a girl child is not without laudable reward. So, tomorrow morning, I would like to see you all bring your girls to enrol in school'.

The Chief's statements struck a deep chord with me because they described the path I had started, one that aimed to shatter stereotypes, alter perspectives, and spur advancement.

The village was profoundly impressed by the Chief's message. The next morning presented a remarkable scene outside the school: a lengthy queue of parents, accompanied by their daughters, all brimming with eagerness to pursue their education. This sight stood as a potent testament to the capacity to dismantle preconceived notions and ignite transformative change.

But it was the Chief's parting words that struck me.

'Well,' he said, 'you are one of us. You have come to see us and we have given you our time and efforts. You are one of us. If you do not return to offer us assistance, we leave it to your conscience'.

His candid remarks left an indelible imprint on me, serving as a guiding beacon throughout my decades-long career at the UN. It was a defining moment in my career, one that cemented my commitment to translating goals into tangible impact.

Upon my return to Geneva, I promptly briefed my Director, Mr Bhalla, about the mission, filled with a sense of accomplishment and confidence. I narrated the heartening interactions, the authentic connection I had established with the locals, and the promises I had made to personally ensure they received the aid they deserved. The excitement in my voice was palpable as I queried about our plans to equip the women with the much-needed equipment.

However, I was ill-prepared for the jolt that followed. His response was a blend of hesitation and indifference, akin to someone grappling with a foreign language. I eagerly enquired about our next course of action, but his reply doused my optimism with a chilling dose of reality. It was as if he failed to grasp that I was seeking more than just a report—I yearned for a tangible outcome that would bridge the chasm between rhetoric and action.

'This is a research project and the outcome, as stated in the project document is to be a publication, which could come out in your names, and which will advise the governments on the course of actions that they should take to improve the lot of the women'.

'Oh no', I said. 'This cannot be the case'. I was flabbergasted. *'What?'* I thought to myself, *'All this effort was to get a publication to our credit?'*

Tormented by the Chief's poignant words, I found myself making a fervent appeal to him—an appeal imbued with tears and an unyielding desire for transformation. I beseeched him to contemplate the harsh realities that these rural women confronted daily—the ceaseless labour under the merciless sun and the relentless downpour. 'Could we not', I pleaded, 'transcend beyond the realm of mere reports and statistics, and genuinely reach out to these deserving women with a helping hand?'

That conversation, marked by my fervent entreaty, left me feeling emotionally drained and deeply disheartened. The weight of my own emotions mingled with the immense responsibility I felt for those whose voices often went unheard. I could not shake off the sense of guilt that followed me.

A week later, a glimmer of hope emerged when Mr Bhalla summoned me to his office. His words, spoken with a touch of surprise, carried a promise that lifted my spirits. 'I have good news for you', he declared. 'We have some project funds remaining and have secured approval from the donors to use it for a pilot project in villages in Sierra Leone'. As those words sank in, relief washed over me like a soothing balm. It was a ray of light breaking through the clouds of bureaucracy and apathy.

He did not stop there. With an encouraging tone, he revealed another opportunity that was on the horizon. 'And if you're interested', he continued, 'We could begin preparations for a follow-up project in Ghana. The Dutch Government has expressed interest in supporting it'.

I had initially felt uncomfortable and disappointed, but it soon gave way to a newfound feeling of purpose and tenacity. I was reminded that even within the intricate web of multilateral organizations and their protocols, change—however gradual—was in fact achievable.

'What a relief'.

I returned to Fallu, the village I had visited earlier, to deliver equipment for cassava processing to the women. According to our conceptual framework, we were to ensure that this equipment did not get taken over by the men, as was the case with innovations introduced in rural areas. We were thus required to oversee the formation of women's cooperatives, train the women in the use of the equipment and provide basic business training to them.

The village burst into a flurry of celebratory activities and the Women's Cassava Processing Committee was elected, a wave of fulfilment swept over me. My pledge was coming to fruition, and I could almost savour the gratification of witnessing a subtle yet significant transformation in progress.

As my initial two-year tenure with the ILO was nearing its conclusion, I found myself at a crossroads, contemplating my next move. Driven by a desire to see my project meet its objectives, and after gaining the consent of my director to extend my contract, I boldly sought a one-year extension of my university leave of absence. I dispatched the request in late July 1982, filled with optimism yet tinged with a hint of anxiety about the impending decision. I waited for a response.

As time ticked away during the waiting period, I felt an irresistible urge to revisit Fallu. This time around, I was not merely an observer but a catalyst for change. My mission was to ensure that the machinery designed to expedite cassava processing did not just remain intriguing devices. Instead, they were to transform into powerful tools that would empower the women of the community.

In our idealistic blueprint, we had overlooked the deep-rooted traditional structures that dictated the village dynamics. The Village Chief's supreme authority, for instance, was an undeniable force. Our project, aimed at fostering women's agency, found itself at odds with age-old norms that vested all power in the Chief's hands.

However, I was oblivious to the unexpected turn of events that awaited me. Amid our jubilation, the Chief's voice echoed above the merriment. He asserted his right to supervise the equipment, citing its origin from far-off Geneva and his role as the Chief to justify his claim. But the village women, fortified and emboldened by their new tools, stood their ground. They refused to be marginalized. Thus began a power struggle.

Ultimately, the Chief had wielded his authority, confiscated the equipment, and handed it over to a local businessman to operate for profit. In the eyes of the women, their hope and empowerment were being commodified and sold back to them at an exorbitant price. The ensuing protestations echoed their sense of ownership and the essence of what the project was meant to achieve.

The community of Fallu found itself at a juncture where tradition was colliding with change, and the palpable tension was evident. The young men of the village were on the verge of stepping in to support the women, their mothers, who had dared to challenge norms and embrace empowerment. These young men were prepared to reclaim the equipment forcibly, driven by a sense of duty to protect their mothers and their heritage. Upon my return to the community, I could sense the brewing conflict. Recognising that a confrontational approach would only exacerbate the situation, I promptly convened a meeting in the communal court. As we gathered under the vast expanse of the open sky, I endeavoured to bridge the divide between the conflicting parties.

In a surprising turn of events, the Chief stunned us all. He unveiled a suitcase filled with money that had been amassed over the period, in an unexpected display of transparency. He took responsibility for this money, affirming that he had safeguarded it.

As I facilitated the discussion, the Chief's demeanour began to soften. However, the women remained steadfast in their demand, but advocated for the inclusion of at least one male member in their committee, deviating from our initial plan, but recognizing the need for a balanced approach. This unforeseen compromise shed light on the evolving dynamics of the village.

A resolution was reached through mutual understanding among the parties. The women retained control over the equipment, supported by a cooperative organization comprising both men and women. This demonstrated the power of dialogue and adaptability and highlighted how embracing unexpected ideas and navigating uncharted territory are often essential for sustainable change.

At last, I eventually received a response to my letter sent in July 1982 seeking an extension of my leave of absence from the University, which sent ripples through my journey as my commitment to this mission deepened. The letter, dated February 1st, 1983, did not reach me until late March. It stated that I had until February 28, 1983, to return to my post or face being deemed as having abandoned it. So, according to this letter, I had already lost my job at the university.

For me, this letter held a great significance—it was a crossroads of its own. The choice to remain dedicated to the transformative work I was part of meant that I had relinquished the stability and familiarity of my academic career. As the saying in my country goes, 'When you fall into the water, you have to swim'. With this in mind, I forged ahead, undeterred by the uncertainties that lay before me and resolute in my commitment to driving change on a broader stage.

The funding for the project was concluding, and I needed to find a job. It was not easy navigating the murky waters of a job search within the International Labour Organization (ILO). Despite having been given special authority to apply for substantive posts, the issue proved difficult to deal with in reality. I soon learned that there was intense rivalry and rigid standards that frequently did not match my background. Although there were a few open opportunities, there were a large number of candidates. The ILO's distinctive method of choosing candidates through tough competition made things more difficult. Also, the ILO applied strict geographic quotas, based on the size of countries and their financial contribution to the ILO, and this added another layer of complexity.

Just as I was on the verge of losing hope, one morning brought a glimmer of optimism. I received a call from Samir Radwan, a high-ranking official from the Rural Employment Branch at ILO, which was located on the same floor as ours. He extended an invitation to meet him in his office.

'We've been approached by the United Nations High Commissioner for Refugees to help provide self-reliance activities for Ethiopian refugees in Eastern Sudan', he said. 'We've seen that your work over the past two and a half years has been successful in providing employment for the disadvantaged, so we're hoping you'd be interested in working on a team that would be addressing this under a joint ILO/UNHCR project'.

'Would I be interested?' I really did not have a choice, did I?

Stepping into my new role as the Income Generation Activities Expert, I was equipped with the foundational knowledge I had garnered from my previous experiences. At this juncture, I found myself collaborating with a diverse team, their varied skills and backgrounds mirroring the global issues we were striving to address. Azita from Iran brought her unique perspective, while Tony and Janine from the UK contributed their expertise. Under the adept leadership of Samir, our supervisor from Egypt, Abdul Megit, a Somali, further enriched our team dynamics.

Our mission was centred on a significant initiative that involved conducting a labour market survey and a refugee skills assessment. These studies were instrumental in pinpointing labour market gaps and potential employment opportunities in Eastern Sudan, which could be leveraged by Eritrean refugees residing in the region. The Sudanese government had expressed its desire for the local economy in Eastern Sudan to benefit from the refugee presence and had extended its support by allocating land for farming in refugee settlements. With the official approval from the Sudanese Government in hand, we were ready to commence our work.

The warmth and hospitality of the Sudanese people left a lasting impression on me as I embarked on my inaugural journey there. We collaborated closely with the Commissioner for Refugees, Ambassador El Ahmadi, a remarkable individual. His cheerful disposition and ever-present smile seemed to illuminate every room he entered. His playful remark, 'You mean you don't like us in Sudan?' whenever I had to return to Geneva, encapsulated the amiable atmosphere he cultivated. His spirit exemplified the bonds that can form even in challenging circumstances, making working with him a genuine delight.

Our journey took us on a road trip from Khartoum to Eastern Sudan, located northeast of Sudan's central plains, characterized by desert, semi-arid terrains, and coastal lowlands. After traversing this diverse landscape for several hours, we reached El-Gadarif, the capital of Eastern Sudan. This city, nestled amidst mountains on three sides, would serve as our base for the nine-month duration of the project, interspersed with regular trips to Geneva. El-Gadarif was a bustling hub for trade in cotton, grains, sesame seeds, and fodder harvested in the nearby regions. It was a vibrant mosaic of central Sudan's mixed ethnicities. Our initial visit during the rainy season revealed vast pools of water and verdant meadows dotted with various species of acacia trees.

From El Gadarif, we ventured to most of the refugee camps and settlements dispersed across Eastern Sudan. Access was not always straightforward. In several instances, we had to navigate on makeshift rubber dinghies - a daunting prospect for a non-swimmer like myself. We interacted with refugees and conducted market surveys at each refugee site to identify potential activities that could be promoted among the refugees.

We took advantage of our stay in El-Gadarif to visit Kassala, a renowned town positioned on the northern outskirts of Eastern Sudan, nestled near the Eritrean border. Kassala's distinct appeal stemmed from its breathtaking red hills, which rose sharply from the surrounding plains. These hills, like sweeping waves in a stormy sea, produced a stunning panorama, adding to the town's charm. A spring sprang forth cool and pleasant water from one of these hills, thought to have a compelling power, enticing travellers to return to Kassala time and time again. I was enthralled by this natural wonder and the vitality it seemed to provide. I drank the spring water, but I have not returned since that unforgettable experience in 1983.

As our project neared completion, a diverse array of programs surfaced, each designed to guide refugees towards self-reliance. These initiatives were structured around three primary areas of focus. The first approach aimed at integrating refugees into local labour markets, which were grappling with acute shortages due to the emigration of skilled Sudanese workers. Our second suite of activities proposed the establishment of a revolving fund, envisioned as a financial instrument to stimulate both collective and individual small-scale initiatives in areas directly impacted by the refugee presence. Lastly, the final set of actions concentrated on initiating income-generating activities in both rural and urban settings.

This extensive portfolio was devised to directly benefit approximately 55,000 refugees. It encompassed a range of activities including dairy and poultry farming, fishing, beekeeping, electrical and mechanical workshops, handicrafts, woodworking, leatherwork, and secretarial services, among others. As the project concluded in early 1984, we harboured hopes that these activities would not only enhance the lives of refugees but also stimulate local economic growth and instil a sense of empowerment and self-reliance.

After the UNHCR project, I endeavoured to carve out a niche that aligned with my skills and aspirations within the Technology and Employment Branch. I found myself once again in a position to bolster the efforts of the ILO, leveraging my engineering background. This was particularly evident in my engagement with the UNHCR in Sudan. I consistently applied my engineering expertise in this role to address challenges and effect change.

Despite the undoubtedly arduous journey that lay ahead, I was determined to press on. Armed with my skills and experiences, I was resolved to carve out a meaningful trajectory both within and beyond the organization.

'Yvette', Mr Bhalla said, 'When I finished the work on the Sudan project, I have something that would interest you as an engineer'. My eyes lit up.

'I have secured funds for your services for the next three months to work with me to identify case studies of the application of new technologies in traditional activities in developing countries around the world'.

The landscape in 1984 was starkly different from today's, especially in developing countries. Many technologies that are now common were largely unexplored for traditional activities.

This offered me an opportunity to delve into avant-garde subjects like solar photovoltaic technology, which had captivated my interest during my tenure at the Fourah Bay College, the potential of personal computers, biotechnology, satellite technology, and microelectronics to support established practices in industries such as metal extraction, weaving, or even biogas production piqued my curiosity.

This exploration culminated in an ILO publication entitled *Blending of New and Traditional Technologies,* which I had the privilege of co-editing. This project encapsulated my final three months at the ILO and left me with a sense of accomplishment upon its completion. I realized that my work transcended technology; it was about empowering communities and bridging the divide between innovation and time-honoured practices.

Chapter 9

On "Loan" from ILO to UNHCR, the United Nations Refugee Agency

As a result of the appreciation of my work in Sudan, the UNHCR signed a Memorandum of Understanding ILO, under which I was to be sent "on loan" to UNHCR to serve as an expert in income generation, in a bid to boost their efforts at promoting self-reliance of refugees.

Expert in income generating activities

Within the framework of the UNHCR's comprehensive strategy to address refugee challenges, there are three long-term solutions that are prominent: voluntary repatriation to the country of origin when conditions allow, local integration in the host country subject to mutual agreement, and resettlement in a third country. While these solutions are pursued, the UNHCR places a strong emphasis on fostering self-sufficiency among refugees. This strategic approach aims to empower refugees to actively contribute to their own well-being and that of the local economy, thereby alleviating the burden on both the UNHCR and host countries.

In this role, my primary responsibility was to identify and seize opportunities for implementing self-reliance projects among refugees. This encompassed initiatives that not only eased the pressure on humanitarian aid but also equipped refugees with the skills, resources, and means to sustain themselves and their families. By promoting self-sufficiency while working towards long-term solutions to displacement, we aimed to foster resilience, dignity, and a sense of agency among displaced individuals.

Upon my appointment to the UNHCR technical division, I was inundated with requests from regional bureaux and country offices worldwide. They sought my assistance in promoting self-sufficiency initiatives for refugees. Driven by the growing recognition of self-sufficiency's value, I felt compelled to respond to these requests and share my expertise. Consequently, my schedule quickly transformed into a whirlwind of field missions that took me to all corners of the globe.

In the year 1986 alone, these missions consumed a whopping 186 days of my time. Each journey presented its own set of problems and opportunities, ranging from collaborating with varied communities to developing methods that went beyond agriculture-focused solutions. My colleague in the technical area was an agriculturist, and my job was to find non-agricultural work opportunities.

However, finding acceptable career possibilities was frequently like looking for a needle in a haystack. The regions in which refugees found themselves were typically remote, with limited access to vital production supplies and essentially non-existent markets. The reality was different in the cities, but as daunting: high unemployment rates, strong competition for jobs against local nationals, and limited options. I attempted to construct paths toward self-sufficiency within these difficult settings, a process that required both ingenuity and tenacity.

Working as an Evaluation Officer

In the later stages of my career with UNHCR, I embraced a new role as an evaluation officer, which proved to be immensely rewarding. This position offered me a panoramic view of UNHCR's multifaceted activities, enabling me to delve into various sectors and derive insightful observations. Armed with these evaluations, I was able to strategize for the enhancement and refinement of our programs. An added satisfaction was the fact that my suggestions were taken seriously by the upper management, often leading to tangible changes in programme direction. However, the realm of evaluation is not without its complexities. In an organization like UNHCR, which operates much like a close-knit family, my honest assessments were not always welcomed by programme managers. Some of my well-intentioned proposals were seen as criticisms and were met with resistance or even hostility from programme managers and their teams, who occasionally failed to appreciate the insights that an "outsider" like me could offer.

At the onset of each year, we would compile a list of countries slated for evaluation, a list that would subsequently receive approval from the Evaluation Committee. However, Country Representatives and Desk Officers were not always receptive. The mere inclusion of their programmes on this list would sometimes elicit questions like, 'Why my programme?' This reaction mirrored the inherent defensiveness associated with having one's work scrutinized, reminding us of the delicate balance we had to maintain in conducting these evaluations.

As I embarked on my evaluation missions, I repeatedly encountered one challenge: the deliberate withholding of information. I recall how my colleague Klaus Wulff, a very enthusiastic Dane and I transformed into amateur detectives. Driven by determination, we would work into the early hours of the morning, remaining at the office long after everyone else had departed. We would meticulously sift through files late into the night, uncovering hidden truths that had been concealed from us during the day. Despite these hurdles, our commitment to transparency remained steadfast.

However, my unwavering dedication to honesty in my assessments came with a price. Friendships were strained and relationships frayed as some began to suspect that I was being used to gather evidence against them. It was an uncomfortable situation that tested both my resilience and commitment to my principles. The strain eventually became overwhelming, prompting me to explore other options. After four years as an evaluation officer, my former boss at the technical section, Omar Bakhet announced his departure to take up a UNDP job. His position became vacant, and I seized the opportunity to apply for it. I was selected for the post, and in August 1990, I assumed the role of Chief of the Programme and Technical Support Section, or PTSS for short.

This new position put me in charge of a diversified and brilliant staff of twenty professionals from ten different nations. They specialized in a wide range of subjects, including health, nutrition, education, agriculture, physical planning, water supply, sanitation, engineering, the environment, and economics. The task was challenging, but the idea of leading this vibrant team filled me with excitement and resolve. It was a watershed moment in my UNHCR career, one that would determine my destiny for years to come.

Chief of the Programme and Technical Support Section

As the Chief of the Programme and Technical Support Section (PTSS), my responsibilities were extensive. We were tasked with supervising all on-ground technical operations, which encompassed the development of UNHCR policies and plans across various technical domains. A key responsibility was providing guidance and advice to our field-based colleagues on technical matters, a role I found deeply fulfilling. Our duties expanded to include coordinating planning efforts across diverse technical areas. A critical aspect of our mission was evaluating requests for technical assistance from over 100 countries, and I was committed to devising efficient methods to deliver the necessary support. To augment our capabilities, we maintained a roster of technical consultants who could be called upon at short notice to lend their expertise.

My interactions with my team members were largely positive. While some found the transition in our professional relationships challenging, I remained dedicated to fostering an atmosphere of respect and collaboration. Despite assuming a supervisory role, I made concerted efforts to preserve the rapport we had established over time. However, one individual seemed particularly resistant to working under a black woman's supervision.

This burly, pompous man appeared bewildered by the notion of a black woman in a leadership position. His actions reflected his scepticism, making my initial days as his supervisor challenging. However, one day, I decided it was time for an open dialogue. The air was heavy with anticipation as I invited him into my office.

I addressed the issue head-on, speaking in a firm yet empathetic tone. 'I understand the discomfort you might be experiencing, given my background as a black woman and our age difference', I stated. 'However, I want you to understand that despite our differences, I am your superior. I am here to lead and guide and I need your cooperation'.

His surprise was palpable as if my words had upended his world. Yet, this candid conversation managed to bridge the gap that had previously existed between us. Remarkably, our relationship transformed following this encounter. It served as a valuable lesson in communication, respect, and mutual understanding and he evolved from being a sceptic to an ally and friend. It was yet another testament to how overcoming preconceived notions and biases can pave the way for a collaborative foundation.

Involvement in major refugee emergencies

When I returned to head the technical support section dynamics relating to technical experts had undergone a significant shift. The technical specialists, once perceived as operating on the fringes, were now recognized as an integral part of UNHCR's operational machinery. Our experts' roles had gained recognition, and we were no longer battling for relevance. Instead, we found ourselves under pressure to deliver critical insights and contributions to field projects. Coinciding with this shift was the emergence of a new division—the Emergency Response Unit. Collaborating closely with this newly formed entity was crucial as we strategized and responded swiftly to crises. I was entrusted with the responsibility of being a key member of the emergency task forces, managing our response operations on the ground and participating in pivotal decision-making processes.

Despite my work not necessitating direct field trips, my involvement in these emergency task forces proved to be immensely rewarding. It allowed me to immerse myself in the intricate processes of developing and implementing refugee programs, contributing my ideas and experiences towards their successful execution. This marked a stark contrast to my previous role where I had been a bystander or stepped in post-facto to review programs developed by others.

Leading these emergency task forces was a moderately built American man, Eric Moris, who wore his concerns like a badge. His irritation was palpable, particularly when he observed any delays in the actions of various section heads. His urgency mirrored the high-stakes environment we were operating in—a region where swift decisions were often the difference between life and death, and key to alleviating the hardships of displaced communities.

'Our situation is nothing short of an emergency', he would repeatedly tell us. During our heated talks, this chairperson, a committed smoker, would frequently chain smoke, his cigarette smoke combining with the tension in the room.

The onset of the first Gulf Crisis, following Iraq's invasion of Kuwait, coincided with the early days of my new role. This marked the initiation of UNHCR's newly formed emergency response systems. Amidst this turmoil, my division was entrusted with the task of formulating contingency plans for prospective refugee camps in countries anticipating an influx of displaced individuals. To achieve this, I dispatched technical teams to Jordan, Syria, and Türkiye. However, due to the unpredictable nature of events, the swift resolution of the conflict ensured that these camps were never established. The conflict ended in February 1991, largely due to the massive mobilization and overwhelming power of foreign forces, under the umbrella of *Operation Desert Storm*.

The subsequent year saw a massive refugee crisis resulting from the ongoing conflict in Somalia. The country's unrest led to a surge of people seeking refuge in Kenya and Somalia. Approximately 150,000 individuals sought sanctuary in the northern regions of Kenya, near the border town of Liboi. However, the Kenyan government deemed it necessary to relocate them further inland, selecting Dadaab for this purpose. My division was responsible for planning for the Dadaab camps, which involved sending a team of specialists to Kenya to execute the task. This was another challenging phase in my UNHCR career, where my team and I grappled with the complexities of planning a safe haven amidst chaos and displacement.

In 1991, a spark of violence ignited in the former Yugoslavia, signalling a unique emergency unfolding in the heart of Europe. Despite this setting demanding a new set of technical skills, we managed to deploy professionals capable of providing assistance on emergency shelters and infrastructure restoration. The emergence of a severe crisis on European soil exposed the limitations of our refugee relief solutions. During this period, we found ourselves advocating for resource allocation for necessities like underpants, acknowledging that refugee needs were more multifaceted than we had previously assumed.

In my mind, I could not help but reflect, 'This should apply to African refugees as well'. I made a vow to advocate for equal treatment, to ensure that refugees on the African continent received the same level of consideration and support as those in Yugoslavia.

During my tenure as chief of the technical unit, the most gruelling experience was the horrific conflict in Rwanda in 1994. We at UNHCR had been closely monitoring the situation in Rwanda, and when the call came to prepare for a potential influx of 50,000 refugees, we diligently worked to devise a plan. My technical experts journeyed to Goma, Democratic Republic of the Congo, to formulate this comprehensive plan. They meticulously explored potential sources for building materials and camp equipment, laying the groundwork for camp expansion. With our plan in place and ready to implement our model emergency response, we felt equipped to effectively respond to the anticipated crisis.

However, when the situation in Rwanda escalated into an actual genocide, the scale of the influx far exceeded our projections. Our camp, designed to accommodate 50,000 individuals, was overwhelmed within a week as nearly a million refugees flooded across the Goma border. We were taken aback by the enormity of the humanitarian disaster unfolding before our eyes. Faced with such an unprecedented task, we grappled with the daunting question of how could we possibly manage and respond to such a massive influx.

The atmosphere in the emergency task force sessions was

charged with urgency, akin to a simmering cauldron. Refugees were streaming across the border like a tidal wave, inundating our well-laid plans. Our preparations had tragically fallen short for the magnitude of what was about to unravel before us. A torrent of phone calls poured in from governments and media outlets worldwide, each demanding answers and action. The situation was rapidly spiralling into an extraordinary crisis. Then, as if the challenges were not formidable enough, cholera reared its dreadful head, compounding the disaster.

Amidst this chaos, Eric's voice rang out across the table, his words underscored by anger and urgency, 'We need three doctors to be deployed by tomorrow'. It was a raw, unfiltered depiction of the colossal challenges looming ahead of us. With time running out and pressure mounting, we embarked on a relentless campaign of phone calls, scouring the globe for experts who could be mobilized at a moment's notice. However, despite our unwavering determination propelling us forward, identifying available professionals on such short notice proved overwhelming. The clock was ticking relentlessly, but returning to the task force meeting without a resolution was simply not an option.

I remember those sleepless nights vividly, my mind consumed by the seemingly insurmountable challenge of securing the consultants needed to fly to Goma. Even as this endeavour consumed every waking moment of my life, an underlying worry persisted. It was evident that having experts on-site would not fully resolve the situation unless they had access to the necessary tools and facilities. This stark reality was an uncomfortable truth to voice during intense task force discussions.

Our office transformed into a hub of activity with phones ringing incessantly and an unmistakable sense of urgency permeating the air. Reaching out to donor countries and organizations became an endless task as we sought the resources needed to address the escalating catastrophe. The urgency of the situation was widely publicized in media outlets and responses from contributors were swift and at times unexpectedly generous. Some even proposed deploying military resources for assistance. However, directing their well-intentioned aid in the most beneficial manner posed a challenge. Amid a flurry of appeals and offers, we found ourselves delicately balancing the acceptance of aid and ensuring that the assistance provided was truly suitable for the situation at hand. Walking this tightrope was difficult, and our reluctance to accept certain contributions left some donors discontented and restless. One specific incident stands out: the German military was ready to deploy an extremely advanced water treatment plant, a marvel of technology, which required daily infusion of expensive chemicals that we could not afford. However, our pragmatism prevailed as we emphasized that our real needs were simpler necessities like chlorine and large water storage tanks. This distinction was crucial because, in view of the absence of silt, the lake water only required basic treatment.

Many donations from "do-gooders" had to be turned down because they were inappropriate. Some of these included some nuns who wanted to send buffalos to the camps in Goma "to provide milk for the children", without thinking of the required consumption of scarce water by buffalos. There were also containers of clothing, including high-heeled shoes, being offered.

To put some order in the response, we systematically produced our assessment of the technical sector's needs and disseminated it to all those eager to assist. Our message underscored the inefficiency of shipping unsuitable commodities to the disaster area, as these items not only strained the limited airport handling capacity but also diverted resources from more pressing needs. As we managed the influx of well-intentioned individuals and groups, each eager to make a difference in their own way, it became a continuous struggle, akin to a tug-of-war.

Over time, coordinated efforts eventually brought the cholera outbreak under control. The hastily established camps were gradually taking shape, offering a glimmer of hope amidst the chaos. During one of our task force meetings, when things seemed to be improving, Eric, our ever-direct task force leader, posed a tough question to Sylvanna Foa, our outspoken head of communications, as to why the progress in controlling the cholera outbreak did not receive press coverage.

Sylvanna, known for her direct and honest communication style, responded without hesitation. 'You need to understand, Eric', she replied in a firm yet somewhat resigned tone. 'Bad news sells well. Good news rarely makes the front pages'.

Her remarks echoed a fundamental truth about media dynamics. It served as an unexpected lesson, reminding us how the media landscape often prioritizes sensational and disturbing stories over those of progress and perseverance. It was as if a curtain had been lifted, revealing the complexities of media coverage and the frequently harsh reality of public perception.

Working with partners in providing assistance in the technical sectors

In my role, I found myself liaising and coordinating with a diverse array of entities, including UN agencies, non-governmental organizations, and governments. These interactions were about more than just paperwork; they were about translating our technological expertise into tangible actions on the ground. One aspect of my job involved developing UNHCR's contributions to the Consolidated Appeal Process (CAP) for the countries under our purview. These publications served as blueprints for our interventions in critical sectors such as health, engineering, social services, education, and water supply. It was an intricate process of weaving together data, research, and strategies, all aimed at making a meaningful difference in the lives of refugees and displaced individuals.

However, my responsibilities extended even further. I was part of an initiative to bridge the gap between refugee aid and long-term development activities. This involved collaborating with key United Nations agencies such as UNFPA, UNDP, and UNICEF. Our objective was to advocate for a more sustainable approach to humanitarian relief—one that not only addressed the immediate needs of refugees but also laid the foundation for their long-term well-being. Amid these high-stakes discussions and strategic planning sessions, I found myself representing UNHCR on numerous international platforms. A notable milestone was my participation in the 1994 United Nations International Conference on Population and Development (ICPD) in Cairo. Standing alongside fellow delegates from around the world, I understood the significance of our collective efforts to shape policies that would impact the lives of millions.

Chairing the Working Group on the situation of women in UNHCR

As I transitioned into the realm of middle-level management, a new set of responsibilities awaited me, each presenting unique challenges and opportunities to effect lasting change. One of the most significant roles I assumed was as Chair of UNHCR's Permanent Working Group on the Situation of Women, a pivotal position that came my way through the nomination by the esteemed High Commissioner, Sadako Ogata.

When I delved into this role, a glaring issue became apparent. The statistics on the representation of women within UNHCR's professional ranks were telling. Women constituted a mere 20 per cent of professionals, a proportion that dwindled further up the career ladder. With the United Nations setting a target of achieving 30 per cent representation of women across its entities, it was clear that UNHCR was falling short.

My task group was assigned a year to compile a comprehensive report and was entrusted with two critical tasks: firstly, to propose practical solutions to rectify the gender imbalance, and secondly, to identify unique challenges faced by women within the organization and devise strategies to address them.

A detailed examination of personnel statistics painted a grim picture. The male majority in senior positions held indefinite contracts, making it challenging to effect gender balance through attrition. However, a potential solution emerged amidst this predicament. With the global refugee crisis escalating, new employees were being recruited to meet the increased demand. Could this influx be strategically leveraged to enhance female representation? Our ambitious proposal suggested just that: prioritizing the recruitment of women for these burgeoning roles.

In its simplicity, this concept seemed almost audacious, but it held the potential to inch the percentage of women closer to the targeted goal. We were apprehensive that it might appear too radical, but it was an essential recommendation if only to underscore the practical challenges we faced.

Our investigation uncovered a systemic issue: women often entered UNHCR at lower levels than their male counterparts, even when they were equally qualified and vying for identical roles. The gender disparity in promotion rates was starkly evident, with women typically waiting longer for advancement. As we sifted through these specifics, it became clear that our endeavour extended beyond merely reforming regulations—it involved changing attitudes, dismantling ingrained biases and affirmative action.

With a mix of anticipation and apprehension, I stood before the senior management committee, ready to present the culmination of our rigorous research and deliberations. The room was filled with accomplished senior managers, predominantly men, their stern expressions and probing gazes dominating the space. I was acutely aware that my forthcoming proposal would challenge established norms and potentially stir emotions.

The gravity of the situation weighed heavily as I navigated through the comprehensive presentation, outlining the numbers, analyses, and strategies. The figures underscored the glaring gender disparity within UNHCR, while our discussions highlighted the critical need for innovative solutions. As I neared the conclusion, I made a recommendation that had been brewing in my mind for some time. My heart raced.

'The path to achieving gender balance', I said, pausing to collect my thoughts, 'requires a decisive step- a temporary freeze on male recruitment'. A strange silence crept in the room, broken only by the faint shifting of papers and the tapping of pens. I could almost feel the weight of the room's collective gaze on me, their scepticism palpable. In that tense silence, I wondered whether I had gone too far or if my bravado had shifted the scales from pragmatism to impracticality. As the seconds passed, my hopes for a positive response began to fade. Just as uncertainty began to creep in, a voice of authority and resolve broke through the silence- Madame Ogata's.

Madame Ogata thought for a brief while. 'Then let us do so', she said decidedly, looking at the director for human resources.

And it was true. The idea was accepted by the senior management committee, which was guided by Madame Ogata's unwavering dedication to change. A procedure was put in place that required directors to prioritize female candidates for open jobs. This new approach required directors to justify every decision to propose a male candidate over a female counterpart, essentially shifting the burden of proof onto them.

This initiative was met with apprehension. Inherited prejudices and assumptions prevailed, and one of the reasons given for the preference of male staff to fill positions was that women were predisposed to taking maternity leave or time off for caring for family and therefore should not be given priority. But tenacity paid off, and the system of checks and balances resulted in a transformational outcome: we met our target for the female representation of 30 per cent, within a year.

Chapter 10
My Deployment to the Field

The UNHCR's rotation program significantly impacted the lives of its employees, orchestrating transfers from one duty station to the other every two to four years. This rhythm kept the pulse of change alive for most, a symphony of new locations, cultures, and challenges. However, a distinct melody played for those labelled as "experts," including myself.

When I moved from ILO to UNHCR, I was recruited as an "expert" and was not subject to rotation. While this ensured that I remained in Geneva, providing stability for the family, it also meant that I faced the annual uncertainty of contract renewals and promotion to a higher grade remained a distant dream. However, the consistency in my children's education was a priceless reward.

The stability offered by "expert" status was not without its challenges. Our small enclave of technical professionals had an aura, a sense of exclusivity that over time morphed into an attitude of superiority that began to chafe against the fabric of our larger UNHCR community. Jealousy and frustration simmered beneath the surface, exacerbated by perceived favouritism. By 1993, whispers of reform had grown into a thunderous clamour from both administrative corridors and the staff union. The winds of change ushered in the decision of rotation for all, including experts - a chorus of voices asserting that all must share in the experience of serving in the field, learning firsthand about the obstacles faced by refugees and those on the frontlines.

As an engineer, I thrived in managing a team of specialists, offering critical technical advice, and designing camps and settlements that housed displaced people. The thought of leaving this role and swapping it for field postings to advance in my career did not immediately intrigue me. The years had woven a tapestry of skills, and venturing into unknown territory felt like starting a new book. Yet, the crescendo of change was inescapable. As expert status was re-evaluated and calls for rotation echoed through the halls, I found myself at a crossroads. The notes of the expert's song were giving way to a broader chorus of service.

As the winds of change swept through UNHCR, the day arrived when the list of open positions, the annual compendium was unveiled as usual. My heart pounded a little faster with each passing line as I perused the pages. There it was, nestled amid the comments: my own post, which had become a haven for me, a safe refuge for my knowledge. With options before me, I weighed my next steps. Faced with a decision, I took a leap of faith and decided to apply for my own post. I submitted my application with fingers crossed, each keystroke echoing a silent plea. The desire for consistency and a sense of belonging was palpable. Could the winds of change spare me this time? I could only hope. A month later, the news arrived as dawn painted the sky anew. My pulse quickened as I read the words before me- I had succeeded. Relief washed over me as uncertainty evaporated like morning mist. I had secured my job back, at least for another year.

But time has a way of weaving its threads anew, and soon enough, vacancy's cadence returned. My post reappeared on the list like a familiar refrain. This time though, my director Gerald

Walzer invited me to his office for what promised to be a pivotal conversation. As I began to make my case, it was clear he was not buying it this time around.

'Listen', he said to me, 'I can no longer justify you remaining in your post in the face of mounting pressure for you to be treated like all other staff. So, you must accept to be sent to the field'.

As the chapters of my career unfolded, an epiphany struck me. Fourteen years had elapsed since I first stepped into the embrace of Geneva, my sanctuary as I navigated the labyrinth of UNHCR's mission. During those years, my children had blossomed like seeds into saplings, each finding their own paths and interests. The rhythm of my life had shifted, and the anchor that had once grounded me in Geneva was loosening.

The chapters of my journey were etched with lines of guidance, evaluation, and coordination, skilfully woven into a mix of experiences. However, the experience of steering a program from the helm was a blank canvas yearning for fresh strokes within this rich tableau. This call resonated within me, compelling me to embark on a new quest and heed the call of an unexplored experience.

A new chapter began on a brisk day in January 1995. My passport to navigate new waters was my application for the position of Deputy Regional Representative in Addis Ababa, Ethiopia. The intricate network of responsibilities that came with the position intrigued me, as did Ethiopia's stunning landscapes.

The UNHCR Regional Office in Addis Ababa served not only the refugee programme in Ethiopia but also as a liaison office with other African intergovernmental organizations, the Organization of African Unity (OAU) and the United Nations Economic Commission for Africa (ECA); hence the office bore the responsibility of advocating for UNHCR's interests within these influential organizations.

I felt a sense of purpose when I penned my application for the position. As I watched the intricate web of activities that constituted Ethiopia's programme unfurl before my eyes, it resembled a vast tapestry with technical threads ready to be woven together. It was an image that resonated with my years of integrating multiple inputs into a cohesive program. Reflecting on my previous role as an evaluation officer, I remembered how I had assessed and modified the Ethiopian program through policy recommendations, demonstrating my intimate familiarity with its fundamentals. The idea of establishing a regional technical team and decentralizing program assistance from Geneva sparked my excitement.

On February 28, 1995, I received a letter informing me of my appointment—signalling the beginning of a new chapter in my life. My promotion to director was announced in a subsequent letter on June 16, 1995—confirming that the path ahead would be both an opportunity and a challenge. Poised to leave Geneva on July 1, I was brimming with purpose, engineering pragmatism, and policy insight—ready to assume the role of managing a significant refugee program. I embraced Ethiopia's challenges with confidence that success lay ahead.

Deputy Regional Representative in Ethiopia

Stepping onto Ethiopian soil after leaving Geneva's warm summer was a jolt, a stark reminder that Addis Ababa's climate was vastly different from what I had grown accustomed to. This metropolis, perched on a plateau and nestled at an elevation of 2,300 to 2,600 meters, was the fifth-highest city globally and the highest capital in Africa. This distinction sent an unexpected shiver down my spine.

The night-time wind greeted me as I disembarked the plane like an unwelcome guest. The temperatures were significantly lower than the averages I was used to in West Africa, dipping as low as 10 degrees from June to August. To my surprise and disappointment, I realized that in my eagerness to embrace my new role, I had likely overlooked the advice of Heywote, my best friend and an Ethiopian national, who had cautioned me to equip myself for the cold weather. Although I had visited Ethiopia before, it was in April and in a warmer part of the country than Addis Ababa. The notion that an African nation could be this chilly had never really crossed my mind. Suddenly, it seemed like a glaring oversight that my luggage contained lightweight summer clothing.

I received a dinner invitation from Dr Dawde, an Ethiopian physician with whom I had supported the establishment of an indigenous African non-governmental organization. This was not just any dinner; it was a meeting of minds with a shared goal. His organization, the Africa Humanitarian Action (AHA), was born out of the dedication of like-minded individuals in the wake of the atrocities of the 1994 Rwandan genocide. AHA served as a key source of humanitarian relief for refugees, internally displaced people (IDPs), and local populations across the continent.

That evening, we engaged in extensive discussions about the challenges Dr Dawde faced while steering AHA during its formative years. Despite my best efforts to concentrate, the persistent cold of the Ethiopian night gnawed at my thoughts. The chill seemed to permeate every cell in my body, serving as a distracting reminder of how unprepared I was. We dined and conversed, but my thoughts kept circling back to the unexpected cold that had come to visit me.

Back in my hotel room, I found myself grappling with a seemingly trivial issue: how to stay warm. I longed for the comfort of my belongings, but they were in transit from Geneva, thousands of miles away. As I lay there contemplating the unusual weather of this new place, it struck me how out-of-place hailstones pelting rooftops during rain seemed, given my preconceived notions of Africa. The irony was not lost on me: while spending years analysing events and making informed judgments, I had underestimated the simple task of adequately preparing for my personal journey.

My new boss, David Lambo, was a very likeable and enthusiastic individual, with a blend of cultural sensitivity and caution. A man of both British and Nigerian descent, his affable demeanour exuded a strong sense of political astuteness. Upon arrival, he openly shared his views with me, sensing the delicate approach we required with the Ethiopian authorities.

'Yvette', he began, his words carrying the weight of shared heritage, 'Our actions could easily be interpreted through the lens of regional relations. We must tread carefully'.

He had assumed the post of Regional Representative after the death of his beloved son, and it was as if he was trying to bury his sorrow in hard work. His office transformed into a whirlwind of vigour and determination, punctuated by his constant readjustment of his ill-fitting spectacles—a sure sign that the conversations were intensifying. We often had heated discussions due to our differing priorities. David's desire to appease the authorities was driven by the intricacies of government interactions. My focus, on the other hand, was on the impactful execution of our programme, ensuring that resources were utilized effectively.

Our international staff was an exceptional team of individuals, a group of brilliant minds meticulously chosen for their roles. We came together as a formidable group in this Ethiopian crucible. George Okoth Obbo, a young Ugandan lawyer who served as our protection officer, was one example that stood out. His presence added depth to our team, and we seamlessly integrated protection and assistance to create one of the best field programs. Then there was Heywote Haimeskal, a formidable force in the field of gender equality. Her passion for her work shone through, leaving a lasting impression on all of us. Her tragic passing in 2005 left me devastated. Our exceptional team was rounded out by Kwame Boafo, our administrative officer, and Daisy Buruku, our repatriation officer. Each strand came together to form a collective mission.

A group of competent Ethiopian colleagues worked in our office, including Kassa Lakew, our knowledgeable IT specialist, and Amarech Makonnen, my dedicated and hardworking secretary. Our interactions extended beyond strictly business-related conversations, resulting in a close-knit group that felt more like a family. Their consistent attention, enthusiasm, and commitment to the programme's success were a blessing.

Ethiopia's landscape was unique compared to many other countries. Unlike other regions where foreign non-governmental organizations were dominant, Ethiopia's government took the lead in protecting refugees and organizing aid. The Administration for Refugee & Returnee Affairs (ARRA), UNHCR's Ethiopian counterpart, played a pivotal role in this collaboration. This setup had its benefits as well as challenges.

Firstly, the government's active participation ensured that they fully accepted their responsibilities for determining refugee status and addressing sensitive cases—with our support. Additionally, this connection garnered crucial support for our programs from various ministries. However, there were costs associated with this collaboration. The funding of administrative expenses, which were unusually high, fell on us while the government took charge of operational aspects.

We did experience certain pressures throughout program execution due to the interconnected nature of our relationship. We frequently complied with requests from the government, even though it occasionally gave me cause for concern. This intricate balance between our objectives and governmental expectations resurfaced and shaped the trajectory of our efforts.

During my assignment, Abraha Abraha, an intimidating figure, presided over ARRA. Anyone who encountered him would be wary due to his stern demeanour and persistently furrowed brows. His thunderous warnings echoed with authority when disagreements arose, and his piercing gaze conveyed an unshakeable resolve. His presence was so daunting that I frequently questioned if working with him would be successful. Such was the aura that hung over me since I knew that conflict with governments often resulted in recall and isolation at UNHCR.

Fortunately for me, Abraha's rule was brief, and Atto Ayele—a middle-aged, soft-spoken antithesis to his predecessor—took his place. Our partnership was a breath of fresh air, marked by honest communication and shared compassion. We were able to make significant progress thanks to this noticeable change as we collaborated to attain our common goals.

In Addis Ababa, I frequently encountered delicate asylum situations. One incident that stands out involved a person connected to the Lord's Resistance Movement, a group infamous for its violent actions in Northern Uganda arrived at my office when Mr Lambo was away. His safety hung in the balance until his status could be determined. Wracked with uncertainty, I reached out to ARRA. In a testament to the swift and cooperative action that could be taken, when necessary, they arrived at my office within minutes to securely transport him to a safe haven, where he could await the proper procedure for his status determination.

At that time, the goal of self-reliance for Somali refugees residing in eight camps in Eastern Ethiopia was limited. Our focus shifted to preserving and enhancing their well-being. However, challenges continued to loom large. Water supply was a recurring issue that necessitated us trucking water over long distances to deliver to the Aware camps. Between 1988 and 1991, following the overthrow of Siad Barre's government in Somalia, these refugees, most of whom were from North West Somalia, sought asylum in Ethiopia. By 1996, North West Somalia had seen some semblance of tranquillity, leading the region to formally declare its independence as Somaliland.

The majority of the estimated 230,000 refugees in eastern Ethiopia embarked on a journey to return to Somaliland, even though many others whose places of origin were close to the border, continued to shuttle back and forth between the newly self-declared republic of Somaliland and Ethiopia, to receive the essential aid still being distributed at the camps. In 1996, when there were only 60,000 registered refugees left, it was decided to properly repatriate them and close down the camps. The groundwork for this large operation was laid in 1995, but obstacles caused by intermittent crises within Somalia prevented it from being launched until April of 1997. Tripartite negotiations between the governments of Ethiopia, the authorities of North West Somalia, and UNHCR paved the way for the repatriation process.

I vividly remember accompanying the first group on this return journey from Teferi Ber camp, located not far from the north-eastern town of Jijiga. On the historic day of February 18, 1997, a convoy of six buses transported nearly 200 Somali refugees, including 35 families, 25 kilometres to dispersion sites in north-western Somalia. From these hubs, they would continue their journey to their various home areas. Each family received a stipend of 200 Ethiopian Birr (about $30) for travel and a nine-month supply of food.

That morning, as the repatriation kits were distributed, I witnessed an inspiring scene. The refugees, with smiles on their faces, waited in line patiently, eagerly anticipating their aid and supplies. They shared a sense of purpose as they boarded the buses, knowing they were finally going home. I joined the convoy and followed their journey. The arrival at Hargeisa, the capital of North West Somalia, was exhilarating. Welcoming groups from various origins had gathered to greet their returning compatriots. The ensuing embrace was a touching reunion that defied words, a beautiful blend of love, warmth, and tears of joy.

Our arrival in Hargeisa unveiled a peaceful environment that had seemingly resumed its rhythms of normalcy after years of warfare—a stark contrast to our impressions of a war-ravaged country. The scenario was one of impressive organization, showcasing a government that maintained solid control and worked towards a clear future goal despite its lack of international recognition. The city's expansion, partially financed by proceeds from cattle trade with Middle Eastern nations, was evidence of a thriving economy.

Delving further into its historical backdrop reveals that North West Somalia had been governed by the British, separating it from the sections of Somalia under Italian rule. When these areas gained independence, the idea to unite them into Somalia met with some opposition, at the time, especially from the population of the North West. Now, during Somalia's turbulent period, in the wake of the overthrow of Siad Barre, they chose secession and declared themselves as a separate country, Somaliland. However, their efforts to gain international recognition were in vain. The fact that this haven of tranquillity, within a turbulent region, was not recognized as such, struck me as fundamentally unjust. Where was the "peace dividend" that the international community was supposed to offer as compensation for peace efforts? Here was a place that personified peace, yet its efforts went unnoticed. The repatriation efforts continued with unwavering dedication. Through our repatriation efforts, almost 10,000 refugees had reached their country of origin by June 1997.

Sudanese refugees were housed in four camps in the western region of Ethiopia. The rich soil in this area made it suitable for agriculture. However, our attempts to secure government-owned land for refugee-driven agriculture with the goal of promoting self-reliance encountered difficulties. A constant influx of southern Sudanese refugees entered Ethiopia throughout my tenure there. I had the opportunity to evaluate the circumstances of these refugees when visiting the Fugnido camp, and our response included providing them with shelter and relief materials within the camp.

During one of my visits, I travelled to regions in the Tigray Province where returning Ethiopian refugees from eastern Sudan were being resettled. This journey led me to a fascinating location: a hidden settlement nestled in the mountains. The Tigrayan People's Liberation Front, under the leadership of Meles Zenawi, had meticulously planned their audacious attack into Addis Ababa from this very spot in order to overthrow the Derg government and depose President Mengistu in 1991.

Navigating the challenging mountain terrain required more than an hour of our time and demanded tenacity. We ascended to a cave skilfully carved into the rock. This cave had served as Meles Zenawi's home and administrative centre during those pivotal times, and it was surprisingly well-equipped with necessities like power and water supplies. The operational maps adorning the walls of this historically significant room seemed to echo the strategic planning of that courageous assault. I found it hard to comprehend how such a defensive stronghold could be constructed in such difficult terrain, amidst the chaos of war.

However, the journey back to our vehicle proved to be beyond my capabilities. I felt drained and apprehensive that it might be too much for me to handle. In this moment of exhaustion, a young boy, no more than eight years old, offered a helping hand. Observing my struggle, he stepped in to assist, demonstrating the tenacity and spirit that permeated these settings. I could not help but admire the exceptional agility and adaptability of the rest of the team as I trailed behind them while they navigated their way through the mountains.

'Let me help you', he said, giving me his hand. I needed the help.

The repatriation of Ethiopians still living as refugees in eastern Sudan was a crucial task within the larger context of the Ethiopian program. The process of assisting returnees was a thorough undertaking that included a variety of crucial support systems. This contained an income-generating award of EB 1,500 (US$200) for every household as well as food rations for nine months that were professionally coordinated by the World Food Programme (WFP). Additionally, funds for transportation of EB 180 per person were made available to help these returning families with the expenditures of getting from dispersion facilities to their ultimate locations. The delivery of non-food goods like kitchen utensils, blankets, and plastic tarpaulins also facilitated the transfer back to their country of origin.

The one-time lump sum gift allotted to each returning family was determined regardless of the family size, creating an unusual loophole. Some returnees pragmatically recognized that they could exploit this framework to their advantage. As a result, the typical family size decreased to as low as two people, as they divided their families to maximize the benefits. This phenomenon caused concern and necessitated careful consideration.

I had a candid conversation with my boss, David, and shared my observations. I suggested a different strategy, recommending that we recalculate the allocation based on an individual rather than a family measure. He acknowledged the logic behind this change but expressed concerns about potential government reactions. He was apprehensive about possible discord since many government officials belonged to the same ethnic groups as the returning refugees. This scenario presented a complex balancing act where the imperative of equitable support clashed with the sensitivity of regional affiliations.

As the person in charge of the program's daily operations,

I understood that I needed to take swift action in light of the pressing reality of dwindling funds. I saw an opportunity to address the issue when David was away on a trip to Geneva. I took matters into my own hands and wrote a letter to the government informing them that reintegration payments would henceforth be distributed on a per capita basis. However, upon David's return, the Commissioner for Refugees expressed his displeasure with this decision, leading David to revoke my decision and withdraw the letter I had sent to ARRA. Even though disagreements like this were commonplace, it was a disheartening turn of events, as I held great respect for David's commitment.

This incident acted as a starting point for reflection about my position within the organization. I started to crave the chance to run a programme on my own, to be in charge of its direction and to exercise autonomy. When the Representative in Kenya, Alain Peters, was promoted to oversee the Africa Bureau in Geneva, the opportunity to finally do so materialized in January 1997. I grasped the opportunity to apply for his post. I was selected and was formally appointed to the position on April 2, 1997.

As my journey progressed, I came to a fork in the road. With the promise of a new chapter in my career, this new chance drew me to Kenya. After only two years in Ethiopia, I made the choice to discontinue my pursuits there, winding up outstanding projects and getting ready to move to Nairobi in August 1997. My professional journey's evolving story was characterized by difficulties, personal development, and a steadfast dedication to the goal of humanitarian service.

Representative to Kenya and Somalia

August 1997 marked a poignant arrival in Nairobi, accompanied by a heartfelt departure from Addis Ababa. The transfer was emotionally charged, reflecting the deep connections I had forged during my time in Ethiopia. After bidding farewell and receiving well wishes, I embarked on the next leg of my journey, arriving in Nairobi to commence a new chapter in assuming responsibility for over 400,000 refugees in Kenya.

My tenure in Nairobi was an intriguing experience. The office had secured the rental of my predecessor's former residence, located in the affluent neighbourhood of Muthaiga, known as Nairobi's diplomatic district. The house, which was the property of the government of Oman, was situated alongside residences of ambassadors of Italy, Sweden, Türkiye and Belgium. Upon my arrival, I was taken aback by the house's beauty; initially, it seemed somewhat incongruous for a UNHCR representative, but then I understood that Nairobi's security dynamics and the delicate nature of refugee programs necessitated this decision. The reports of carjacking and other security concerns underscored the need for vigilance, and the government ensured a high level of protection in this diplomatic enclave.

For someone like me, living alone with only my Ethiopian housekeeper, Belaynesh, ensuring a safe environment in Nairobi was crucial. Living in Muthaiga provided not only physical security but also mental peace in a city where safety was paramount. The mansion itself was impressive, evoking images of opulent homes from television series such as Dallas. It was a sprawling two-story building with six independent suites, a large kitchen, and a grand reception hall. It boasted of a twin staircase. The enormity of the house left me awestruck and made me feel both daunted but protected within its walls.

Nairobi had all the hallmarks of an ideal duty station: it offered excellent amenities, pleasant weather, and striking architecture. Despite the city's undeniable charm, security concerns always cast a shadow over it and limited its appeal. This overshadowed its many positive attributes, including its vibrant metropolitan environment and stunning natural scenery.

One could relish the thriving cultural scene, indulge in

the diverse culinary offerings, and soak up the multicultural ambience in this dynamic cityscape. However, despite its vibrant appearance, daily life was punctuated with incidents of burglary and carjacking. These were not merely speculative events relegated to hearsay; they represented a stark reality that many people, including those within my own circle, could attest to. Colleagues and acquaintances shared personal accounts of security incidents, and firsthand accounts of security issues from office staff painted a realistic picture.

Just three weeks after my arrival in the country, I had an unsettling wake-up call to this fact. The scene of this particular incident was the UNHCR office located in Eastlands in the heart of the city. My peace was disrupted at four in the morning by the anxious crackling of the radio announcing a call from my security officer. The sombre hour mirrored the disheartening news I was about to receive.

'Good morning, Yankee Sierra', he started. We had adopted the NATO phonetic alphabet for our radio calls. 'There has been a burglary in the office'.

'A burglary?' I could not understand.

We had a very impressive security system with a reputable security company with a wired alarm system and nine security officers guarding the building. In addition to this, a twenty-four-hour duty driver and a vigilant radio officer lent an extra layer of protection. The ensemble of precautions seemed impervious, a bulwark against any threat that might dare to breach our fortified defences. The question echoed in my mind, finding a voice as I asked, 'Whatever happened to the system?'

'Well, they were all tied up', was his reply. 'I will come now to pick you up, because we need a waiver to allow the police to enter the building, due to its diplomatic status'.

He arrived promptly, and together we embarked on the silent

drive to the office. The gravity of the situation hung heavy in the air, rendering words unnecessary. Upon reaching the office, I was met with a sight that seemed straight out of a surreal crime thriller. The audacity of the intrusion was evident in the sight of immobilized staff members and security officers.

The aftermath of the breach was quite revealing. The clocks that had once adorned the reception area were missing, as if time itself had been disrupted. But what truly caught our attention was the missing equipment. Computers, copiers, and fax machines— all essential for our operations—had been removed from their places, leaving behind a silent trace of their absence.

However, it was the sight of the office safes that held everyone's focus. These once secure vaults had been subjected to relentless pounding until they lay open and exposed. The items they had once safeguarded were nowhere to be found. It appeared that the robbers were well-versed in our financial operations. It was no secret that we played a role in allocating funds for the UNHCR program in the Great Lakes area, particularly in post-war Rwanda. Disbursements reached up to two million dollars daily. Despite the high demand for funds following war and genocide, we had implemented stringent procedures.

We had devised a method to safeguard the money, collaborating with the bank to collect any leftover cash at the end of each day and transfer it to the secure confines of a bank vault for storage. Unaware of this precaution, the attackers had exerted considerable effort trying to open the safes. Their efforts yielded only a collection of personal items belonging to UNHCR employees who were working tirelessly to aid recovery operations in Rwanda. In their pursuit of financial gain, they had unwittingly met their match with a combination of diligent planning and cooperative security measures.

Their method of infiltration was audacious and unnerving in its aggressiveness. The robbers had cunningly begun by intimidating the gate sentries, cloaking their intentions with an air of urgency. They fabricated a situation involving an urgent medical emergency within the compound, prompting the duty officer to open the door to the building out of necessity. Seizing this opportunity, they exploited this vulnerability and once inside, chaos ensued as guards were quickly overpowered and restrained.

The mystery deepened with new information. According to security personnel stationed on the rooftop of the building, the alarm system, which should have immediately relayed signals to the central headquarters of the security company, had malfunctioned. Shortly after, a startling discovery was made- the wiring for the alarm had been deliberately damaged and then concealed with tape. The implication of an inside job was hard to dismiss.

The police were summoned but their conclusion, before even inspecting the premises, came as a surprise to us. They immediately concluded that this was an inside job. The security officers, along with the UNHCR duty driver and radio operator, who were Kenyan nationals, fell under suspicion. They were swiftly detained for what the police termed "questioning". The step seemed as a normal step in the investigations, but when by the end of the day, none of them had returned, we began to worry and I contacted headquarters to inform them about this incident.

Trepidation grew as the hours passed. The staff union's chairperson came to my office and expressed concern over the non-return of our radio operator and duty driver. In response, it was decided that I would visit the police station to find out where they were. We set out on a mission with the driver that took us to a number of nearby police stations but could not locate them. We eventually found their location in one police station, some distance away, but the officer-in-charge had gone home for the night and was thus unavailable and they could not be released, in his absence, which was an unforeseen roadblock that prevented us from succeeding. We were forced to go home reluctantly, with the unfolding events shrouded in mystery. The chapter was yet unfinished, but the prospect of learning the truth awaited on the horizon.

The next morning, the Kenyan staff members gathered in the meeting room in protest. A sit-down strike had been called as a show of support for their jailed co-workers. For me, who had just arrived to take up the position of UNHCR Representative in Kenya, this was a baptism of fire. I could see the dissatisfaction in the eyes of the staff and prayed that I would be able to secure the release of their colleagues.

I returned to the police station after promising them firm action. The officer in charge welcomed me and informed me that the prisoners were being treated as suspects and would be the subject of an investigation to see if charges would be brought against them. I insisted on seeing them, so I could talk to them myself.

They were escorted into the room, and it was clear from their unkempt appearances that the experience they had been through had left its mark. They had obviously been manhandled and their features were bruised. Imagining how they were treated shocked and infuriated me. I noticed a bump on the forehead of the radio operator, whom I had been informed, had a heart condition. They were in a very different physical condition than the people who left the office the day before.

My resolve intensified—justice must be served. Their release became a paramount mission. The echoes of the staff's unwavering support reverberated in my mind, propelling me forward. The pursuit of truth and fairness became a personal commitment.

The officer-in-charge was insistent. 'We have to carry out our investigations unimpeded', he said. 'A burglary has been committed and it is our job to bring the offenders to justice'.

My appeal for their release was unanswered, and a terrifying conclusion struck. I was troubled by the idea of going back to the office and confronting my worried and irate local colleagues. I urgently contacted the Ministry of Foreign Affairs to request their assistance. The limitations of their power in problems involving Kenyan nationals and law enforcement were repeated in their answers. A dropped case would be the only reason for their release, according to conversations with the police that ensued.

I made a critical decision to prioritize my relationship with the local staff and the effectiveness of the programme over the challenges of pursuing a case. Although there was a risk of repercussions from headquarters for not filing a police report, the acceptance and trust of the local staff were crucial for successfully managing the complex programme in Kenya. So, I took the difficult decision to request that the case be dropped. The financial implications of this decision eventually prevented the replacement of stolen property without a police report, due to United Nations financial regulations. We were compelled to do without the stolen equipment while maximizing the limited resources still available.

Regrettably, security incidents were common, underscoring the unstable environment. The importance of vigilance was highlighted by incidents such as carjacking that left employees trapped in their cars' trunks and even an assault on a security guard just outside the office.

With Kenya's unique strategy, at the time, UNHCR was given control over refugee operations, including status determination, with the government overseeing our efforts. While this afforded us some autonomy, it also complicated the programme's management.

The refugee populations in Kenya were primarily located in two regions. The Dadaab camps—Dagahaley, Ifo, and Hagadera—to the east provided asylum to Somali nationals. The Kakuma camp, situated further south, housed a diverse group of refugees, predominantly from southern Sudan but also including Ethiopians, Rwandans, and Ugandans. Both groups received support in the form of care and maintenance. These camps were situated in dry, infertile areas of the country, offering little opportunity for farming or other self-reliance projects.

Interestingly, I was involved in the establishment of the Dadaab camps. During a trip to Kenya in 1992, while I was head of UNHCR's technical section based in Geneva, the roots of my involvement were planted. I participated in selecting the Dadaab site at that time. A small village called Liboi, near the Kenya-Somalia border, was where the initial wave of refugees was located. Working with our program support division, I assessed their needs and identified suitable land at least 20 kilometres away from the border due to security concerns for both the government and refugees. The government suggested the final location, which I promptly agreed to. Upon returning to Geneva, I coordinated with technical specialists in my team to plan and design the camp. This led to an accelerated construction process in response to the government's insistence on relocating refugees away from the border. Fast forward five years, and I found myself in an unusual situation—tasked with managing the operations of the very camps I had helped establish.

In stark contrast to many situations that had developed spontaneously, these camps were a microcosm of vibrant life that had been meticulously planned to ensure smooth operation. The entire camp buzzed with activity; and, on weekends I would retreat to stay in the staff quarters. I humorously referred to these retreats as "voluntary absence for relief from company", drawing a parallel to Voluntary Absence for the Relief from Isolation (VARI) which was offered to personnel in remote locations, such as Dadaab. It was a priceless respite from the daily grind.

I routinely received invitations to attend the large commemoration events staged on national holidays while serving as the UNHCR Representative in Kenya. It was not wise to take the decision to not attend lightly. Even though I might not have understood the speeches given in Swahili, I would patiently listen to them while secretly wishing that President Moi would not use the word *wakimbisi,* which is Swahili for "refugees," in his remarks. Any mention of this subject would surely mean that there were problems that would make things more difficult for me. I understood the political significance of my appearances in these parades, as a way to maintain good relations with the government, which was crucial for the protection of and assistance to refugees.

Kenya commemorates Madaraka Day as the day it gained independence from British colonial rule. The centrepiece of the celebrations is the President's Madaraka Day address, delivered during the event and attended by diplomats. At the parade in 1998, President Arap Moi focused on Kenya's security situation. He attributed a series of violent robberies that shook the regional capital of Garissa and Nairobi to Somali refugees. In a highly inflammatory speech, he also threatened to deport all Somali refugees back to their war-torn country.

I felt immense pressure to respond to such a stance. I spent the evening contemplating how to handle the situation. As the new day dawned, my phone was incessantly ringing with calls from NGOs, human rights groups, and UN colleagues. They urged me to take a firm stand and remind the President of Kenya's obligations under the Refugee Conventions—to provide sanctuary to those fleeing violence and persecution—in order to remind him of Kenya's commitments on the global stage.

As I considered their suggestions, I realized the complexity of the situation. While I recognized the need to advocate for refugees' rights, I also understood the importance of maintaining the refugee asylum system. After careful thought, I chose a different course of action that prioritized ensuring that refugees continued to enjoy asylum in Kenya.

Later that day, as I expected, I was summoned by the President himself to the State House. I faced a significant challenge as I needed to convey our commitment to assisting refugees while managing delicate national security concerns.

Everyone working in refugee and security settings was aware that weapons and ammunition were readily available just across the border. Personal accounts revealed a thriving arms trade along the road. Naturally, this situation led to concerns about weapons entering Kenya. A careful examination of news about armed attacks in Kenya revealed an intriguing trend: those arrested for these crimes were not of Somali descent. This insight painted a more complex picture: while it was possible that the guns originated from Somalia, it was likely that they had been imported into Kenya and were being used by local criminals.

At the State House, I met with the President in person. Accompanying him were the Foreign Minister and Minister of Social Welfare. The President's anger was palpable.

In a firm voice, he said, 'Go tell Kofi Annan I want the Somali refugees out of Kenya. The UN can set up camps for them inside their own country. We have extended our hospitality to refugees, but when our national security is jeopardized, I am compelled to evict them from Kenya'.

I managed to keep my cool and decided that it might not be the best strategy to explicitly refute his statement that the refugees were the criminals behind the reported incidents. Instead, I chose to respond strategically and delivered a speech that I had meticulously crafted in my mind during the course of the preceding night.

First of all, let me thank you Mr. President, on behalf of the High Commissioner for Refugees, Madame Ogata, for generously hosting refugees and for the important role that you are playing in negotiating peace in the Horn of Africa Region. We appreciate your concern about national security and we would not like to see this compromised. UNHCR will not condone refugees breeching national security and in fact, any refugee that is caught with firearms or committing crimes would lose his refugee status. This is why we would be willing to assist you, in whatever way possible to monitor and police the refugee camps and the Garissa District, in general, to weed out any refugee who is abusing his asylum status.

There was a moment of silence and one could feel the tension drop.

'So, what do you propose?' he asked.

'I propose that I go on a mission with the Head of the Police to the regional capital of Garissa to assess the needs of the police force to maintain law and order in the district and determine how the UNHCR could provide necessary assistance. We could leave tomorrow'.

By the time I finished speaking, the mood of the President had changed. He even called his photographer to take a picture of us together. Refugee asylum was saved for now.

As a result of our evaluation, UNHCR acted swiftly to acquire 10 Land Cruisers, night visors, and other crucial security equipment for the Garissa police. Considering the stakes—ensuring the continuation of sanctuary for a refugee population of over 200,000 people, primarily composed of weak women and children—this was a rather tiny expenditure. I was proud to share the results with our implementing partners and my colleagues at the UN. I had avoided cornering the Kenyan government by navigating the situation satisfactorily.

The Kakuma Refugee Camp was formed in 1992 as a result of cooperation between the Kenyan Government and UNHCR and was located in the northwest of the country of Kenya, close to Lake Turkana. The arrival of the famous "Lost Boys of Sudan", who made the extraordinary trek on foot from southern Sudan, across difficult terrain to seek sanctuary in Kenya, gave it notoriety. As they travelled to Kenya, satellite photographs were taken of their amazing journey, and their fascinating narrative attracted the attention of the world, generating funding for the camp's expansion.

The bulk of those living in the camp were Sudanese refugees, Dinkas and Nuers who belonged to two significant South Sudanese ethnic groups. Intergroup disputes between these two communities were a recurring issue within the camp. I made multiple visits to the camp to negotiate and ease tensions, because of this situation. How these groups, who were both subject to persecution in their home countries, struggled to come to terms while residing in a safe haven outside of their countries remained incomprehensible.

Even though my official title was UNHCR Representative to Kenya, I was given the role of serving as UNHCR Representative to Somalia, with the exception of North West Somalia, as part of my job responsibilities. North West Somalia had its own dedicated representative headquartered in Hargeisa. Dominik Langenbacher, a Swiss native who served as the United Nations Resident and Humanitarian Coordinator for Somalia, oversaw UN coordination activities, as Nairobi functioned as the base for all UN agencies working in Somalia, and was the location of the UN Country Team for Somalia. He also served as the head of the Somalia Aid Coordination Body (SACB); an organization that brought together all parties involved in aiding Somalia.

During Dominik's absences, he often delegated me to serve as the Resident and Humanitarian Coordinator, entrusting me with the oversight of UN activities. When Dominik departed, I assumed his role as the acting resident and humanitarian representative for a six-month period until a successor was appointed. Concurrently, I took on the critical role of the United Nations Designated Official, responsible for managing security throughout the UN system in Somalia.

In my role as the Designated Official, I was directly responsible for the security of UN personnel, their families, and organizational resources. This was particularly crucial given Somalia's volatile and conflict-prone environment. The role demanded meticulous decisions to ensure the safety of both the team and resources in a country beset by the challenges of war and instability.

I had a group of seasoned security experts at my disposal while serving as the United Nations Designated Official in Somalia, and they were willing to share their knowledge and advice. But putting their recommendations into action was frequently difficult, especially when it included limiting the movements of foreign employees in a dangerous place like Somalia. This was especially true when organizations like the World Food Programme (WFP) wanted to provide the populace with necessary supplies, but the security officers advised that the security situation in a particular area was not conducive.

In such situations, I had to stand firm and prioritize the security advice of professionals, even if it led to resentment from affected parties. For example, when the Special Representative of the Secretary-General arrived from New York intending to visit Somalia, the security team expressed concerns about his safety due to the prevailing conditions. To navigate this, I arranged meetings for him in Nairobi with the individuals he intended to meet in Somalia. This approach enabled him to achieve his goals while avoiding a potentially hazardous trip.

One particular story stands out in my recollections. A member of staff of the United Nations Conference on Trade and

Development (UNCTAD) was involved in an odd occurrence in Baidoa, which became an entertaining episode. Following a slap of an international official by a Somali, the traditional court had offered two possibilities for recourse: a bride or a camel. At a management meeting of the UN Team, I found myself leading discussions of this dilemma. We all agreed that receiving an apology was insufficient and that we should not set a precedence of condoning infractions. Notwithstanding the official's apparent hidden interest in the wife option, we decided to accept the camel which had considerable cultural significance to Somalis. The camel was housed on the UNCTAD property and provided milk for local staff.

The August Terrorist Attack on the United States Embassy

An important incident that occurred while I was in Kenya was the devastating terrorist attack on the US Embassy in Nairobi in August. I had found myself in the US Embassy for a meeting with the ambassador just a week before this horrible tragedy. However, the US Marines in charge of security abruptly barred my access. They insisted that they had not received the necessary memo from the ambassador's office, announcing my arrival. I offered my business card as the UNHCR Representative and had the secretary of the ambassador vouch for me over the phone, but I was made to wait outside for thirty minutes until she could send a memo to the security desk. I had thought at the time that this was strange, but the events that occurred a week later, made clear the reason for precautions by the marines.

I had a meeting with the ambassador regarding her upcoming trip to the Dadaab refugee camps. Initially, she had requested only one security guard to accompany her. However, during our conversation, she abruptly asked for two additional seats on the plane for extra security officers. This posed a logistical challenge as our small 12-seater jet to Dadaab was often fully booked. In the end, I had to make the tough decision to bump off two of my staff members from the flight to accommodate the extra security personnel, much to their disappointment. For logistical ease, I also suggested that she bring forward her trip from Friday to Wednesday. The real reason for this timetable modification was rather more private. That Friday, my dear friend Heywote, was coming to see me, and I had previously planned for us to visit the Nairobi National Park, but I did not disclose this as the reason for the change of date to the ambassador.

On that Wednesday, as promised, I went to Dadaab with the ambassador. The three security guards who were with her were quite diligent and thorough, searching the camp thoroughly as we moved forward. Although I valued their dedication to security, I could not help but think that their vigilance was a little excessive. Nevertheless, we made it back to Nairobi without incident, and our paths split apart at the airport. On hindsight, I realized that the intensified vigilance must have been a result of suspected terrorist action.

On that ill-fated Friday, Heywote and I left for the park. As we left my house and reached the end of the street, we encountered a flurry of vehicles speeding in the opposite direction. Alarmed voices implored us to avoid the city due to a recent catastrophic explosion. After being informed about the significant loss of life, we heeded their advice, retraced our steps home, and immediately turned on the TV to grasp the extent of the incident.

The information was both terrible and shocking. The sights on the TV were horrifying; the United States Embassy had been the subject of a terrible attack. I could not help but go back to the previous week, when I had been sitting in the Embassy's lobby, awaiting the required authorization to enter, and two days before, when the US security officers were patrolling the camp during my visit with the ambassador.

I moved right away in response to the urgent request for supplies for the assault victims. I made the decision to drive to the UNHCR warehouse to get blankets and medical supplies, which we then took right away to the Kenyatta Public Hospital. It was a little, but significant, gesture to support individuals impacted by the tragedy, and it made me think about the crucial role that humanitarian groups play in dire situations.

Chapter 11
Change from Humanitarian to Development Work

During my fifteen years of working for the UNHCR, I witnessed firsthand the humanitarian situation of populations, especially in Africa. My roles varied from being a technical expert and evaluation officer to advising and managing UNHCR programs in three African nations with significant refugee populations. I dedicated myself to ensuring that refugees received necessary care and maintenance relief. Additionally, I facilitated the establishment of self-reliance activities for refugees and returnees, whenever possible.

I understood that despite the assistance we gave, the refugees living in our camps were not content, even though they were generally faring better than the local inhabitants. The haste at which they would return to their countries of origin when the conflicts ended, was an indication that they preferred home, even if they would be poorer there. Indeed, whoever was it who said, 'There is no place like home?'

When these refugee situations were closely examined, it became clear that many of the conflicts were primarily brought on by a lack of development. I kept asking myself, 'How could I make myself more meaningful?'

Coincidently, while I became increasingly reflective of the need to address the root causes of conflicts, that led to displacements, in 1998, the United Nations Secretary-General published a landmark report to the Security Council entitled, *The Causes of Conflicts and the Promotion of Durable Peace and Sustainable Development in Africa.* The report was presented to the Council on September 25, 1997, to consider the need for a concerted international effort to promote peace and security in Africa. During that time, there were conflicts in 14 of the 53 nations that make up Africa. They accounted for half of all war-related deaths worldwide that resulted in no less than eight million refugees, returnees, and displaced persons. The report attempted to bring the components of the UN system, peace and security, human rights, and development, together, for the first time, to prevent conflicts.

In presenting the report to the Security Council, the Secretary-General said, 'For the United Nations, there was no higher goal, no deeper commitment, and no greater ambition than preventing armed conflict so that people everywhere could enjoy peace and prosperity. Preventing (such) wars was no longer a question of defending States or protecting allies. It was a question of defending humanity itself'.

Reading this report, I became convinced that the best way to prevent displacement and refugee outflows was to address the root causes of conflicts. I decided that the only option was to work on development, despite my lack of academic qualifications and experience in the field of development. My work with the ILO opened my eyes to how technology could foster micro-level development. As an evaluation officer, I prepared the first UNHCR report on refugee aid and development, gaining experience in linking humanitarian and development work. My role as head of the UNHCR technical section bolstered my confidence in coordinating various inputs to achieve development goals. My stint as a United Nations Resident and Humanitarian

Representative in Somalia reaffirmed my ability to positively influence development issues.

When the United Nations Development Programme decided to open up the post of resident coordinator to staff from other UN agencies in 1998, I had the opportunity to put my skills to the test. This led to my application to participate in the first UNDP session for the assessment of staff across the United Nations, willing to serve as resident coordinators. I was accepted and took part in the first-ever assessment program for potential resident coordinators outside of UNDP.

The assessment exercise took place in Turin, Italy, in November 1998. This assessment turned out to be very thorough and engaging. The assessment results indicated that I would be an appropriate choice to serve in the capacity of country resident coordinator. Following the assessment, the first offer that was made to me was to serve as a resident coordinator in Belarus, maybe because of my knowledge of the Russian language. This was hardly what I was looking for. How could I use my efforts to promote development in Europe to the exclusion of countries in Africa? In any case, I did not know how readily a black woman would be welcomed to serve in that capacity in Belarus. I therefore turned it down.

Then I was made a second offer, this time in Africa, in Eritrea. This was more interesting. A compatriot of mine, Herbert Macleod, had served in that capacity and gave me positive feedback on his experiences there. The Eritreans were difficult to deal with, but they were honest and committed to reconstructing their nation. I could not wish for a better placement. Once I agreed to this placement, the request for approval by the Eritrean government was sent by UNDP. While waiting for approval, I considered the practical realities of working in Eritrea. When my two brothers unexpectedly passed away, within a week of each other, while I was working in Ethiopia, I had adopted their children, Josephine, who was twelve, and Ambrose, who was four, from them. I was worried about their schooling and tried to see how I could keep Josephine at boarding school in Nairobi and made a formal request to that effect. This was being considered at the same time that I was waiting for the "agrément" from the Eritrean government.

I was in this mindset, hoping that things would work out, when a friend of mine in New York gave me, a vacancy notice after learning about my interest in African development. It was a post as coordinator for Africa at the United Nations Department of Economic and Social Affairs (UNDESA). As I lacked direct experience in development, I believed that my prospects of being selected for this position were slim. I also imagined that there would be intense competition for such a position at the UN headquarters. But one item in particular caught my attention. The incumbent of this post was to be responsible for monitoring the implementation of the 1998 Secretary General's report on the causes of conflict. I considered that it would be a great opportunity if I could work in this capacity. So, I applied for the post. After all, I had nothing to lose. I was on a job with a permanent contract and was being actively considered for another.

Much to my surprise, I was invited for a phone interview. My preparation was rigorous, delving into all relevant topics to ensure I was well-versed if shortlisted. I found myself immersed in research on development issues and pertinent political matters, thanks to the access that one now had to the internet. The interview panel consisted of Mr Nitin Desai, the Indian Under-Secretary-General (USG), and his Italian deputy, Mr Patricio Civili and Angela King, the Jamaican Assistant Secretary-General for gender issues. Despite the interview going well, I remained sceptical about my chances. However, I must have left a positive impression as I was subsequently invited for a face-to-face interview in New York.

In April 1999, I travelled to New York for this interview, and I realized that I was the only one invited to it. I was thrilled. I had spent the entire night researching the subject of African development. I had the idea that the USG had already made up his mind because the interview was not as in-depth as the one over the phone. I was to become the next Special Coordinator for Africa and Least Developed Countries at DESA.

I began to feel guilty about potentially leaving the position in Eritrea to which I had been assigned, pending the Eritrean government's approval. A month had passed since the UNDP made the request, but there was still no response. The opportunity to work on African development issues at a global level within the United Nations Secretariat in New York was undeniably more attractive, especially considering it was at a higher professional level than the Eritrean post. After the interview, I confessed to Angela King that I had committed to accepting the Eritrean position.

"But you have not yet been recruited to that post, have you?" she responded. Even though she did not say so, I concluded that my chances were good to get the New York Post. "Hang in there," she said as I left her office.

A month later, I received a fax message. It read: *We are pleased to inform you that you have been selected to fill the post of Special Coordinator for Africa and the Least Developed Countries at the United Nations Department of Economic and Social Affairs.*

Just a couple of days before, I had received the news from the UNDP that the government of Eritrea had accepted me to serve in the capacity of Resident Coordinator in Eritrea. However, my request to keep my adopted daughter in boarding school in Nairobi had been rejected by the UNDP administration.

The choice was clear. New York, here I come.

Special Coordinator for Africa and the Least Developed Countries

I arrived in New York to take up my appointment on November 1, 1999. The Office of the Special Coordinator for Africa and the Least Developed Countries (OSCAL) was a small unit within the Department of Economic and Social Affairs (DESA). It was established in 1992 with the intention of enlisting worldwide assistance for the growth of Africa and the least developed countries (LDCs), with the long-term objective of assuring their full inclusion into the international community as equal participants. Through the coordination of inputs from the UN and other bodies, the Office facilitated intergovernmental debates and negotiations on Africa and LDCs. In its advocacy capacity, it examined numerous problems and developments pertaining to the development of Africa and encouraged communication between African nations, LDCs, and their development partners.

My boss, Mr Nitin Desai, was distinguished-looking, with his salt and pepper hair. He saw his role as one that was described at the creation of the department, namely "providing substantive support to the normative, analytical, statistical, and relevant technical cooperation processes of the United Nations on economic and social affairs".

The office of the special coordinator had a modest staff of five economists and development specialists. There was Emmanuel Goued Njayick, a Cameroonian, who was my de facto deputy. He was a stockily-built, greying man in his late fifties. He had worked in the office since it came into existence in 1992. He always waited for everyone to speak before slowly delivering his opinion, like an old African sage. He was highly devout, which accounted for why he did not appear to harbour any resentment toward me for getting hired for the position for which he had applied.

Then there was Ruth Engo, another Cameroonian who looked

majestic in her short hair with streaks of grey. She had served as the head of the labour department in her country. Her main passion was making the case for the recognition of Africa-based NGOs. Raj Bardouille, a Dominican national, was conscientious and was always searching for solutions. Leslie Wade was a young woman from St. Kitts and Nevis who was tall, slim, and had short hair as well. She was a bright spot, on grey days, since she was highly knowledgeable, intelligent and patient. Abraham Joseph a grey-haired Indian was the fifth staff member in the office. When Emmanuel retired in 2000, Eloho Otobo, a Nigerian national, who was erudite in issues of African development, replaced him.

Advocacy for African Development

My role encompassed overseeing United Nations programs for Africa and managing the creation of reports on Africa for intergovernmental bodies, drawing on inputs from thirty-two UN entities. I was also tasked with scrutinizing various multilateral and bilateral initiatives aimed at the development of Africa and the Least Developed Countries. Additionally, I led the promotion of South-South and trilateral cooperation and initiated catalytic activities pertinent to African development.

The United Nations has Economic commissions in all regions of the world. In addition to the Economic Commission for Africa (ECA), there was the Economic Commission for Asia and the Pacific (ESCAP), the Economic Commission for Latin America and the Caribbean (ECLAC), the Economic Commission for Europe (ECE), and the Economic and Social Commission for Western Asia (ESCWA). However, one thing I did not realize when I applied for the position was that Africa was the only continent that had an office covering development issues at the UN in New York. This office was created as a result of a General Assembly resolution that African members had campaigned for, in order to guarantee that advocacy for Africa received the attention it merited. I soon realized that the existence of this office was not appreciated by the then Executive Secretary of the UNECA, Mr K.Y. Amoako, a charismatic Ghanaian and seasoned economist, who felt that his authority was being usurped by such an office, especially because the office did not report to him.

Acknowledging his qualifications to play a lead role in African development, I tried desperately to work with him and benefit from the knowledge amassed in ECA, as I saw my role was mainly for advocacy and coordination of reports on behalf of the Secretary-General, but I was rebuffed and the relationship did not build up as I had hoped.

In contrast, all other offices within DESA focused on global thematic issues such as statistics, sustainable development, and policy analysis. Mr Desai even questioned the existence of an office, dealing with regional issues, the only one of its kind, within his department. I believed that working within DESA offered a unique advantage for Africa. In an era when face-to-face interactions were standard, it enabled me to voice Africa's concerns, considering it was the world's least developed continent.

I had arrived in New York in the final year of the United Nations New Agenda for the Development of Africa in the 1990s (UN-NADAF), a programme that was drawn up by the United Nations and approved by the UN General Assembly, and assumed responsibility for the final evaluation of it. The majority of African nations appeared to be oblivious to the existence of this agenda. This astonished me because the United Nations General Assembly had endorsed it as a development plan for Africa in 1990. There was a problem. It was evident that the African nations did not feel a sense of ownership over the agenda, which was, after all, created by UN agencies and submitted for approval to the General Assembly. I immediately felt that a change was required to enable the countries themselves to take their development into their own hands, with support from the UN entities. The final evaluation of UN-NADAF would present an opportunity for change, and the task lay squarely on my shoulders.

The evaluation of UN-NADAF was assigned to a team of development specialists, with my office offering substantive organizational support. The team of eight was led by Professor Botchwey, a dedicated and diligent scholar from Ghana who taught at Harvard. The analysis they conducted presented a grim scenario. Africa's growth performance averaged a mere 4 per cent over the period, covered by UN-NADAF, while overseas development assistance saw a decline of over 40 per cent. Debt reduction initiatives fell short of expectations, with only four countries reaching the prescribed level for debt cancellation. Progress on trade was minimal.

Among the lessons learned were, first and foremost, that conflict and development were mortal enemies. A number of countries were in conflict in Africa when this evaluation was being undertaken. In addition, the model of international development cooperation needed to be revised from the dominant thinking that had guided it in the preceding two decades. Finally, the commitments made must be kept by all parties, and there should be sustained advocacy for African development. There is a need to increase the efficiency and relevance of the United Nations, in this regard.

Over the years, the Organization for African Unity (OAU) had drawn up its own development programmes. These included the Lagos Plan of Action (1980); The African Charter on Human and People's Rights (1981); The African Charter for Popular Participation in Development (1990); The Abuja Treaty establishing the African Economic Community (1991); and the Conference on Security, Stability, Development, and Cooperation Solemn Declaration (2000). But, as for the UN initiatives, these plans had remained documents that were not translated into the actions advocated in them and have suffered the same fate as the UN programmes. Therefore, what resulted was a profusion of unfulfilled ambitions for the development of Africa.

In 2001, while the final evaluation of UN-NADAF was being undertaken, a new initiative emerged from Africa. The New Partnership for Africa's Development, or NEPAD, which was a merger of two plans for the economic regeneration of Africa, the Millennium Partnership for the African Recovery Programme (MAP), led by Former President Thabo Mbeki of South Africa in conjunction with Former President Olusegun Obasanjo of Nigeria and President Abdelaziz Bouteflika of Algeria; and the OMEGA Plan for Africa, developed by President Abdoulaye Wade of Senegal. At a summit in Sirte, Libya, in March 2001, the Organization of African Unity (OAU) agreed that the MAP and OMEGA Plan should be merged, and New Partnership for Africa's Development (NEPAD) emerged.

Given its relevance to our evaluation exercise in New York, we sought to participate in its development. However, this was met with resistance as the proponents envisioned it as an African-led and owned initiative for Africa. They believed Africa needed to take charge of its own development while seeking external partnerships. NEPAD's primary objectives were to eradicate poverty, foster sustainable growth and development, integrate Africa into the global economy, and expedite women's empowerment. These objectives were underpinned by a commitment to good governance, democracy, human rights, and conflict resolution. The proponents recognized that upholding these standards was crucial for creating an environment conducive to investment and long-term economic growth.

By offering an African-owned development framework as the basis for cooperation at the regional and global levels, NEPAD aimed to attract more investment, capital flows, and finance. This was good news to me, although I was left in limbo, as I was involved in the exercise, which was expected to come out with a UN successor program for UN-NADAF.

While the UN in New York was not involved in the drawing up of NEPAD, the UN Economic Commission for Africa had a voice, but there was some disagreement, and it was not given the key role it had expected to assume in its implementation. Instead, a separate secretariat was to be set up in Pretoria. Part of the terms of reference for the evaluation of UN-NADAF was to recommend a successor arrangement to it. It soon became evident that this would not make sense, and rather, the United Nations should support the African initiative. This was the main recommendation that came out of the review, and the assessment team concurred.

Mr Amoako and Mr Desai saw that the change-over to support NEPAD was a good opportunity to get rid of my office, OSCAL and campaigned in this regard. However, the African delegates in New York soon realized that that would result in reducing Africa's voice within the UN Secretariat, and they invoked the General Assembly resolution that created OSCAL. It was established by a General Assembly decision, and the only method to shut it down was also by a resolution from the General Assembly. It seemed unlikely that such a resolution would pass.

We were engaged in drawing up the draft resolution to be adopted by the General Assembly at the end of UN-NADAF. It was clear that there was no point in the United Nations coming up with a "rival" initiative to NEPAD, and the resolution sought to get support and partnership for NEPAD. The big question was the future of OSCAL. I must admit that I was rather nervous, as the abolition of the office would mean that I would need to seek alternative employment. I would not have to leave the UN, as I was at the secretariat on secondment from UNHCR, and with an indefinite contract, I could always return.

However, in addition to the consideration I had, that sparked my move from humanitarian assistance to development, my involvement in the evaluation made me believe that I could contribute in a meaningful way to the development of my beloved continent. I was eager to stay and continue working in New York, as a result of the fresh momentum brought about by the approval of NEPAD.

The negotiations for the resolution were intense. The African countries were adamant that the voice of Africa in New York had to be strengthened, rather than weakened by the abolishment of an African office in the secretariat. Several Western countries saw this as an opportunity to cut down on administrative costs in New York, as part of the ongoing attempts to streamline the budget of the UN.

On the eve of the day that the resolution was to be presented to the General Assembly, the negotiations went on till the wee hours of the morning. At last, sometime around 2 a.m. the chair gave the final version. It confirmed that the UN, rather than spawning another new initiative, should throw its weight behind NEPAD. It also requested that the Office for Africa report directly to the Secretary-General, at the level of Under-Secretary-General, two levels above that of the post that I occupied. As a result of this, the Office of the Special Adviser on Africa was created.

Work with Least Developed Countries (LDCs)

If my role as coordinator for Africa placed me at loggerheads with ECA, my role as coordinator for LDCs did the same with the United Nations Conference on Trade and Development (UNCTAD). UNCTAD had a strong office on LDCs and was the only UN entity that did comprehensive reviews of the situation in LDCs. It was for this reason that they were given a key role in the preparation of the third United Nations Conference on LDCs.

The Secretary-General of UNCTAD was Mr Ricupero, a bald, middle-aged Brazilian economist of high standing. With the third international conference for LDCs taking place in Brussels, he thought UNCTAD should be assigned the responsibility for LDC development. However, this resulted in controversy with the LDCs themselves, who felt that efforts for the development of LDCs should not be restricted to analyses, even if these were thorough. They understood the need for political engagement with LDCs and valued New York's role in that regard.

Again, I was caught in the middle. As the focal point in the DESA for the Third United Nations Conference on the Least Developed Countries in Brussels in 2001, I advocated for the need to have a comprehensive and holistic approach to the problems of LDC, going beyond trade.

I believed that considering trade to the exclusion of everything else was not desirable, and that, in order not to compete with UNCTAD, I would concentrate on a subject that I knew best – energy. Energy, which was indispensable for all aspects of development, was a major problem in LDCs, and to highlight the fact that LDCs cannot hope to provide for their economic and social needs or benefit from trade concessions without adequate energy supplies, I commissioned a report on the situation of energy, which was completely ignored by UNCTAD. I was a key contributor to the planning and execution of the LDC Conference in Brussels, creating various background documents for the event.

I was inclined to support UNCTAD taking the lead on LDC development, recognizing that my small office could not effectively shoulder this responsibility. However, UNCTAD viewed me with suspicion due to my advocacy for the LDC office to be based in New York. The negotiations for the conference's outcome document were fraught with tension, but ultimately, the LDCs prevailed. A decision was made to establish a separate LDC office in New York, led by an Under Secretary General reporting directly to the Secretary-General, a decision which was not appreciated by UNCTAD.

General Assembly Working Group on Africa

The 1998 Secretary General's report on the Causes of Conflicts and the Promotion of Durable Peace and Sustainable Development in Africa, produced for the Security Council, failed to get the Council's attention since it went beyond what they regarded as its jurisdiction. It was promptly forwarded to the Economic and Social Council. The General Assembly had called for regular reports on the implementation of this report to be provided to it, and this responsibility was given to the office for Africa, within DESA, OSCAL.

The lack of cooperation among the key pillars of the United Nations - peace and development, and human rights and development - was something I found perplexing. These pillars largely operated in isolation. I had optimistically hoped that this report would bridge the gap, but this proved unfeasible. I remember proposing a joint meeting of the Security Council and the Economic and Social Council, only to be met with laughter from colleagues. It was then that I realized even the mere suggestion of such collaboration was discouraged.

In 2001, the General Assembly established an open-ended ad hoc working group to monitor the implementation of the 1998 Secretary General's report on Africa, with my office serving as the substantive secretariat. The working group convened for two-week sessions annually, presided over by an ambassador. I believed this role should be assigned to a non-African ambassador and advocated for an ambassador I greatly admired to assume this position. In the working group's inaugural year, I successfully secured the chairmanship for the Singapore ambassador, Ambassador Kishore Mahbubani, whose work and apolitical stance in New York had greatly impressed me.

Another consideration I had was that Africans could benefit from the Singapore experience. At independence, Singapore was at the same level of development as many African countries. I believe that the remarkable success it had made since then might serve as an example and inspiration to African countries. This working group was led the next year by Ambassador Ban Ki Moon, who eventually became Secretary General of the United Nations.

One major frustration I had playing the monitoring role for this report and servicing the working group was the lack of comprehensive consideration of the recommendations of the report, which were aimed at a holistic approach to address the root causes of conflicts in Africa. My role was thus reduced to collecting input from thirty-two United Nations entities to prepare the annual report to the General Assembly.

Office of the Special Adviser on Africa

After the LDC Brussels conference, the United Nations Office of the High Representative for the Least Developed Countries, Landlocked Developing Countries and Small Island Developing States (UN-OHRLLS) was set up. The process of selecting the Under Secretary General commenced, and I remember one of my staff members, Mary, an Iranian who had strong political connections, coming to see me.

'Mrs Stevens, do you want us to lobby for you to get this position?' she asked.

This took me by surprise, as I had never considered it. Firstly, this position was at the Under Secretary General level, two levels above the level I occupied at the time. Secondly, vying for this post would confirm the belief held by many that I had lobbied for the post of head of the Office to be based in New York, for personal reasons. Thirdly, our office still held the mandate for Africa, and there was still a lot to do in advocacy for African development. We were, in fact, in the middle of the final evaluation of UN-NADAF and NEPAD had just been adopted.

'Thank you', I said to her. 'I will concentrate on Africa, which in any case has thirty-two of the forty-six, least developed countries. There is still plenty to do'.

In 2002, as a result of the General Assembly resolution, OSCAL, the African division within DESA was abolished and replaced by the Office of the Special Adviser, led by an Under Secretary General, Ambassador Ibrahim Gambari. The office also had a provision for a director position, which was advertised. In May 2003, I was appointed as the Director of the Office of the Special Adviser on Africa.

In this role, I had numerous responsibilities including setting up the office and filling open positions. We also aimed to establish a sector to assist NEPAD. Having a new boss was reassuring. In DESA, my previous boss, Mr Nitin Desai, was not very supportive of the office and even advocated for its abolition under the influence of his counterpart, Mr Amoako of ECA. Now, under the leadership of an African dedicated to the African cause and who had served as an ambassador of Nigeria in New York, we were ready for action.

The New Partnership for Africa's Development

The first major task we had was to convince the African countries to bring NEPAD to the United Nations. As a result of the frustration of African countries over the implementation of the United Nations initiatives for the development of Africa, the United Nations was mainly dropped from its finalization, and even the Economic Commission for Africa, which played a role in the early stages of its development, had been left out by the time the program was adopted.

In drafting the resolution at the end of the evaluation of UN-NADAF, we had put in a provision that the United Nations should not develop a continuation program for UN-NADAF but should support the ownership by African countries of their development, and promote partnerships among international actors, as affirmed by NEPAD. We argued to the African delegates that leaving out the United Nations General Assembly would be a huge mistake and that, because the New Agenda for the Development of Africa in the 1990s had come to an end, NEPAD could take its place. This would allow for scrutiny of how countries were meeting their commitments for Africa to take place within the ultimate intergovernmental body, the General Assembly. In the end, we succeeded in replacing UN-NADAF with NEPAD as a standing item in the United Nations General Assembly. The Office of the Special Adviser for Africa was thus entrusted with the responsibility of preparing annual reports on the implementation of NEPAD for the General Assembly.

The Tokyo International Conference on African Development (TICAD)

Perhaps the only initiative on south-south cooperation that was not bilateral but involved the United Nations was the Tokyo International Conference on African Development (TICAD). In the aftermath of the end of the Cold War, when African countries found themselves abandoned by other countries, Japan took the initiative to organize what became known as the Tokyo International Conference on African Development (TICAD). Two TICAD conferences (TICAD I and TICADII) were held in 1993 and 1998, respectively, and during my period as Director for Africa, the third such conference (TICAD III) was being planned to take place in 2003.

The Steering Committee for TICAD III consisted of the Japanese government, the United Nations, the United Nations Development Programme, the World Bank and the Global Coalition for Africa. The World Bank, even though listed as a member of the committee, never attended the meetings in

New York. First, as the Special Coordinator for Africa and Least Developed Countries, and later as Director of the United Nations Office for the Special Adviser for Africa, I assumed special responsibility, as the representative of the UN Secretary-General in the Steering Committee for organizing TICAD III.

During our preparations for TICAD III, significant transformations occurred in Africa. The Organization of African Unity evolved into the African Union, and the New Partnership for Africa's Development was established. These two pivotal movements underscored the importance of African nations taking charge of their own development. They advocated for a shift in perspective, urging other countries to engage with Africa as partners rather than mere donors.

One thing that struck me at the time was the absence of representatives from Africa within the Steering Committee. This led to a lot of misunderstandings and I had to act as a go-between of the African ambassadors in New York and the Japanese Mission organizing the conference. As the representative of the Secretary-General, I had to reconcile the aims and objectives of the Japanese government with the expectations of African countries. African countries saw this conference as the medium by which Japan would announce, in concrete terms, its contribution to the priorities of NEPAD, while the Japanese stressed that TICAD was not a funding conference, but that the TICAD process should be seen as playing a catalytic role in translating philosophy and priorities into tangible projects in areas such as human resources development and socio-economic infrastructure. According to the Japanese, the ceaseless efforts under the TICAD process had steadily contributed to African development by presenting unique views on African development and new grounds for partnership.

In the Steering Committee, I endeavoured to echo the sentiments of the African delegates and advocated for the inclusion of the African Union as a member. Collaborating with the Japanese in this context was a unique experience. The committee meetings were often quiet. The Japanese representatives would communicate their government's decisions, attentively listen to the inputs from other committee members, and nod in acknowledgement without providing immediate feedback, citing that the matters "would need to be referred back to Tokyo".

I grew vocal about the need of including Africans in conference preparation and questioned the proliferation of preparatory meetings, whose costs were being considered as Japanese overseas development to Africa. My outspokenness was not well received. At one time, Ahmedou Ould-Abdallah, the Executive Secretary of the Global Coalition for Africa and my predecessor as Director for Africa in the Secretariat, pulled me aside to warn me.

'Be careful what you say at these meetings', he told me. 'The Japanese are not happy with your interventions, and if they report you to the Secretary-General, you could be in big trouble'.

Notwithstanding this warning, I continued to raise the issues that I thought were important, and even though I received no direct reaction, I was never held to account or reprimanded by the Secretary-General. The conference was held in Tokyo, and His Excellency Mr Junichiro Koizumi, Prime Minister of Japan, introduced three pillars of Japan's assistance to Africa, namely, "human-centred development, poverty reduction through economic growth, and consolidation of peace". He also outlined a new objective of extending a total of one billion US dollars in grant aid assistance to directly benefit the people of Africa in areas such as health and medical care, education, water, and food assistance. He concluded that the most important theme of TICAD III was to bring together the knowledge and experiences of the international community in African development in support of the New Partnership for Africa's Development (NEPAD).

To my satisfaction, the recognition of ownership by Africa and its partnership with the international committee made it obvious that the African Union needed to be incorporated as a member of the TICAD steering committee, and this was done after TICAD III.

By the end of 2003, I had the feeling of fulfilment that the important functions which I took up at the level of director when I was assigned to New York in 1999, were now being assumed by two individuals at the level of Under Secretary General, as a result of the recognition that greater attention needed to be directed to the development of Africa and the Least Developed Countries.

Chapter 12

United Nations Assistant Emergency Relief Coordinator and Director for Humanitarian Assistant in Geneva

After five years working at the United Nations Secretariat in New York, and having contributed to the transformation of bodies required to address development in Africa and Least Developed Countries in New York, I decided that I needed to get back to humanitarian work. When the post of Assistant Humanitarian Coordinator and Director of the Geneva Office for the Coordination of Humanitarian Assistance became vacant, I applied for it and was selected. I also wanted to return to Geneva before retiring, to enable me to apply for residence in the city that I loved, after my retirement. I also had two of my children and their families residing there.

In the briefing by my new boss, the United Nations Relief Coordinator, Jan Egeland, the young charismatic, energetic and enthusiastic Norwegian, before leaving New York, he told me that following a recent restructuring of the office, the Geneva office would henceforth focus on natural disasters, thus leaving the more complicated and complex emergencies to the New York office.

'Responding to natural disasters would be less demanding than wars and conflicts, and thus would be a fitting calm before my retirement', I thought. Indeed, a review of my job description revealed that the tasks assigned to me would not present any challenges. It read:

Contribute to the formulation of OCHA's overall strategies as well as to the overall management of the Office's activities and operations; be responsible for the overall management of the OCHA Geneva Office; formulate and implement the substantive work program of the OCHA Geneva Office; oversee the programmatic and administrative tasks necessary for the functioning of the Office, including preparation of budgets, the assigning and monitoring of performance parameters and critical indicators, report on budget/program performance; prepare inputs for results-based budgeting; evaluate staff performance (PAS), interviews of candidates for job openings; and evaluate candidates. Responsible for OCHA working relations in Geneva and Europe on a daily and ongoing basis. Exercise functional management responsibility for the Donor Relations Section, the Emergency Services Branch, as well as the Administrative Office in Geneva; direct OCHA's overall work on disasters caused by natural hazards. Serve as the Chair of the Inter-Agency Standing Committee (IASC) Working Group and, in this capacity, spearhead the work program of the Working Group and its Subsidiary Bodies. Coordinate the Humanitarian Response Review to ensure a more timely and predictable response to disasters.

It turned out that the next year was going to be the *annus horribilus* of natural disasters, characterized by some of the most devastating disasters the world had had to face. The Indian Ocean Tsunami and the South Asia Earthquake were two of the most serious of these. Until my retirement in August 2006, I was not able to fully unpack my personal belongings shipped from New York in 2004.

In my new job, I assumed the chairmanship of the Working Group of the Inter-Agency Steering Committee (IASC), an inter-agency forum for coordination, policy development and decision-making involving the key UN and non-UN humanitarian partners. The United Nations General Assembly created it in 1991 as the principal forum for inter-agency coordination of humanitarian aid. The members of the IASC are the heads or their designated representatives of the UN operational agencies (United Nations Development Programme(UNDP), the United Nations Children Fund (UNICEF), the United Nations High Commission for Refugees (UNHCR), the World Food Programme (WFP), the Food and Agricultural Organization (FAO), the World Health Organization (WHO), The United Nations Human Settlements Programme (UN-HABITAT), the UN Office for the Coordination of Humanitarian Affairs (OCHA) and the International Organization for Migration (IOM). In addition, there was a standing invitation to the International Committee of the Red Cross, (ICRC), the International Federation of the Red Cross and Red Crescent Societies (IFRC), the UN Office of the High Commissioner for Human Rights (OHCHR), The United Nations Population Fund (UNFPA), the Special Rapporteur on the Human Rights of Internally Displaced Persons, and the World Bank. The NGO consortia, International Council for Voluntary Agencies (ICVA), InterAction and The Steering Committee for Humanitarian Response (SCHR) were also invited on a permanent basis to attend. The Emergency Relief Coordinator chaired the IASC; however, there was no differentiation in terms of the involvement of the various participants. This group was unique in the UN system, as the only body pooling together the United Nations humanitarian organizations and other humanitarian actors to address humanitarian issues.

The IASC Working Group, comprising policy directors or equivalents from IASC organizations, primarily focuses on humanitarian policy. As the Assistant Emergency Relief

Coordinator, I chaired this group, which proved to be one of the most challenging tasks during my tenure at the United Nations. Over half of my time at OCHA was dedicated to chairing the working group. Preparations for the working group meetings were intense and time-consuming, involving thorough discussions on agendas, meticulous verification of documents, and efforts to alter established or perceived opinions. The working group's recommendations were presented at the principals' meetings of heads of the participating entities for adoption by the heads of respective member organizations. During my tenure, a total of five IASC principals' meetings took place.

The small IASC Unit in my office consisted of staff from UNICEF, first Kirsi Madi, a Finn and later Marilena Viviani, an Italian. Both women were very hardworking and dedicated and served as strong support for me at some of the most difficult moments at the IASC.

Despite all IASC members being humanitarian organizations, their diverse interests and differing mandates and approaches made it challenging to mediate negotiations. For example, the ICRC representative would consistently preface discussions by asserting their special mandate and non-obligation to adopt any group decision. This became such a routine that I would humorously echo this statement before yielding the floor to the representative.

Despite these hurdles, we successfully finalized inter-agency guidelines in several critical areas. These included the use of in-country self-assessment tools for natural disasters, Human Rights Guidance Notes for Humanitarian Coordinators, Operational Guidelines on Human Rights and Natural Disasters, and Guidelines for Gender-Based Violence Interventions in Humanitarian Settings. These guidelines were made available in English, Arabic, French, and Spanish.

2005 – "Annus Horribilis" for natural disasters

Indian Ocean Tsunami of 2004

On Christmas Eve 2004, I arrived in Geneva to begin my new work. I spent Christmas with my daughter and family, as well as my sister, Yamide, who was visiting from London. We woke up early on the morning of Boxing Day, December 26th.

'Can we turn on the TV to find out what is happening in the world?' asked Yamide. I looked at the clock on the wall. It was only 6 a.m.

'Why don't we lie in today and forget about the problems of the world?' I responded as I reluctantly opened my eyes. 'After all, today is Boxing Day'.

She insisted, and I unwillingly turned on the TV. The pictures were unimaginable. The sight of the huge waves was surreal. At first, I thought it must be a horror film. 'Why would they want to show such a depressing film on Boxing Day?' I asked myself. It took some time for the reality to sink in. Certainly, a tremendous natural calamity had occurred—a tsunami. It also took me another minute to realize that this was perfectly up my alley and that it was my responsibility to commence international response coordination—just two days after starting my new job. It was the middle of the night in New York, which meant that my boss Jan Egeland was still in bed.

The first six hours after I jumped out of bed were quite hectic. Before I could pick up the phone to call Rashid Khalikov, the Deputy Director of the Office, he rang me. 'Did you see the TV pictures of the tsunami in the Indian Ocean?' he asked.

'Yes', I replied, 'Why don't you call all the heads of sections, and we meet at the office at 8:00 a.m.'

A huge earthquake measuring 9.0 on the Richter scale rocked the west coast of northern Indonesia in the early hours of Sunday,

December 26, 2004, followed by aftershocks ranging from 6 to 7.3. The epicentre was located thirty kilometres beneath the seafloor and 250 kilometres south-southwest of Banda Aceh. The quake caused a massive tsunami that swept over the Indian Ocean, destroying the coastlines of northern Sumatra, Thailand, Burma, and Sri Lanka, as well as the east coasts of India, the Maldives, and Africa, particularly the Seychelles and Somalia.

Rashid, a robust Russian who had managed the office after my predecessor's departure and was a contender for the Director's post, initially shared a tense relationship with me. However, our shared commitment to humanitarian work brought us together in the face of a significant disaster, and he proved to be highly cooperative. The inaugural meeting of the task force, comprising all of the office's sections and established by me, saw an impressive attendance despite it being the holiday season. Arjun Katoch, an experienced Indian colleague and the standby duty officer for the holiday period, initiated the office's emergency response procedures. The Emergency Response Team, comprised of individuals who had pre-registered for deployment during the holidays, departed for Sri Lanka on a flight at 11:30 a.m. that same day.

Having invoked the emergency mechanisms, I waited until noon (6 a.m. New York time) to call my boss in New York. 'Good morning, Jan', I started in that early morning call. 'There has been an earthquake and tsunami in the Indian Ocean'.

'You mean the Pacific Ocean?' he replied in a condescending tone. 'Earthquakes do not occur in the Indian Ocean'. I should have been offended, but I did not have time. I pondered, 'He must think this West African woman was so dumb that six hours after we got the news, I could not figure out the difference between the Indian and the Pacific Oceans'.

'Well, I replied', trying to maintain a cool head, 'Why don't you turn on your TV?' He later apologized for his reaction.

Since there was no foreign press presence in the disaster areas, all major news organizations relied on the United Nations' office for up-to-date information. I held general press briefings every day and was interviewed each day by a number of media outlets. At the peak of the response, I held more than 30 press interviews a day.

I vividly recall the first press conference I held that morning. Initially, the death toll stood at 20,000. As our evaluation teams expanded their reach, the numbers tragically rose. By December 28, recorded deaths had escalated to 80,000, with many still unaccounted for. By January 8 an estimated 165,000 lives were lost, and the count continued to rise. The final death toll was approximated at 230,000, though some believe the actual number could have been significantly higher.

As the Assistant Emergency Coordinator, one of my duties was to draft appeals for emergency aid. During the press conference on December 28, I outlined the funding needs. I stressed the unprecedented scale of this disaster - it was the largest natural disaster the United Nations had faced in its sixty-year history. I anticipated that the global appeal for funds would be the largest in UN history. The previous record was a $350 million request for relief following the Bam earthquake in Iran on December 26, 2003, which claimed approximately 30,000 lives exactly a year before the Indian Ocean catastrophe. I informed them that an initial appeal would be issued within two or three days once assessment teams returned with a more comprehensive financing plan to be published by mid-January.

The task of first drawing up a Flash Appeal for funding was not an easy one. The enormity of the disaster meant that coordinating the response was beyond the capacity of the Geneva office. Indeed, the whole of OCHA had to be involved. Five United Nations Disaster Assessment and Coordination (UNDAC) teams, comprising forty-four disaster-response experts from 18 countries and four international organizations, were deployed to five of the tsunami-affected countries. 16 UN Agencies, 18 IFRC response teams, more than 160 international NGOs and countless private companies and civil society groups were deployed to affected areas to provide emergency food, water, and medical services to an estimated five million people in need of assistance. Nonetheless, my office was in charge of organizing replies and producing the Inter-Agency Appeal.

On January 6, 2005, the UN Secretary-General launched a Flash Appeal for the tsunami. From January until the end of June 2005, this Flash Appeal sought for US$977 million to assist the important work of 40 UN agencies and NGOs in Indonesia, the Maldives, Myanmar, Seychelles, Somalia, and Sri Lanka.

After the appeal launch, I campaigned for funding within the Geneva-based humanitarian community. I chose to deviate from the norm of conducting briefings and appealing to the established Humanitarian Response Group, which comprised major humanitarian donors. Instead, I opened the campaign to all United Nations Member States. My reasoning was straightforward - the Tsunami was a colossal humanitarian crisis that necessitated assistance from all Member States. Even if contributions from less affluent countries did not match those from larger donors, it would symbolize global solidarity with the affected countries. This decision yielded the desired results, with non-traditional contributors like Equatorial Guinea, Mali, Senegal, Liberia, East Timor, Palau, Jamaica, and Columbia contributing to the Tsunami Response Trust Fund. Consequently, this strategy of opening the United Nations Appeal for Funds to all became a standard practice at the OCHA Office in Geneva during my tenure as Assistant Emergency Relief Coordinator, and continued thereafter.

For the following months, as the number of casualties increased, it became what seemed like a numbers game, and the emphasis was on knowing how many people had died. By May, the tally of deaths had stabilized. I wanted to know what was beyond the numbers and decided to undertake a mission to some of the affected areas to get some first-hand knowledge as to what these figures meant. I visited Thailand and Indonesia.

In Phuket, Thailand, the stench of the bodies combined with the smell of formaldehyde prevailed. It was extremely difficult to identify the corpses, as I learned that they all turned black after a few days in the sea. Initially, the remains were cremated, but after international concern, a morgue with a cold room was established to keep the collected corpses while they were being identified. Many of the deceased were Western tourists, and hundreds of bodies were still to be identified when I arrived.

Personal belongings of the deceased, including watches, rings, and lockets bearing images of loved ones, were displayed on a billboard outside the authorities' headquarters to facilitate identification. Examining these items closely served as a poignant reminder that each statistic represented a real person. These were ordinary individuals who wore clothes, used watches, and cherished keepsakes of their loved ones.

In Banda Aceh, Indonesia, the local population bore the brunt of the tsunami's devastation. I had the opportunity to engage with groups of survivors residing in temporary shelters and listen to their harrowing tales. The men described how they lost not just their homes but also the land on which these structures stood, as the tsunami obliterated entire villages. I spoke with a group of men who survived because they were away from their villages when disaster struck. They shared their terrifying experiences of waking up one day to find that they had lost their entire families and all their life's possessions.

The stories from the women were most touching. They each recounted their experiences when the tsunami struck. The story of one woman stands out: 'My husband, our six children and I were in bed asleep when the wave hit our house. As the wave receded, I watched my family disappear with it, but I was lucky to have hung on to a tree stump in our yard, holding the hand of my baby girl. The force of the water was strong, and I felt that the hold on my baby daughter was weakening. But I was determined to hold on with all my strength. I could not lose ALL of them. However, as the pressure of the water intensified, I had to let go for a moment to maintain my grip. I stretched my hand to reach her again, but she was not there. She had gone too. I should never have let go of her hands. Oh, why did I let go?'

The tears were now dripping down her face—and down mine too.

'Why did I let go?'

South Asia Earthquake

On October 8, 2005, we were jolted awake by a major catastrophe. A colossal earthquake, registering 7.6 on the Richter scale rocked Pakistan, India, and Afghanistan in the early hours. This was the most destructive earthquake the region had witnessed in a century. As per protocol, the UN Disaster Management Team from my office was deployed and took charge of coordinating information-sharing on relief activities carried out by the UN and NGOs.

Nearly four weeks had passed since this massive earthquake had devastated the Kashmir Province of Pakistan. The United Nations had assembled a consolidated appeal for US$500 million to aid in relief efforts. However, funds were trickling in slowly, and we had only managed to amass US$60 million. So, when I was informed by the Public Information Officer that the BBC World Service had invited our Office to participate in a live show called "Talking Point", I seized the opportunity. This was a chance to enlighten the world about the catastrophic situation in Kashmir and underscore the urgent need for resolution, thereby attracting additional donations for our cause.

It was only on the eve of the programme that I grasped how challenging this experience could be. I had previously participated in radio and TV interviews and panel discussions without any issues, usually feeling quite confident as I could predict the questions and prepare my responses accordingly. However, this was going to be a live phone-in show open to audiences worldwide, and it was impossible to anticipate what could transpire.

I was soaking up all the knowledge I imagined I would need until the last minute when I had to rush off to a private studio in Geneva from where I was to participate. I arrived five minutes before the program was scheduled to begin and dashed to the studio just in time to regain my breath before being placed online. I grew nervous, which is rare for me. The presenter, Robin Lustig introduced me as the guest of the show and started by asking me, 'Yvette, why is the UN desperately appealing for money to help victims of the earthquake?' This was simple since it allowed me to discuss the need for donations to convey food and other relief supplies to people through tough terrain, as well as for winterized tents as the typically harsh winter approached. After me, an official from another assistance group said something similar. Everything was going well. Then it was the turn of the then Prime Minister of Pakistan, Shaukat Aziz.

To my astonishment, Mr Aziz began by stating that his government was making all necessary arrangements for aid and expressed gratitude to the international community for pledges amounting to 2.5 billion US dollars. He concluded by asserting that "no Pakistani victim of the earthquake is hungry". I was taken aback. His words were hard to believe. He could have moderated his claims by emphasizing that housing was a more pressing concern than food and that the funds he mentioned were pledged but not yet received, but he chose not to. I found myself thinking, 'Here I am, with a global audience, urgently appealing for more aid that is desperately needed, and the Prime Minister of Pakistan is undermining my efforts. How could I navigate this situation without publicly confronting the prime minister?' I realized I needed to devise a strategy swiftly before the presenter redirected the conversation back to me.

So, as we paused for phone-in interventions and questions, I pondered while still responding to questions. It is amazing how one develops these skills when cornered. At last, I found a way to handle this. I would still make my point without challenging the prime minister. So, I said calmly, 'A disaster of this magnitude, even when it occurs in the most developed countries, needs the support of the international community, and this does not imply weakness on the part of the Government'.

I waited a few moments for this to sink in and then added, 'My particular concern about the lack of funding is related to the UN Appeal, which covers unmet needs as determined jointly with the Government. If we do not get the funds, then we cannot meet our part of the bargain, and people will suffer'. And with that, I breathed a sigh of relief. The point was delivered without hurting the prime minister's dignity, who I later learned, was using this show to reply to some organizations in Pakistan criticizing the government's inability to offer help to its people. I do not know if the TV program helped, but at least I saved an embarrassing situation. Funding for the UN Appeal did pour in later, and the UN could undertake the most urgent actions as planned.

The South Asia Earthquake struck the Himalayas, where the mountainous terrain hindered the transportation of relief supplies to the affected populace. Mountain roads had vanished in spots, causing relief convoys to be stranded. Typically, in emergencies, non-governmental organizations conduct area mappings for relief agencies to plan trips, but access was restricted in this instance. During my tenure at ILO, I studied satellite remote sensing applications and recognized that despite its high cost, it was an ideal solution for humanitarian situations.

Meanwhile, UNOSAT, the United Nations Institute for Training and Research (UNITAR) Operational Satellite Applications Programme, was eager to provide its expertise to assist in the mapping. However, UNOSAT, as a programme of UNITAR, is a project-based organization and does not receive any funds from the regular United Nations budget. The institute was financed entirely from voluntary contributions, so to be included in the response to this disaster, it needed to be part of the United Nations appeal. UNOSAT had established a Humanitarian Rapid Mapping Service in 2003, but this had not been recognized by the humanitarian community, and therefore many within the community were reticent to accept UNOSAT "into the fold".

As Chair of the Inter-Agency Standing Committee, I advocated for UNOSAT's involvement. I arranged a session with UNOSAT to enlighten the humanitarian community about the benefits of satellite technology in relief operations. Ultimately, it was acknowledged that traditional on-the-ground mapping was unreliable.

The session was a success, with UNOSAT demonstrating their crucial role through the periodic satellite maps they procured. These maps unveiled details that ground or aerial photographs could not capture. The extent of building damage was indiscernible from aerial images in which the roofs appeared intact on the ground. Despite the high cost of regular satellite imagery, it was evident that this would be an ideal method for mapping this disaster and future calamities.

UNOSAT was so grateful for my role that they invited me to become their goodwill ambassador after I retired from the United Nations the following year. Due to a lack of finances, I was unable to actively serve in this role. Yet the case had already been made, and I was pleased to have played a crucial role in it.

The Niger Food Crisis

The food crisis in Niger in 2005-2006 was a slow-onset calamity. It was a limited food security crisis in Niger's northern Maradi, Tahoua, Tillabéri, and Zinder areas caused by an early end to the 2004 rains and a locust infestation. This famine was said to have affected 800,000 people. Although the UN's Food and Agriculture Organization had already warned of an upcoming crisis in late 2004, donor support came slowly throughout the first half of 2005.

The situation in the country was dire. Over 2.5 million individuals in Niger, including 32,000 children, were identified as "vulnerable", with the children at risk of death. The United Nations' plea for aid was less than 50 per cent funded. UN Secretary-General Kofi Annan, after visiting President Tandja Mamadou in Zinder in late August 2005, brought the crisis to the forefront. This visit was seen as an effort to highlight the issue and address criticisms of the UN's perceived hesitancy to respond. Donors had provided less than half of the US$81 million that the UN had requested.

I accompanied the Secretary-General and his team from New York on this delicate visit. The then President of Niger challenged the accuracy of the international media's claims about a famine in Niger. He argued that while chronic malnutrition was indeed a problem for the people of Niger, the media had mistakenly and intentionally portrayed common local food habits as signs of a worldwide famine to garner sympathy from donors. To circumvent the controversy, the Secretary-General skilfully employed his diplomatic acumen.

'The debate as to whether this was a famine or a food crisis is irrelevant to those who are hungry and need food. The focus should be on providing immediate assistance to them'.

The visit of the Secretary-General drew the attention of the international community, and humanitarian aid was increased. On January 16, 2006, the UN directed an appeal for US$240 million of food aid for West Africa to feed at least 10 million people affected by the food crisis, with Niger being the worst-affected country.

The humanitarian response review

In light of the problems faced in Darfur and the experience gained from the response to recent emergencies, the Emergency Relief Coordinator (ERC), Jan Egeland, decided to embark on the Humanitarian Response Review in October 2004. In a note to the IASC Principals, the ERC announced the review as follows:

In several humanitarian crises, there is a perceived weakening of the humanitarian capacity to respond to many of the parallel crises that face the current international humanitarian system. The result is that we often cannot meet the basic needs of affected populations. As the Emergency Relief Coordinator, I feel it is critical that we address this concern by reaching a common understanding of both the current response capacity and available expertise, and how we can effectively mobilize and deploy them. This would include a better appreciation of the possible gaps in expertise and resources that exist by sector and the identification of those factors that act as a constraint to the effective and full deployment of humanitarian capacity when needs arise.

To that end, I would like to propose an independent review of the current global response capacity, which I feel requires a level of external support. It is my hope that through this exercise we can jointly identify existing weaknesses and trends in our response and then develop a common plan for addressing these shortcomings, as originally envisioned in UN General Assembly Resolution 46/182. I would wish that the outcome of the review could help us ensure that our response capacity, as UN agencies and NGOs, in terms of human and financial resources, tools and mechanisms - is appropriate to changes in the humanitarian environment. This should ultimately help us meet future challenges through improved response mechanisms and delivery, as well as better-defined accountability for humanitarian action.

In the meantime, I have asked Assistant Emergency Relief Coordinator Yvette Stevens to lead consultations on this process through the IASC Working Group, with technical support from OCHA's policy branch, in the identification of external support for the processes.

The Humanitarian Response Review (HRR), which was undertaken by four independent consultants, was only started in February of 2005, because of the Indian Ocean Tsunami crisis. I had been one of the critics of the shortcomings of responses to humanitarian assistance, so I was pleased when Jan named me as the OCHA coordinator for the project. A team of five consultants, led by Costanza Adinolfi, a former Director General/Head of the Department of Humanitarian Aid of the European Commission, was recruited for this review.

We were all tremendously engaged with the review when the Indian Ocean Tsunami struck on December 26, 2004. I thought the evaluation would be postponed, but our boss, Jan, indicated to senior management that he still wanted the review to go ahead, nevertheless.

After the selection of the consultants, work started in earnest. What was lacking, however, was the full commitment of some OCHA staff both in New York and Geneva to provide OCHA input to the review, in the light of responding to ongoing emergencies. Attempts to discuss substantive issues relating to the review did not achieve much, as this was never viewed as a priority by OCHA staff.

I also encountered some difficulties in securing the participation of the humanitarian actors. To begin with, the initiative came from OCHA rather than the Inter-Agency Standing Committee for Humanitarian Assistance (IASC).

In addition, Ms Adinolfi did not seem to get along well with the other members of the team. She tried to impose her views on them and I found myself having to play the role of arbitrator between the team members. Furthermore, within the office in Geneva, I did not enjoy the support I needed, even if my boss in New York always gave credit for any success that I achieved to my deputy or the "team" in Geneva.

The consultancy period was nearing its conclusion, and the anticipated report was nowhere to be found. Jan was keen to receive the report, but I saw little possibility of that happening. It was evident that due to internal disagreements, the review team could not meet the deadline. Having attended all the meetings and debates with the team, I had a clear understanding of the situation. I chose to take a bold step and overhaul the entire report, incorporating the recommendations that had emerged during the deliberations. I presented this to the team, and much to my delight, only Ms Adinolfi expressed concerns. Despite some intense phone discussions, she eventually agreed, albeit reluctantly, to accept the revised report I had prepared.

This groundbreaking study included various suggestions to enhance humanitarian response, the most important of which were connected to readiness, early warning, and sectoral coordination of humanitarian actors' operations in the field. As a result of the assessment, the United Nations General Assembly established the Central Emergency Response Fund in 2006. Its aims are to promote early action and response to avoid loss of life, enhance response to time-critical requirements, and strengthen core elements of humanitarian response in underfunded crises.

The CERF has a grant facility of US$450 million and a loan facility of $30 million.

To mitigate the issue of sectoral coordination, the review suggested that the IASC should designate lead organizations with sectoral responsibilities. This would hopefully prevent duplication of efforts and competition for limited resources during humanitarian crises. The focus would be particularly on the protection and care of populations affected by disasters. The recommendation was to adopt a cluster approach for response in all priority areas of assistance. This strategy was expected to ensure clear leadership and accountability in key areas of humanitarian response, thereby consolidating their efforts into cohesive clusters.

Upon receiving approval from the IASC, I was entrusted with spearheading the intricate task of developing the clusters. Initially, we referred to these as sectors for coordination. However, I observed that while some sectors like water and health were well-defined, many areas needing coordination, such as early recovery and protection, transcended these conventional sectors. Consequently, I proposed that these areas be termed as clusters. The term "clusters" sparked debates among some members. To circumvent protracted disputes over terminology, I persuaded the IASC Working Group members to concentrate on the essence of the recommendation and consider renaming it later if needed. Interestingly, no alternative name has been proposed to date.

The Cluster Approach was first implemented following the 2005 earthquake in Pakistan, a mere three months after its inception. In the span of twenty-four hours after the earthquake, nine clusters were established. This approach offered the Pakistani government a more structured and consistent liaison with the humanitarian community. Furthermore, clusters facilitated members with opportunities for information sharing and coordination. The nine clusters for the Pakistan earthquake were defined under three broad headings: Service Provision, which encompassed logistics and emergency telecommunications; Relief and Assistance to beneficiaries, which covered emergency shelter, health, nutrition and water hygiene and sanitation; and Cross-Cutting Concerns, with three clusters: early recovery, protection and camp coordination and management.

Management problems at OCHA

I took up my appointment at OCHA just a couple of weeks after a restructuring was announced. The changes were the merging of the operational unit in Geneva and New York, with the unit in Geneva reporting to a director in New York. While the merger indicated in some detail the revised structure for the newly created division, it failed to lay out how this change would affect the work of the Geneva Office in general, or more specifically, the authority of the Director of the OCHA Geneva Office.

The shift of field operations management to New York, coupled with the fact that many Geneva-based functional units were already reporting to New York, diminished the Director's influence over the Geneva office's operations. In this context, I had to depend on the staff members' goodwill to effectively execute the office's tasks, which unfortunately was not always forthcoming.

In this ambiguous situation regarding my role, I took the initiative to delineate how I could optimally function within the existing parameters, given that no immediate change was foreseeable. This decision was met with resistance from some quarters and led to some personal frustration. I realized that I needed to exhibit exceptional assertiveness if I wanted to achieve anything substantial. This assertiveness indeed proved beneficial, especially in coordinating OCHA's initial response to the major natural disasters of 2004 and 2005. The heads of the sections reporting directly to me, Gerhard Putman Kramer, Magda Ninaber, Kirsi Mardi and Marilena Viviani gave me their unflinching support. However, in other work areas, I had less success and ended up personally handling tasks assigned by the ERC, with minimal involvement from some line entities, despite my repeated appeals. This was evident in the humanitarian response review and the development of the Cluster Approach.

My assertiveness, particularly as an African woman, was misconstrued as aggression. My appeals for clarity from New York were met with scepticism. Jan attributed the deteriorating relations between the Geneva and New York offices to me, rather than his organizational structure. Although he did not express this directly, he voiced his complaints to others who relayed them to me. He had hoped that I would unify the two offices, but I sensed his disappointment when I could not. Despite my best intentions, this task was beyond my capabilities.

Upon leaving OCHA, I proposed specific recommendations on how the terms of reference for the two offices could be harmonized to prevent disagreements. However, I am not sure if these suggestions were considered. I have heard that the friction between the two offices persists to this day.

As a single black woman in a high management position within a predominantly white-male institution, my words and actions were often misinterpreted. The presence of racism was palpable, even if it was not overtly apparent.

Another thing to note is that the whole structure in Geneva for dealing with humanitarian issues was tailored towards the traditional humanitarian donors. For example, despite the fact that the majority of the crises were in Africa, Asia, and Latin America, the focus of OCHA briefings was the Humanitarian Liaison Working Group, a group of donors. This was the reason why I broke the chain, following the Indian Ocean Tsunami, when the first and subsequent briefings I gave were not restricted to the HLWG, but to the entire United Nations Member States.

The result was striking. The poorest countries announced pledges, and even though they were small, the fact that they felt that response to catastrophes required a global response was satisfying to me. I continued to invite all Member States to humanitarian briefings during my entire period at OCHA.

Retirement from the United Nations

When I took up the appointment at OCHA, I knew that I had less than two years before the United Nations statutory retirement age of 60. But I felt I was in my prime and had a lot of steam to go on.

My departure from the United Nations was somewhat uneventful. At that time, a General Assembly resolution mandated the compulsory retirement of professional-level staff at age 60. The quotas for regional representation at the United Nations Secretariat were determined by a nation's population size and its contribution to the regular budget. Some influential but under-represented countries believed they needed more space to meet their quotas.

I officially retired from the UN on August 31, 2006.

Chapter 13

Back to the United Nations as Permanent Representative of Sierra Leone

After retiring, I went to Freetown at the end of 2009 and spent nearly three years as a policy adviser to the Minister of Energy and Water Resources and Director of Energy. One day in July 2011, I received a phone call from the office of the President of Sierra Leone.

'This is the Secretary to the President', the voice on the phone was auspicious.

I was baffled since I had no idea what to anticipate. A call from the President's office may indicate that you were in trouble or, on the contrary, that you were being recognized for the outstanding work you were doing. 'May I help you?'

He went on. 'Well, as you may know, the Cabinet has approved the opening of a Sierra Leone Permanent Mission to the United Nations in Geneva'.

'Oh, that is good news', I replied. I had, for years while working for the United Nations, been advocating and campaigning for Sierra Leone to open a Permanent Mission in Geneva, and I had even offered to serve as an honorary ambassador for Sierra Leone after retiring from the United Nations, but this was turned down since the expense of living in Geneva was considered prohibitively high.

After several attempts to convince the Government, I gave up but remained disappointed at the absence of a Sierra Leone Mission in Geneva. This was in view of the fact that while New York is the headquarters of The United Nations, Geneva is what could be described as the "Kitchen of the United Nations". Most of the specialized agencies covering health, trade, telecommunications, meteorology, human rights and humanitarian concerns have their headquarters in Geneva. Geneva is also home to over 200 non-governmental organizations dealing with these issues. Representation of Sierra Leone in Geneva could thus immensely benefit from such a presence. I became interested.

'The President has indicated that he wants someone who knows the United Nations thoroughly to fill the post of Permanent Representative, and you come highly recommended. This call is to ask if you would accept such a position'.

If this offer had come three years before, I would have readily accepted it, but now that I had returned to my engineering career and loved every minute of my job, I was not too sure. After some hesitation, I said, 'I really cannot leave this job I am currently doing because I am in the middle of a number of initiatives aimed at improving power supply in the country'.

'Well', he said, 'Why don't you think about it? I will call you again in two weeks'.

The subsequent weeks were devoted to reflection. On one hand, I found solace in resuming my hands-on engineering responsibilities and being at home with my ailing sister, Hannah, who unfortunately had no children. She had been a significant financial pillar for our family, and I felt it was my responsibility to care for her now that her health was declining. Moreover, after nearly three decades of living as a foreigner in various countries,

I was finally home- a place where I truly felt a sense of belonging, and practising the profession I was educated in.

On the other hand, I thought that given my "insider's" knowledge of the United Nations, I could serve my country in good stead. I thought about a few of the things that could be done in Geneva while keeping in mind President Bai Koroma's Agenda for Change. The Agenda for Change recognized that, in order to reduce poverty, our strategy should include substantial investments in supportive infrastructure, improved delivery of social services, and private sector involvement, and it identified the priorities for addressing Sierra Leone's development needs as energy, agriculture, infrastructure, and human development, including health and education.

Health was a paramount objective, serving as a measure of all successes. Geneva, being the health "capital" of the United Nations, offered an excellent opportunity to garner the comprehensive support needed to achieve our country's health goals. Sierra Leone's presence in Geneva would ensure regular interaction with health institutions such as the WHO, ensuring that all avenues for addressing our health concerns were explored.

Under infrastructure, the development of our feeder roads was crucial for facilitating the movement of goods and people from the remotest parts of our country. The International Labour Office's expertise in labour-intensive work programs could enhance rural road networks while providing valuable employment opportunities for our youth. Youth employment was a challenge highlighted in the Agenda for Change, necessitating engagement with the ILO to devise innovative solutions to our youth unemployment issue.

Good governance was another challenge outlined in the Agenda for Change. A transparent and democratic system, underpinned by respect for human rights, forms the bedrock of effective governance. Geneva offered us the opportunity to benefit from the proceedings of the United Nations Human Rights Council. Sierra Leone could also leverage inputs from organizations such as the World Meteorological Organization, the Secretariat of the International Strategy for Disaster Reduction, and the United Nations Office for Humanitarian Affairs to mitigate the adverse effects of climate change, which we anticipated would severely impact Africa.

Sierra Leone was heavily reliant on international trade for survival and should take a more active role in international trade discussions to ensure that its interests were reflected in the relevant outputs of the World Trade Organization (WTO) and the United Nations Conference on Trade and Development (UNCTAD).

Although I had three of my children and their families in Switzerland, we kept in regular touch through my visits to Geneva and, of course, theirs to Sierra Leone. Given that my children grew up in Switzerland and were married to Europeans, my presence in Freetown provided fantastic motivation for them to visit their origins on a regular basis, which I appreciated. After two weeks, my decision was guided by the consideration of putting my country ahead of my personal interests. When the President's Secretary called again, I answered positively.

'Yes', I started. 'I would be pleased and honoured to serve my country in the capacity of Ambassador and Permanent Representative of Sierra Leone in Geneva. However, I would like to complete the current initiatives I am undertaking as Director of Energy before I take up this appointment'.

Once I made the decision to represent Sierra Leone in Geneva, my enthusiasm was overwhelming. According to the Ministry of Foreign Affairs, the Mission was to be hosted by the Commonwealth Secretariat Small States Office and would benefit from a Swiss grant of 3000 Swiss Francs monthly towards the administrative costs. The Sierra Leone Honorary Consul had promised to provide a car and office furniture and equipment, and the Sierra Leoneans based in Geneva had expressed their support to the Mission. Everything seemed shaky, but I plodded on.

Thus, on September 1, 2011, I travelled to Geneva for the official opening of the Mission. It was agreed that I would need to wrap up my ongoing tasks at the Ministry of Energy and Water Resources before taking up my position as Ambassador. In the meantime, I was asked to find someone to be officer-in-charge until I was able to assume my functions. I moved between Freetown and Geneva from September 2011 to March 2012, while appointing a young Sierra Leonean, Kanyama Dixon-Fyle, to hold down the fort at the Mission. I offered to give her an honorarium, but there was no funding for it, so I had to pay her out of my own cash for the first two months.

We were provided with two rooms with a total area of 48 square meters and given the possibility to use the common facilities at the Commonwealth Secretariat Small States Office at a subsidized rental of 1,800 Swiss francs. But the use of the facilities was expensive. Photocopying costs ten cents a page in black and white and thirty-five cents in colour. In those days, most of the documents were sent by fax, and some could be as big as 100 pages.

Mr Luy a Swiss of medium height and slight build, had served as the Honorary Consul of Sierra Leone for over a decade. It turned out that his promise to personally fund the Mission's setup was in anticipation of his appointment as the Permanent Representative upon its inauguration. However, much to his disappointment I had been appointed instead. Consequently, he only furnished the office with two tables and a few chairs. My son Boris stepped in to supplement the office equipment, procuring second-hand computers, a photocopier, and a high-capacity fax machine.

I could not pay the rent for two months, from September to December, and all transactions had to be done on credit. On December 19, 2011, the first funds were sent to the Mission. I had to clear a lot of bills and cover the Mission's administrative obligations for the next few months because I had no idea when I would again get money from Freetown.

In terms of assistance, all Sierra Leoneans in Geneva were holding substantial positions within international organizations and did not have the time to furnish me with the substantive assistance that was anticipated. I was only able to begin operating properly owing to the assistance of a dedicated Sierra Leonean who was the president of the Sierra Leone Association in Geneva, Mr Claude Stefanopulos and my son Boris. Later, I was able to recruit a hardworking personal assistant locally, Folake Idowu, a Nigerian, who turned out to be a huge asset to the Mission.

I officially assumed my full-time duties in March 2012, but I needed parliamentary approval for my nomination before I could formally present my credentials in Geneva and Bern. I returned to Freetown, initially assuming that the parliamentary clearance process, with the Foreign Ministry's support, would take a week or two. However, this support was not provided. I reached out to the Parliament's clerk, who directed me to the Director of Committees at the Parliament. The Director provided me with a list of documents required in 17 copies for the Parliament's Appointments Committee. These included a copy of my appointment letter, my Voter ID Card, my curriculum vitae, copies of all my academic certificates (with originals to be presented on the interview day), a declaration of all assets (including bank statements for all accounts sworn before a Justice of the Peace), an Income Tax Certificate from the National Revenue Authority, and a Police Clearance Certificate from the Criminal Investigations Department (CID).

Putting together the documents that I had to prepare was

easy, even if time-consuming and I could manage to do this within a couple of days. However, obtaining the certificates from the CID and the NRA proved to be extremely difficult. I first called these offices to become acquainted with the procedures for obtaining these certificates. Within these offices, the sight of stacks of paper files approaching the ceiling was unnerving. The pages popping out of the folders were brown and faded, and I recognized that these offices' records were not stored electronically. To locate anything, officials had to go through these shattered files. I was perplexed as to how they were supposed to provide any credible information on anyone, yet they did.

My initial trips to these entities were fruitless. Every time, I was informed that the persons in charge were not present. Ultimately, after two weeks of daily visits, I was encouraged to offer some incentives to the responsible employees, or risk not receiving these certifications at all; I gave in. I needed to return to Geneva because I had handed the work at the Mission to a volunteer, Mr Claude Stefanopulos, with whom I was in regular contact, but I needed to return since some crucial events were taking place. The incentives were effective.

Finally, I had compiled all the necessary documents for the Parliamentary Appointments Committee. I took them to a public photocopying service to create 17 sets of the 50-page document. I neatly organized these copies into a folder and presented them with pride to the Parliamentary Secretary. However, I was disheartened to learn that due to the pressure of work, my case would only be reviewed in a month. Once again, I was advised to offer some incentive, which I did, resulting in my case being expedited to the following week - a testament to the power of incentives in Sierra Leone.

I was scheduled to appear before the Parliamentary Committee on Appointments and Public Service Vetting of the President at Parliament in Tower Hill. Tower Hill held fond memories for me as a child growing up in its vicinity in the fifties. The hill was the home of the military and was abundant with fruit trees. As children living nearby, we would go there to pick mangoes and often found ourselves being chased down the hill by the soldiers, as we scampered to safety in the neighbouring areas.

It was at Independence that Tower Hill became the home of the Sierra Leone Parliament. The House of Parliament of Sierra Leone is a cubic citadel with a panoramic view of the Freetown harbour. The coffee-coloured building is characterized by sharp geometric forms, with a dome in the middle and a rough concrete surface that reveals the imprint of the structure's wooden frame. The façade is covered in pre-cut pieces of red stone, locally excavated from the hilltop, which gives the building its coffee colour. The building was a gift from Israel for Sierra Leone's Independence in 1961.

I recalled how, in the sixties, after Independence, it was such a pleasure for me to visit Parliament in session and, from the public galleries overlooking the chamber, listen to the speeches of visionaries such Cyril Rogers-Wright, one of the most charismatic politicians in those days, and the many debates. Now, I had to confront Parliament in a different role.

I arrived in Parliament with my sister Hannah, approximately an hour before the interview. I took advantage of the chance to look around Parliament, which prepared me for the interview I was about to face. I wandered around the grounds, admiring the unusual buildings and posing for photos. I gazed down from the hill to take in the panoramic view of Freetown and its natural harbour, which is regarded as one of the best in the world.

I paid my respects at the graves of two influential leaders from our past. The first was Sir Milton Margai, the inaugural Prime Minister of Sierra Leone, and the second was my father-in-law, Siaka Probyn Stevens, the first Executive President. These two leaders collaborated to secure independence but parted ways when Siaka Stevens declined to sign the Declaration of Independence during the constitutional talks in London, deeming the stipulations within its voluminous pages unfair. Consequently, he was incarcerated before Independence Day and had to spend the Independence Day in confinement. Now, they rest side by side. This served as a poignant reminder that despite our differences, we shared a common purpose- to serve our beloved nation. It reaffirmed my commitment to serve my country in any capacity, undeterred by any obstacles that might be placed in my path.

When I entered the structure, I was allowed to peek into the main chamber. Although Parliament was not in session, the view of the chamber reminded me of my childhood, when I was a member of the public witnessing the proceedings from the gallery.

The interview by the Committee was profound. The questions covered the relevance of a mission in Geneva, my background and qualifications for the job, and the issues I hoped to address while in Geneva. It all went extremely well. The questions were good, clear and to the point and I got so engaged and enjoyed the questioning, that I was kind of sad when it ended. Each member of the panel, which consisted of members from all the political parties, gave their sign of approval and said they were more than satisfied with my answers.

The Committee's findings were delivered to Parliament on June 19, 2012, when I seated in front of the whole House. This was an amazing experience. As a nominee, I sat in a designated seat towards the front of the Chamber, lower than the Speaker's podium. I then listened to the Committee's findings, which were followed by a lengthy parliamentary debate. I must say that I was gratified by the complimentary comments from all sides of the House, but what I found humorous was that I was being discussed, without having the opportunity to say anything. Even when one over-enthusiastic MP credited me with achievements that I had not made, I could not correct him. At the end of the debate, "the Parliament passed unanimously by a collection of voices" their approval for my appointment as Ambassador Extraordinary and Plenipotentiary to the Confederation of Switzerland and Permanent Representative to the United Nations in Geneva. All was now set for action.

The presentation of my credentials at the United Nations in Geneva was a simple low-profile event. Returning to the offices in Geneva, which I knew so well, but in a different capacity, was touching. I was required to appear for the presentation of my credentials with a member of staff of the Mission, but since I had no staff, I was accompanied only by my son Boris. We arrived at the office of Kassym-Jomart Tokayev, the Director-General of the United Nations Office in Geneva. On entering the office everything invoked a new feeling of hope. There was hope in the potential of the United Nations to deliver under its three pillars: peace and security, development and human rights. The Director General stood on one side of a United Nations flag, mounted on a two-meter flag pole, and I was ushered to the other side of the flag, from where I officially handed my Letter of Credence from the Government of Sierra Leone.

According to protocol, the Letter of Credence was addressed to Ban Ki Moon, the Secretary General of the United Nations, by the Minister of Foreign Affairs of Sierra Leone. It stated that the Government of Sierra Leone had vested me with, *'full and all manner of power and authority, for and in the name of the Republic of Sierra Leone, to meet and confer with Your Excellency and other appropriate officials of the United Nations and with any person or persons invested with like power and authority by the respective Governments and States represented in the United Nations in Geneva'.*

After handing over my Letter of Credence, the Director

General invited me to sit at the conference table in his office for a conversation. Observing the usual courtesies, he, welcomed me to this new role and noted that, as is usually the case, he did not have to use the opportunity to acquaint me with the work of the United Nations, as *"with your experience, you probably know more than I"*.

After the official ceremony, I decided to take some time to walk along the avenue where the flags of all the 193 Member States of the United Nations were displayed. The flags were planted on a lush green lawn along the avenue facing the *Place des Nations*. Four parallel rows of flags, two on each side of the grass lawn, stretch for around 150 meters, with a paved promenade on each side. Throughout my two years in the *Palais des Nations* during the frantic months of 2005 and 2006, I never had time to visit this location, but on this day, I did. As I proceeded down the avenue, I came to a halt beneath the green, white, and blue flag of Sierra Leone. That brought home to me the new job I had been assigned in the name of my nation, Sierra Leone.

Despite my country being among the smallest in the world, I recognized the importance of leveraging this opportunity to protect my country's interests and contribute to global issues.

The presentation of my ambassadorial credentials to the president of Switzerland had to wait a few months due to the president's fixed calendar for the presentation of credentials. On November 23, 2012, I had the honour of presenting my Letters of Credence to the President of the Swiss Confederation for 2012, Her Excellency Mrs Eveline Widmer-Schlumpf.

Upon arrival at the West Wing of the Federal Palace in Bern, I was welcomed by the Head of Protocol, who introduced me to the President. I presented my Letter of Credence and extended fraternal greetings from His Excellency Dr Ernest Bai Koroma, the President of the Republic of Sierra Leone.

In the ensuing discussion post-ceremony, the Swiss President highlighted the longstanding bilateral relations between Switzerland and Sierra Leone, tracing back to our country's independence in 1961. I expressed gratitude for Switzerland's humanitarian aid to Sierra Leone during our civil war and conveyed Sierra Leone's interest in fostering collaboration with Switzerland in areas such as investment, high technology, education, and trade.

The presentation of my Letter of Credence to the World Trade Organization came much later, as the Sierra Leone Embassy in Brussels had been accredited to the WTO, and it was only after I was well-installed in Geneva that this accreditation was transferred to the Mission in Geneva. It was thus that I presented my Letter of Credence to the Director General of the WTO, Mr. Pascal Lamy, in January 2013. I was now equipped with a triple mandate as Ambassador to Switzerland, Permanent Representative to the United Nations, and other Organizations in Geneva, and Permanent Representative to the World Trade Organization.

With the Mission's limited personnel, human rights were not one of the priorities I expected to focus on while serving as my country's representative in Geneva. What I did not know at the time was that Sierra Leone had applied, through its Mission in New York, to become a member of the Human Rights Council for the period 2013–2015. When I learned about this, I tried to protest, but it was too late. We were elected to the Council by the United Nations General Assembly in October 2012.

I confess, this development did not sit well with me. Throughout my twenty-eight-year work at the United Nations in various roles, we viewed human rights as a "thorn in the flesh" when interacting with governments. I recalled instances when working as a member of the UN Country Teams, we deliberately excluded human rights officers from sensitive discussions to avoid stirring up issues that could negatively impact our relations with the government. I remembered having to disregard pressure from human rights activists to reach a peaceful resolution that ultimately prevented the refoulement of Somali refugees while I worked as a UNHCR Representative in Kenya.

Moreover, given that I had no assigned staff and was responsible for covering over 20 intergovernmental bodies in Geneva to address what I considered as critical issues including health, trade, and labour, my involvement at the Council could hardly be prioritized. Consequently, on February 25, 2013, I found myself reluctantly dragging myself to my first meeting, as a bona fide member of the Human Rights Council.

I had never been in the Human Rights Council Chamber at the *Palais des Nations* before. As I entered, I was struck by the majestic image it presented. The stimulating design gave me a sense of the high ideals for which the Council stood – preserving and protecting the human rights of all as defined by the 1948 Universal Declaration of Human Rights and all other human rights instruments since then. The Chamber is in the form of a circle with a unique ceiling painting created by the Spanish abstract artist Miquel Barceló. The dome consists of many layers of paint of different colours, composed of pigments from across the globe and sprayed onto the ceiling to create stalactites whose colours vary according to the different perspectives. According to Barceló, 'All of it is a sea upside down, but it is also a cave- the complete union of opposites, the ocean surface of the Earth and its most concealed cavities'.

I do not know if this inspiration contributed to influencing my attitude toward human rights, but as I participated in the first few sessions of the Council, I slowly became interested in its work, as it dawned upon me that it covered all areas of life from a human rights perspective. I thus became very active in its deliberations.

At one of my first meetings, as I sat down to listen to the

speeches, I opened the webpage of the Council, and something struck me. It was a quotation by the then Secretary General, Ban Ki Moon, which read:

'The Human Rights Council should be the voice of the voiceless'.

This prompted me to think. 'How could I, through my membership in the Council, bring out the plight of people around the world whose rights were being violated daily?' I would like to think about this as the moment I became a "human rights convert".

Representing the "voice of the voiceless" both in my country and around the world, thus became the focus of my attention, not only at the Human Rights Council, but in all the sectors I covered in Geneva.

The Voice of the Voiceless at the Human Rights Council

The Human Rights Council's agenda may be daunting, spanning both thematic and country-specific problems. Meetings ran non-stop from 9 a.m. to 6 p.m. each day during the sessions, making participation difficult for an ambassador without assistance. I found myself waking up at 5 a.m. every day to prepare for meetings and sitting in meetings without eating or even going to the restroom during key discussions and, especially during voting sessions because there was no one to replace me.

Understanding the need to prioritize, I chose to focus on a few themes and address country-specific issues at the Universal Periodic Review, where the human rights situation of all United Nations member countries was evaluated. Bringing these issues to the Human Rights Council was a crucial catalyst for action. While there was more work to be done, progress had been made on each of these issues I chose to concentrate on, since 2013. To raise an issue at the Human Rights Council, one must first identify and form a core group of interested parties among member and observer states. Following discussions with stakeholders such as other governments, non-governmental organizations, and civil society, this core group drafts a resolution to be submitted to the Council during one of its sessions. The draft resolution is then presented to the Council, allowing members to express their stance on it. If none of the forty-seven Member States object, the resolution is passed by consensus. However, any Member State can request a vote on the resolution. In such cases, a public vote is conducted, and the resolution is adopted by a simple majority.

While taking part in all the discussions at the Council, I decided to focus on several causes, which included: people living with albinism; child, early and forced marriage, and lethal autonomous weapons, among others.

People living with albinism

My colleague, the then Permanent Representative for Somalia, Ambassador Yusuf Mohamed Ismail, initially sought my support to highlight the plight of people living with albinism at the Council, as Somalia was not a Council member. My research revealed that these individuals face discrimination globally, with the most severe conditions in Africa. Media reports shed light on their predicament. In some African cultures, they were believed to possess mystical powers, and their body parts were coveted for good luck, often leading to ritualistic mutilations, or even killings.

I embraced this cause with enthusiasm, despite encountering resistance when introducing it to the Council. Several African Ambassadors were hesitant, fearing it might cast African nations in a negative light. However, I was resolute that precisely because the issues faced by people with albinism were most acute in Africa, the African Group should spearhead a resolution. This resolution would aim to appoint an independent expert to study the problems in various countries and propose recommendations to nations and the international community on alleviating the suffering and threats to these individuals' human rights.

I also encountered some opposition outside of the African Group. Some Western countries argued that we should not create new human rights roles because there were already over eighty such positions. Work on people with albinism should be incorporated into existing mandates, such as the one on disabled people's rights. This seemed inappropriate to me, first because people with albinism were not disabled, and second because the Special Rapporteur on the Rights of People with Disabilities was overburdened, and could not deal with the problems of persons living with albinism with the intensity this called for.

My work to convince my colleagues was thus all cut out for me. I had long and emotional meetings with colleagues, both collectively and individually. I was severely handicapped in my efforts, as I had only my personal assistant, Folake, who happened to have a law degree, and a visiting fellow from Sierra Leone, Cassandra Labor, as the only staff I had to do all the groundwork. A young lady, Ikponwosa Ero, a person living with albinism who worked for a Canadian NGO, *Under the Same Sun,* also assisted me.

My desire was to present this as an African Group resolution, but halfway through the session of the Council, after days of trying to convince my fellow Ambassadors, I began to lose hope. Should I go it alone, as Sierra Leone and lobby the other 46 Members of the Council for support during a vote, in the hope that a simple majority would support the resolution? I knew this was a risk I was not willing to take since if the vote was lost, it would effectively terminate my efforts and leave the concerns of individuals living with albinism unanswered at the Human Rights Council.

In a desperate last-minute effort, I again decided to do a

last round of persuasion. Eventually, just at the point that I was about to give up, the African Group decided to present the draft resolution as the core group. The resolution was passed unanimously. My efforts had paid off.

At the last meeting of the Council session, I decided to make, what I considered to be my victory speech. As I sat there waiting for my turn to speak, I looked around at the jam-packed chamber. I took the floor.

'Mr President, Sierra Leone takes the floor to express its satisfaction at the adoption of resolution A/HRC/28/L.10 on the Independent Expert on the enjoyment of human rights of persons with albinism, by consensus yesterday—a proud day for this Council. People living with albinism exist all over the world. They suffer from discrimination, violence and atrocities that prevent them from enjoying their human rights. Unlike other groups of people, they are particularly targeted, in some parts of the world for being who they are.

Press reports bear witness to these atrocities, underscoring the severe human rights violations inflicted upon these individuals, including the infringement of their most fundamental right - the right to life. A quote from the United Nations Secretary General, featured on the homepage of this Council, resonates deeply: "All victims of human rights abuses should be able to view the Human Rights Council as a forum and a catalyst for action." This assurance will bring comfort to tens of thousands of people living with albinism worldwide. They will express their gratitude to the Human Rights Council for serving as their voice in combating stigmatization, discrimination, violence, and atrocities perpetrated against them.

Our hope is that all persons with albinism would live in a world that would treat them as equal members of society; a world that would recognize their talents and capacities; a world that would recognize and address their challenges; a world in which they would live in peace and without fear. Thank you, Mr President'.

Ambassador Yusuf Mohammed was away in Mogadishu, and I was pleased to have reported to him by email that the resolution had been passed.

'Thanks for your efforts, Yvette. For as long as I live, I will always fight for the rights of people living with albinism', he replied. Unfortunately, he was killed in a bomb attack on his hotel, only a couple of hours after I made this statement at the Council.

As a sequel to this resolution, several stakeholders have taken action. The African Union and individual countries have adopted action plans and are prosecuting violators of the rights of people living with albinism. Increasingly, steps are being taken to address their health problems. The Independent Expert, a person living with albinism, has been most influential in this regard.

Child, early and forced marriage

Another issue that I passionately engaged with was the matter of child, early and forced marriage. Although this subject was under discussion in various forums, I firmly believed that the Human Rights Council needed to intervene, given that it represents one of the most severe infringements of women's and girls' human rights. I was heartened to discover that several other countries shared this interest, leading us to establish a core group within the Human Rights Council dedicated to addressing this pressing issue.

This was a statement I made at the 24th Session of the Human Rights Council, when I introduced a resolution on the subject.

'Mr President, It is with great pleasure that Sierra Leone presents the draft Resolution on: "Strengthening Efforts to Prevent and Eliminate Child, Early and Forced Marriage: Challenges, Achievements, Best Practices and Implementation Gaps" on behalf of the core group comprising: Argentina, Canada, Ethiopia, Finland, Honduras, Italy, the Maldives, Montenegro, the

Netherlands, Poland, Sierra Leone, Switzerland, and Uruguay, and over 100 co-sponsors, for consideration by the Human Rights Council.

Child marriage, early marriage, and forced marriage are prevalent practices worldwide. These practices infringe upon human rights as they prevent individuals from leading a life free from violence and adversely impact the enjoyment of fundamental human rights, including the right to education and optimal health. While some countries have recognized this issue and enacted laws prohibiting underage and forced marriages, the practice persists. Factors such as gender inequality and detrimental cultural norms have been identified as contributing causes. Additionally, poverty and lack of education are often associated with early and forced marriages.

It is apparent that efforts must be increased to address this violation of human rights by some of society's most vulnerable populations, and this draft resolution seeks to commence action in this area. This is a procedural resolution in which the Council agrees to have a panel discussion on enhancing efforts to prevent and abolish child, early, and forced marriage at its 26th Session, addressing challenges, accomplishments, best practices, and implementation gaps. It requests that the OHCHR create a report and distribute it to states prior to the panel discussion in order to inform states' participation in the panel discussion. It also asks the OHCHR to compile a summary report of the panel discussion. The Council will show its support by adopting this Resolution.

The process of developing this draft resolution has been quite inclusive. The core group was able to enhance the substance of the draft resolution after two well-attended open sessions. The vast and multi-regional character of the core group and co-sponsors demonstrates the depth of our common desire for action on this issue. The number of young lives impacted by this practice is staggering, as is the impact on their lives. Every year, fourteen *million females marry too young. As a result, this matter merits the Council's attention, and we urge the Council to approve this resolution by consensus'.*

The resolution was unanimously adopted, placing the issues of child, early, and forced marriage firmly within the human rights framework. This action by the Human Rights Council catalysed further initiatives by the African Union, states, non-governmental organizations, and civil society to intensify their efforts on this issue. I had the privilege of moderating a panel discussion convened by this resolution, aimed at sharing best practices from around the globe to combat this menace. The panel concurred on the need for additional measures to address the problem from a human rights standpoint. The discussions yielded a wealth of effective practices, offering valuable insights into successful strategies for tackling child marriage, early marriage, and forced marriage.

Much has been achieved since the passing of this resolution in 2014. Change did not just happen at the international level. An increasing number of countries have developed comprehensive national strategies to address this problem. By the end of 2015, Burkina Faso, Ghana, Mozambique, Nepal, Uganda, and Zambia had finalized strategies, initiatives or action plans on child marriage, while Egypt and Ethiopia continued to implement their existing strategies. There has also been increasing cross-country reflection about lessons learned from national initiatives to end child marriage, for example at the Girls Not Brides Global Member Meeting in May 2015, and at the Africa Girl Summit in November 2015.

Countries acted on commitments to increase the legal age of marriage to eighteen, and several countries took steps to improve their legal frameworks. One of the critical measures to address child marriage was banning marriage under the age of 18. The African Union and the Government of Zambia held the first-ever African Girls' Summit on Ending Child Marriage, bringing together governments, civil society, youth, UN agencies and dignitaries from across Africa, to recognize child marriage as a key priority for Africa's development agenda. The African Union campaign to prevent child marriage in Africa has been extended for another two years, and African states have established an African Common Policy on Child Marriage.

The Chibok Girls

On the night of 14 to 15 April 2014, 276 female students aged between 16 and 18 were abducted by the Islamic terrorist group Boko Haram from the Government Girls Secondary School in the town of Chibok in Borno State, Nigeria. At the first session of the Human Rights Council after the night of the attack, I had believed that the President of the Council would at least say something denouncing this kidnapping during the session, considering that the Council gives a lot of attention to the rights of women and girls and even dedicates a whole day each year to women's rights. When he did not, I approached him to ask why this was not the case.

'We have a tight schedule', he said.

I decided to speak to the Head of the Mission in Nigeria, but he just waved me aside.

'The Nigerian government is handling this, so there is no need to bring it up at the Human Rights Council', was his response.

I needed to think quickly because we were approaching the session's last meeting. Whom should I seek help from? Then it occurred to me: 'How about the female ambassadors?' Women Ambassadors gathered on the fringes of Human Rights Council sessions to arrange activities, although this only happened before the June sessions of the Council, when the one-day summit on women was conducted. We also got together for social events every now and then.

I decided to try to get the women ambassadors on board, and every female ambassador was supportive of the move and the actions that I proposed and agreed to be a part of the initiative. Firstly, we had to request the floor on the last day of the Council session. There was no way the President of the Council could refuse a request by the "Group of Women Ambassadors" and we were given a slot.

What happened was spectacular. I asked each woman Ambassador to take a photograph holding the "BRING BACK OUR GIRLS" placard and send it to me, which they did. I was to deliver the statement, which everyone had endorsed. The statement read:

'We the Group of Women Ambassadors in Geneva would like to express our utmost dismay at the unprecedented abduction of over 200 young girls from their school in Chibok, Northern Nigeria, and the subsequent announcement by Boko Haram that they are being sold as sex slaves. Such an action runs against all the values that we stand for and we cannot stay silent.

This also runs contrary to the provisions of numerous international treaties, agreements and resolutions including those passed before this Human Rights Council. Notably, Articles 3, 4 and 5 of the Universal Declaration of Human Rights. Articles 4 and 5 clearly state; and I quote: No one shall be held in slavery or servitude; slavery and the slave trade shall be prohibited in all their forms. No one shall be subjected to torture or cruel, inhuman or degrading treatment or punishment.

We fully agree with the comments of the UN spokesperson in Geneva, Mr Rupert Colville, when he said, and I quote: "We warn the perpetrators that there is an absolute prohibition against slavery and sexual slavery in international law. These can under certain circumstances constitute crimes against humanity." We therefore call on all Member States to stand firmly united in the universal condemnation of this action.

We urge the Nigerian Government, with the support of the international community to continue to do all it can to ensure the speedy release of these girls and their safe return to their families, and to hold the perpetrators of this heinous act – as well as their collaborators – accountable by bringing them to justice. Our girls must be freed! They must be immediately released – without preconditions and returned to their families. Our girls must be allowed to finish their studies and their exams, and to live normal lives in their communities. Them and their families need our solidarity and we join our voices with theirs, loud and strong:

BRING BACK OUR GIRLS!'

As I made the statement, pictures of the Women Ambassadors holding the placard flashed on the screen one after the other. The whole hall was transfixed. You could hear a coin drop.

The goal of bringing the issue to the Human Rights Council was met, and both the Nigerian delegation and the Council's President were forced to release follow-up remarks denouncing the occurrence. Following that, a resolution would be adopted during the Council's next session.

The Voice of the Voiceless – Disarmament

Lethal Autonomous Weapons Systems

It was the second session of the Human Rights Session that I was participating in June of 2013. Extrajudicial Executions were certainly not one of the issues that I wanted to focus on. Many other countries had far better information on the matter. Yet, on the eve of the discussion, I had gone to bed but decided to read the Special Rapporteur on Extrajudicial Executions' Report. What I read shocked me—the report was on what he called "Lethal Autonomous Robotics", or "Killer Robots", as the non-governmental organizations would like to call them.

"I cannot let this subject go by without a comment", I thought.

I did have some knowledge on automation, even if it was outdated, as I had done my Master's thesis at the Imperial College in London on the automatic control of some electrical power system equipment. The technology had changed, but the basic principle of pre-programming equipment to take autonomous actions remained the same. While automation was beneficial in terms of dependability and speed, it took on a new dimension when used as weapon that maimed and killed humans. It was my responsibility as a member of the Human Rights Council to intervene in this matter.

So, I spent the rest of the night putting together a statement for the debate.

'Mr President, my delegation would like to first of all thank the Special Rapporteur on Extrajudicial Executions for his comprehensive report. The Special Rapporteur on Extrajudicial Executions focused his report on Lethal Autonomous Robotics (LARs). The development of LARs is now becoming increasingly prevalent, and it is but timely that such a technology be viewed under a human rights lens.

From the military standpoint, the use of drones is considered advantageous in terms of saving the lives of the combatants of the attacking side during wars. It is also argued that robots can be programmed to minimize errors and reach their targets with a high degree of accuracy. But robots are machines and as we have seen, can indiscriminately kill innocent victims, including women and children.

The international instruments in International Humanitarian Law are clearly targeted at conventional warfare and the use of robots raises questions about accountability. Who is to blame, when a breach of these laws occurs through the use of these robots? In addition, we have seen with semi-automatic devices that these robots that can be deployed outside conflict zones to hit targeted individuals, who have been considered to be terrorists, but who are not tried through due processes. What are the implications of this under International Human Rights Law? Could this be considered as "extrajudicial execution?" Furthermore, as with all other technology, these robots can fall into the wrong hands and used indiscriminately. How does the international community guard against that to safeguard the right to life of the victims? These are all questions, which need to be answered, before the use of autonomous robots becomes widespread.

My delegation agrees with the recommendations that the Human Rights Council should call on all States to declare and implement national moratoria on at least the testing, production, assembly, transfer, acquisition, deployment and use of LARs until such time as an internationally agreed upon framework on the future of LARs has been established and that the High Commissioner convenes a multi-sectoral High-Level Panel as a matter of urgency, to take stock of technical advances of relevance to LARs; evaluate the legal, ethical and policy issues related to LARs; propose a framework to enable the international community to address effectively the legal and policy issues arising in relation to LARs, and make concrete substantive and procedural recommendations in that regard. Thank you'.

The debate was a heated one. The big military powers sent their military personnel to contribute to the debate. The main points they brought out were that these weapons did not exist and that this was not a matter for the Human Rights Council but should be referred to the Convention on Certain Conventional Weapons, whose purpose was "to ban or restrict the use of specific types of weapons that are considered to cause unnecessary or unjustifiable suffering to combatants or to affect civilians indiscriminately". I was rather perplexed that a matter that concerned the right to life could not be discussed at the Human Rights Council but I resolved that I would follow the consideration of this issue "wherever it took me". It was thus that I found myself in the disarmament forum in Geneva.

The transition from human rights to disarmament was sobering to me. The vocabulary employed in such assertions was utterly unfamiliar to me, and the apparent lack of concern for human rights issues was astounding. The language included words like "neutralize", which I later understood to mean simply "kill". Things moved at a snail's pace, and I realized that this would apply to the question of Lethal Autonomous Weapons Systems (LAWS), the terminology that was adopted by the Convention on Certain Conventional Weapons (CCW).

Between 2014 and 2018, more than eighty countries participated in a total of seven meetings on the subject at the CCW. Three informal meetings of Experts were held in 2014, 2015 and 2016. The 2016 Fifth Review Conference of CCW High Contracting Parties decided to establish a Group of Governmental Experts (GGE) on LAWS with a mandate to assess questions related to emerging technologies in lethal autonomous weapons systems. The formal GGE has met on the subject three times, in 2017 and 2018. I was privileged to have been appointed as a "Friend of the Chair" for the three informal meetings.

Experts spoke at length on the technological, legal, human rights and military implications of the technology during these talks, offering solid background information on the issue. I used every chance to express my dismay that computers, no matter how properly designed could be given the authority to take human lives.

In the realm of weapons systems and the use of force, it was increasingly evident that a normative boundary needed to be established to delineate what was collectively acceptable. At the 2018 Convention on Certain Conventional Weapons (CCW) conference, a majority of the participating nations recommended transitioning from exploring this issue to drafting a legally binding document on the use of fully autonomous weapons before the end of the year. While this was not achieved, there was a glimmer of hope. A broad consensus has emerged among nations on the necessity of retaining human control over weapons systems and the use of force. Furthermore, by the end of the year, twenty-six countries had officially endorsed the call to ban Lethal Autonomous Weapons.

The Secretary General of the United Nations has since called upon States "to ban these weapons, which are politically unacceptable and morally repugnant".

Most recently, on December 22, 2023, the UN General Assembly (UNGA) adopted Resolution 78/241 concerning lethal autonomous weapons systems. This resolution expresses concern about the potential negative consequences and impact of Autonomous Weapons Systems (AWS) on global security and regional stability. It also affirms that international law, including the UN Charter, international humanitarian law, and international human rights law, applies to autonomous weapons systems. However, as with all disarmament issues, progress remains slow.

The Voice of the Voiceless – Health

The Ebola Crisis

I had seen a terrifying documentary video about a haemorrhagic fever epidemic somewhere in Africa, so when I learned that the Ebola virus illness had reached Guinea in March 2014, I quickly phoned the World Health Organization's Director General to request an appointment. She was out of the country, so I met with the Deputy Director General, a Ghanaian, at my request.

'There is no need to be scared', he assured me. 'We have had a number of outbreaks of Ebola in the Democratic Republic of the Congo and Uganda, and we have been able to suppress it with a minimum number of casualties. Everything is under control'. The way he dismissed my fears was so emphatic, that on my way back to the office, I felt that I might have overreacted to the news. As the days went by, the news got worse and worse. Then the virus spread to Liberia—still no evidence of its control that the WHO had assured me about. And then, on May 27, 2014, the news broke that the Ebola Virus Disease had reached Sierra Leone, with five people being diagnosed after attending a funeral in neighbouring Guinea. By August, the disease was spreading like wildfire. WHO was treating this as a medical emergency that fell uniquely within its mandate and was holding briefings mainly for health experts in Geneva, while guarding the responsibility for action to itself like a mother hen covering her chicks.

During one of these briefings I attended, I emphasized that the situation had escalated into a humanitarian crisis. I advocated for a more aggressive publicity campaign to highlight the severity of the outbreak and attract necessary support and funding. When I realized that WHO was intent on sidelining other actors, I knew I had to intervene.

However, the primary catalyst for my action was an alarming article by a German doctor that appeared on social media. He suggested that the three countries affected by the virus were doomed to extinction, and the world should focus solely on the neighbouring countries to prevent further spread. The impact of reading this article was profound. This was my homeland, and these were my fellow citizens being consigned to oblivion. The thought of standing by idly while this transpired was unthinkable.

My experience as an Assistant Disaster Relief Coordinator at the United Nations taught me that the "secret" of Ebola needed to be revealed. So, I returned to my former office, the Office for the Coordination of Humanitarian Aid, to persuade the then Director, who had served as my Deputy and was then my successor, to hold a briefing for United Nations Member States in Geneva.

The first Member States Briefing, which was held in August 2014, attracted over 200 participants. I addressed the meeting:

'Madame Director General WHO, Director of OCHA, Ambassadors and Distinguished Representatives of Permanent Missions in Geneva. Sierra Leone would first like to thank you all for your presence here today. This is a sombre moment for my country and we are counting on all the support that we can get to address this scourge, which is plaguing our country.

As you are aware, Sierra Leone emerged from a most gruelling conflict in 2002, after 11 years of war. This war had a devastating effect on our already fragile infrastructure and services. Since the end of the war, we have set out to aggressively pursue ambitious goals to progress, including the Agenda for Change (2007-2012) In 2013 President Ernest Bai Koroma launched the Agenda for Prosperity (2013-2017), the first part of moving towards an objective of achieving middle-income status by 2035.

We have witnessed slow but steady progress. We have succeeded, inter alia, to reduce absolute poverty from 70 per cent in 2002 to 52.9% by 2013. Our Human Development Index increased from 0.273 in 2002 to 0,374 in 2013. We have set up a free healthcare programme for pregnant and lactating mothers in 2010 and the results in terms of maternal and child mortality rates have been remarkable.

On the economic front, with our focus on the improvement of infrastructure and attracting investments, mining activities have been resumed and expanded and our economic achievements are set to take off. We recorded Real Gross Domestic Product (GDP) growth of 15.2% in 2012 after expanding by 6% in 2011. According to the African Development Bank, in a statement in earlier this year, and I quote, "the outlook for the Sierra Leone economy remains positive in the current and medium terms, with sustained economic growth, falling inflation, and improved fiscal and external positions".

It is clear that Sierra Leone has set the stage towards economic progress – and it is at this moment that this formidable enemy –

Ebola has struck – " below the belt" so to speak. We are facing a war – yet another war and failure is not an option. There is too much at stake. First and foremost, lives are being lost as we speak, and unless the disease is contained, many lives will be lost, needlessly.

In addition, in the health sector itself - a worrying concern over the Ebola scourge is, in addition to its direct effects, its potential to affect the overall health of the population. The gains of the free health care programme are seriously under threat as some people are shying away from frequenting health facilities, for fear of being misdiagnosed as Ebola patients or of catching Ebola at the facilities. On the part of the health workers, following the demise of their colleagues including the country's only virologist, Dr Khan and logistical challenges in the prevention and control of the Ebola infection, have reduced motivation to work. In short, many people stand to lose their lives not only from Ebola but from the traditional curable ailments such as malaria.

Furthermore, the Ebola outbreak is giving rise to humanitarian needs caused by loss of family members, sometimes breadwinners; the suspension of economic activities at state and community levels and lack of mobility, and these will also need to be addressed. Finally, the Ebola crisis can adversely affect our macro-economic activities. This could result in major companies or projects suspending their activities and our well-earned gains risk being reversed'.

I continued.

'We need to address the problem of Ebola in a robust, comprehensive and coordinated manner. But we desperately need the assistance of the international community, in a true spirit of solidarity. Yes, borders can be closed, flights suspended and other measures taken to protect populations outside Sierra Leone. But we cannot be abandoned.

We extend our profound appreciation to all those who have assisted us in one way or another till now – particularly the WHO and the MSF. We thank those who have made pledges – but pledges made today, to be implemented sometime in the distant future will not save lives or reverse the economic hardships that we risk facing. We therefore appeal to all to urgently assist us now.

We welcome in-kind assistance for our urgent needs. Currently, these include experienced personnel, trainers for local staff, PPEs, basic drugs, and logistics support to ensure the smooth movement of personnel and supplies to the various districts and to improve mobility of personnel for purposes of surveillance. As the President said, and I quote: "We are a resilient people. Sustainability of our actions for prosperity depends on winning this battle". BUT WE CANNOT DO IT ALONE – WE NEED YOUR HELP – AND WE NEED IT NOW. I thank you'.

This briefing focused the world's attention on the seriousness of the Ebola outbreak in West Africa. Several ambassadors admitted that they were unaware of the gravity of the situation or the significant early support offered to combat the Ebola epidemic, such as by Cuba. As a result of this briefing, announcements of assistance such as from China and South Africa were initially revealed in Geneva.

In January 2015, I was one of the active negotiators for the resolution to strengthen WHOs capacity to end the crisis and to give WHO the tools it needed to cope with future outbreaks of endemic diseases.

The Voice of the Voiceless – Trade

The category of Least Developed Countries (LDCs) was officially established in 1971 by the UN General Assembly with a view to attracting special international support for the most vulnerable and disadvantaged members of the UN family. The criteria used for this classification are poverty, human resource weakness and economic vulnerability. These countries exhibit the lowest indicators of socioeconomic development. They represent the poorest and weakest segments of the international community. They comprise more than 880 million people (about 12 per cent of the world's population), but account for less than 2 per cent of the world GDP and about one per cent of global trade in goods. As of December 2012, 46 countries were classified as LDCs. LDCs can graduate from this category when they reach the established threshold to do so.

The World Trade Organization recognizes the UN list and is committed to taking measures that can help LDCs increase their exports to other WTO members and attract investment. My focus during my tenure as Permanent Representative to the WTO was on giving LDCs, including mine, a voice in the deliberations at the Organization and advocating for greater international assistance for them to enable them to derive maximum benefit from trade.

As I assumed the role of Permanent Representative to the WTO, negotiations were underway to ratify the Trade Facilitation Agreement, marking the WTO's inaugural agreement since its establishment in 1995. The Trade Facilitation Agreement outlines the procedures and regulations that govern the movement of goods across international borders, aiming to reduce delays and associated economic costs, enhance efficiency, and uphold legitimate regulatory objectives. These discussions necessitated a robust representation from Least Developed Countries (LDCs) to ensure their interests were safeguarded within the agreement's provisions.

Trade facilitation yields comprehensive economic advantages for LDCs by diminishing transaction costs, boosting business efficiency, and augmenting consumer welfare. It guarantees freedom of transit, a crucial aspect for landlocked nations.

Enhanced transparency not only fosters a more conducive business environment domestically but also aids local companies aspiring to penetrate foreign markets. Furthermore, trade facilitation facilitates the integration of LDCs into global value chains and their subsequent advancement.

In the negotiations, it was important that flexibilities be accorded to LDCs to ensure that they were not unduly penalized in the enforcement of the multilateral agreement. This called for "special and differential treatment" for these countries. The main flexibilities that were being negotiated by the least developed countries included progressive implementation of commitments made under this Agreement, linking implementation of substantive measures conditional on the adequate provision of technical assistance and capacity building, as well as an early warning mechanism and grace period for LDCs.

At the WTO, preparations for negotiations are done in groups. There were over twenty such groups and Sierra Leone belonged to four of these – the LDC group, the African Group, the African, Caribbean and Pacific countries with preferences in the EU (ACP) and the G90 group. Without any staff at my Mission to provide backup support for the negotiations, I sought the help of a Trade Expert at the Commonwealth Small States Office, Mr. Fevrier, to explain to me the technical issues relating to this agreement. Armed with the knowledge and advice he provided, I engaged actively in the negotiations and joined both the expert and ambassador discussions. I was even nicknamed "Expert Ambassador" by the experts.

Negotiations were long and intense. Each clause of the draft had to be agreed upon by consensus, and with 154 Members of the WTO, this was not easy. In the main negotiating room, the Chairman of the Negotiating Committee, the Director General of the WTO, Mr Roberto Acevedo, would read out the text of each clause, and one by one, Member States and representatives from the various groups would give their comments, which almost always were not unanimous. As a result, the Chair would suggest a compromise wording, and we would be divided into breakout rooms by group. Because I was alone, I stayed with the LDC group. If no consensus was achieved when we reconvened, we would split apart again, and this may continue indefinitely until a text acceptable to each group was found.

This meant that talks continued all night as the day of the Ministerial conference at which the Agreement was to be adopted approached. I recall one meeting that started at 3 p.m. and continued until 7:30 a.m. the next morning. We had to rely on the slot machines because there was no restaurant or café open, and one day we succeeded in entirely emptying them. All ordinarily unpleasant items, in those machines, such as bland soups, were consumed.

The ninth WTO Ministerial Conference (MC9) (Bali) adopted the Trade Facilitation Agreement, which has now been ratified by the Sierra Leone Parliament. The results of the negotiations were satisfactory to the LDC group in terms of the flexibilities and the provisions for technical assistance and capacity building.

In 2014, the LDC group chose me to serve as Chair of the Board of the Expanded Integrated Framework for Trade-Related Aid for the Least Developed Countries (EIF), a global development initiative committed to addressing LDCs' trade capacity requirements. The EIF consists of a Steering Committee, a Board, and a Secretariat. The EIF Steering Committee is the highest-level body of the EIF and is responsible for setting the overall policy direction of the program, reviewing its effectiveness and ensuring transparency, while the EIF Board is responsible for managing the program and taking key operational decisions. It thereby reports to and implements the EIF Steering Committee's policies. It is made up of three LDC representatives, three donor representatives and one representative each from the core agencies, the EIF Executive Secretariat and the EIF Trust Fund Manager. The EIF Board makes funding decisions under the EIF Trust Fund and monitors, reviews and evaluates country-specific progress and operations.

In partnership with LDCs themselves, donor countries, the World Trade Organization, the World Bank, the World Health Organization, the International Monetary Fund, the United Nations Conference on Trade and Development, the International Trade Center, the United Nations Industrial Development Organization, and the World Tourism Organization, EIF provides financial and technical support.

The first phase of the program delivered 141 projects totalling US$140.7 million across fifty-one countries. One hundred and five of these were to support trade and development capacity while 36 helped countries address supply-side constraints to increase their capacity to trade internationally. I became the Chair of the Board at a time when the first phase of the Framework was ending and there was a need to make the case for a second phase. I had my work cut out for me.

People who were familiar with international organizations would recognize the difficulty in coordinating the activity of multiple separate groups. During my chairmanship, we were able to secure an agreement on a new program for the second phase, with a budget ranging from $274 million to $320 million over a seven-year period. We had to raise the funds for it.

I worked with the Executive Director of the EIF, Ratnakar Adhikari from Nepal, a dedicated and hardworking individual with vast experience on trade issues. Together, we had briefing sessions with traditional and non-traditional donors to convince them of the need to support LDCs to graduate from LDC status. At the WTO Fifth Global Review of Aid for Development, in July 2015, the Chair of the Steering Committee, Ambassador Daniel Blockert of Sweden and I launched the new phase. It was well received, and even though it was not a pledging event, Norway announced its intention to contribute US$10 million.

In the margins of the 10th WTO Ministerial Conference in Nairobi, a Phase 2 Pledging Conference was held. Fifteen donors pledged a total of US$90 million, with a commitment to make further contributions in the future. While this amount was enough to start the activities of the second phase, I was really disappointed that, in spite of all the efforts I put into it, we could not raise more funds at the pledging conference, and I noted at a WTO meeting:

'The Enhanced Integrated System does not receive the support it deserves by the entire membership of the WTO. In the meetings of this body, most members proclaim the importance of addressing the concerns of the Least Developed Countries, but only a few of them have contributed to this important initiative'.

I called on all developed countries and developing countries in a position to do so but have not yet done so to contribute generously to the EIF.

I joined the International Gender Champions (IGC) network in 2015. The IGC is a leadership network that brings together female and male decision-makers determined to break down gender barriers and make gender equality a working reality in their spheres of influence. The initiative was co-founded by former UN Geneva Director-General Michael Møller, former US Ambassador to the UN in Geneva Pamela Hamamoto, and Women at the Table CEO/Founder Caitlin Kraft-Buchman. As part of my contribution to the IGC cause, I co-chaired a Trade and Gender Impact Group together with the Ambassador and Permanent Representative of Iceland, H.E. Harald Aspelund, and the Executive Director of the International Trade Center, Arancha Gonzales. We had as an objective, to look closely into steps that needed to be taken both within and outside the WTO to address gender issues relating to trade.

We proposed launching a Gender and Trade Declaration at the Eleventh World Trade Organization Ministerial Conference in Buenos Aires in December 2017, with the goal of increasing the visibility of trade and gender issues and identifying several key areas to make trade policies more "gender-responsive". Sharing experiences on gender-responsive policies and initiatives, for example; exchanging best practices and methodologies for studying trade policies and their effects on women; and collecting gender disaggregated data were among the measures.

What I assumed would be appreciated by all WTO members, proved difficult to implement. Nearly twenty years after the fourth World Conference on Women in Beijing, and despite the lip service paid to inclusiveness, the reluctance to issue a proclamation was difficult for me to understand. 'WTO discussions are sufficiently convoluted. Please do not add another dimension to them', some members of the African Group warned me.

Hence, once again, it was evident that we needed to launch a broad effort to persuade WTO members to sign the declaration. We briefed, lobbied, and appealed to the consciences of member nations that made token efforts to address gender concerns. Much to my astonishment, they stated unequivocally that it could not be deemed an official WTO document. We decided to pursue it regardless because we thought it had the potential to bring attention to gender and trade concerns, leading to some action to solve them.

In Buenos Aires, the Declaration on Trade and Gender was adopted on the margins of the conference with 120 signatories from member states. Even though it was not an official document, it turned out to be the only outcome of that conference.

I am now pleased to announce that the efforts of the core group at the WTO, with the help of partners, have yielded positive results. No less than six seminars have been held, covering topics such as Financial Inclusion Seminar, Women in Digital Trade,

Women and Trade in Trade Agreements, Women in Global Value Chains, Enhancing Women Entrepreneurs' Participation in Public Procurement and Gender-Based Analysis of Trade Policy.

The WTO Secretariat launched the WTO Gender Research Hub in May 2021 to deepen understanding of the impact of trade on women and gender equality. The Hub serves as a knowledge-gathering platform where the latest research is shared.

Its membership includes trade and gender researchers and experts from the WTO Secretariat, seven international organizations and regional organizations (Economic Commission for Latin America and the Caribbean, International Monetary Fund, International Trade Centre, Organization for Economic Co-operation and Development, United Nations Conference on Trade and Development, United Nations Economic Commission for Africa, World Bank), four members of the WTO's Chairs Programme (Mexico, Chile, Barbados and South Africa) and eight universities. Gender experts from the private sector, non-governmental organizations and think tanks are also invited, on an ad-hoc basis, to present recent findings from current research, to share new perspectives and to expand multidisciplinary research on trade and gender issues.

In spite of the initial resistance to bring up gender issues at the WTO, the efforts of our International Gender Champions contact group on trade and gender are yielding positive results that would assist women traders worldwide.

The Voice of the Voiceless – Intellectual Property

The World Health Organization estimates that there are over 314 million blind and visually impaired people worldwide, with 90 per cent of them living in poor nations. According to a WIPO survey conducted in 2006, less than sixty nations have limitations and exclusions clauses in their copyright laws that provide particular provisions for visually impaired people, such as Braille, big print, or digital audio versions of copyrighted literature. According to the International Blind Federation, less than 5 per cent of the million or so books written worldwide each year were made available in forms accessible to visually impaired people.

In June 2013, I was invited by the Moroccan government to participate in the final stages of negotiations, at the World Intellectual Property Organization's Diplomatic Conference, to conclude a Treaty to Facilitate Access to Published Works by Visually Impaired Persons and Persons with Print Disabilities in Marrakesh. After ten days of negotiations, the *Marrakesh Treaty to Facilitate Access to Published Works for Persons Who Are Blind, Visually Impaired, or Otherwise Print Disabled* was adopted.

'The purpose of this Treaty is to provide the necessary minimum flexibilities in copyright laws that are needed to ensure full and equal access to information and communication for persons who are visually impaired or otherwise disabled in terms of reading copyrighted works, focusing in particular on measures that are needed to publish and distribute works in formats that are accessible for persons who are blind, have low vision, or have other disabilities in reading text, in order to support their full and effective participation in society on an equal basis with others, and to ensure the opportunity to develop and utilize their creative, artistic and intellectual potential, not only for their own benefit but also for the enrichment of society'.

The treaty requires countries that ratify it, to adopt national law provisions that permit the reproduction, distribution and making available of the published works in accessible formats by ensuring limitations and exceptions to the rights of copyright holders. It also provides for the exchange of these accessible formats across borders by organizations that serve people who are blind, visually impaired, or print-disabled. This sharing of works in accessible formats aims to increase the overall number of works available because it would eliminate duplication and increase efficiency.

Before the advent of this convention, the onus was on national governments to decide the permissibility of restrictions and exceptions, resulting in a wide disparity in the exclusions stipulated in national legislation. While several countries permit free private copying, only a few provide exceptions for scenarios such as remote study, and these exceptions are strictly confined to the respective country.

The agreement aims to reassure authors and publishers that their works will be safeguarded against unauthorized use or distribution beyond the intended recipients. It encourages its signatories to collaborate in fostering cross-border exchanges. The parties are committed to expediting the accessibility of published works, and this collaborative effort will be a significant stride towards realizing that objective.

The Treaty had particular relevance to Sierra Leone, as I noted in my statement at the end of the conference.

'In concluding this Treaty, we have addressed a key human right of a group of disabled persons. Article 4 Clause 1b of the Convention on the Rights of Persons with Disabilities, which entered into force on May 3, 2008, requests governments to "take all appropriate measures, including legislation, to modify or abolish existing laws, regulations, customs and practices that constitute discrimination against persons with disabilities". Article 21 of the same Covenant covers the right of the disabled to access information.

For Sierra Leone, this Treaty is timely. Sierra Leone ratified the Convention on the Rights of Persons with Disabilities in October 2010 and passed its Persons with Disabilities Act in 2011. It has now started the process of drawing up action plans for addressing the issues contained in the Act. The application of this Treaty will be an important contribution to the implementation of this Act'.

The support and encouragement of Stevie Wonder had a great impact on the negotiators. He had supported this initiative during the five years of negotiations before this conference. At the start of the conference, he promised in a televised statement to personally come to Marrakesh to treat participants to a free concert if the Treaty was adopted. As the negotiations progressed during the week, it was not clear that this would indeed be the case, as interest groups representing the blind on the one hand and the publishers and authors on the other struggled to convince the negotiators to reach a balanced text that would take into account the concerns of all sides. In the end, after intense negotiations, this was achieved and the text was adopted by acclamation. Stevie Wonder did keep his promise and treated delegates to a touching concert on the last evening.

Showcasing religious tolerance in Sierra Leone

The Special Rapporteur for Religious Freedom appeared before the Human Rights Council at one of my first meetings there. I listened to his report, which emphasized the global prevalence of religious hatred. I came to understand that Sierra Leone's record of religious tolerance was excellent. After the presentation of his report, I made the following statement.

'Sierra Leone takes note of the comprehensive report of the Special Rapporteur on Freedom of Religion or Belief and would like to make a brief comment on Sierra Leone's experience with religious tolerance.

The Constitution of Sierra Leone and other laws and policies protect religious freedom, and the government generally protects this right and does not tolerate religious intolerance. Chapter III, Section 24, of the 1991 Constitution guarantees all citizens the freedom to observe their own religious practices or to change religions without interference from the government or members of other religious groups.

According to Government estimates, 60 per cent of the population is Muslim, 10 per cent Christian and 30 per cent is indigenous. Groups that constitute less than 2 per cent of the population include Baha'is, Hindus, Jews, and practitioners of indigenous and other religious beliefs, mostly animists. Most Muslims are Sunni. Evangelical Christians are a growing minority, with conversions primarily by members of other Christian denominations. There are also a small number of members of the Church of Jesus Christ and Latter-Day Saints (Mormons). Many citizens practice a mixture of Islam or Christianity with indigenous religious beliefs and are known fondly as "Chris-mus", a derivative of "Christian and Muslim".

The Ministry of Social Welfare, Gender, and Children's Affairs is the government body responsible for religious matters but has no mandate to recognize, register, or otherwise regulate religious groups. Religious groups that seek public recognition by the ministry are required to complete a form to register with the Government. In practice, most churches and mosques are registered with the government as well as with an independent religious organization, such as the Council of Churches of Sierra Leone, the Evangelical Fellowship of Sierra Leone (which represents many evangelical churches and denominations), or the United Council of Imams (which has registered 2,350 mosques).

The most prominent religious civil society organization, the Inter-Religious Council (IRC), is composed of Christian and Muslim leaders. Some recent misunderstandings between Muslims and Christians in the East of the country were promptly solved by members of the IRC. The government permits religious instruction in all schools. The government requires a standard Religion and Moral Education (RME) curriculum in all public schools through high school, which covers Christianity, Islam, and other religions.

In addition, instruction in a specific religion is permissible only in schools organized by that religious community or denomination. Private schools are not required to use RME, although many Christian schools do.

Religion does not play a role in either ethnic identity or political affiliation, and candidates for President have generally chosen a running mate of a different religion, although there is no requirement to do so. The recent civil war was not fought on religious grounds, and all factions comprised a mix of people from different religions. Unlike some countries in the world in which religion is so often seen as dividing and tearing apart the population, it unites Sierra Leoneans. Intermarriage among Christians and Muslims is common, and it is quite usual for marriages between Christians and Muslims to take place without either party forcing the other to convert. They simply hold two ceremonies: one in the mosque and the other in the church. Many families have both Christian and Muslim members living in the same household. Sierra Leone observes all major Muslim and Christian holidays, and most citizens celebrate all religious holidays, regardless of sect or denomination, both at home and in houses of worship.

Religious tolerance in Sierra Leone has recently received widespread recognition. In September 2012, the United States Department of State rated Sierra Leone highly for international religious freedom in its sixth annual International Religious Freedom Report.

Mr President,

Sierra Leone is a small country that we believe has experience to share in the area of religious tolerance. But we are not taking this for granted. We need to be vigilant to ensure that recent developments in the sub-region do not affect our long history of religious tolerance. In conclusion, my delegation would like to invite the Special Rapporteur to visit Sierra Leone to determine if lessons could be learned from the Sierra Leone experience. I thank you'.

As a result of my invitation, the Special Rapporteur visited Freetown and gave this account of his visit, in a press conference afterwards.

'Religious diversity is not only a reality in Sierra Leone; it is widely seen and cherished as an asset on which to build community life from the local to the national level. I visited mosques and churches located in close vicinity to each other, at times on the same compounds, and I heard numerous stories about people attending weddings, funerals and other religious ceremonies across denominational differences. People generally express an interest in religious festivities across denominational differences. While many Christians join Muslims in celebrating the end of Ramadan, Muslims join Christians, for instance, in Christmas celebrations.

Religious tolerance comprises both inter-religious and intra-religious relations. While most interlocutors emphasized the amicable coexistence of the Muslim majority, estimated at 60 to 70 per cent of the population, and the Christian minority, estimated at 20 to 30 per cent of the population, there is also a remarkably positive and relaxed attitude towards intra-religious diversity. The Muslim population is composed of Sunnis, Shias and Ahmadis. Manifestations of mutual hostility between those different branches of Islam are unheard of in Sierra Leone. The same holds true for the diversity of Christian communities, which, inter alia, comprise Anglicans, Roman Catholics, Lutherans, Reformed Protestants, Methodists, the New Apostolic Church, Seventh Day Adventists, Baptists and charismatic groups. The Sierra Leonean population furthermore includes small numbers of Baha'is, Sikhs, Hindus, Buddhists, Mormons, Jehovah's Witnesses, and other communities, none of whom seem to have encountered serious difficulties when practicing their faiths.

Moreover, people can freely change their religious affiliation. Conversions are a common phenomenon and can go in all directions. I heard quite a number of stories of people who grew up in a Muslim family and were later baptized as Christians with the unreserved blessing of their parents. I met a woman originating from a Muslim family who even became a Reverend in the Methodist Church. Likewise, others told me they stemmed from Christian families and later turned to Islam, again with the full approval of their families. Some have kept their original first names after conversion, with the result that a person carrying a typically Muslim first name may nonetheless be Christian, or the other way around. In short, religious pluralism in Sierra Leone is dynamic pluralism in the sense that religious communities can grow and develop. People generally do not encounter problems when bearing witness to their faith in private or in public'.

The Secretary-General of the International Association for the Defence of Religious Liberty, D. Liviu Olteanu, invited me to join the international platform on "Religion, Peace and Security" launched by the association and the UN Office for Genocide Prevention, at the end of the Global Summit on "Religion, Peace and Security" hosted in November 2016 at the United Nations in Geneva. The Secretary General of the United Nations also commended the strong commitment of Sierra Leone in favour of interreligious dialogue, as a good example to be emulated throughout the world.

Chapter 14
My Recall From the Post of Ambassador

'No matter how full the river is, it still wants to grow'.
- Congolese Proverb

The general elections were held in Sierra Leone in March and April 2018. The Presidential run-off after the first round was held in April, and President Maada Bio was declared the winner. He was from the opposition Sierra Leone People Party, so after the results, I knew that I would be replaced. What I could not imagine was that it would be so sudden. Three weeks after his election, on the night of April 25, I had gone to bed and inadvertently left my phone on. When it rang to give an alarm of a WhatsApp message, I was tempted to look at it, and there was a message that read, "Sierra Leone Government- Executive Order No 2".

I had to open it quickly. I was curious to know what it contained. I scrolled through it, and I read the many headings, and because I was sleepy, I thought that I would just note them and put them aside for detailed reading the next day. So, I scrolled through the headings, vehicle purchase, wage-bill control, payment for fuel, telephone and internet services, overseas travel, contract prices, and new contracts, and then I stopped short. At the end of the list was the heading- Embassies and High Commissions. I had to read this. The first point related to revenues collected by embassies and high commissions, but the second read:

'All political appointees in Sierra Leone's diplomatic missions overseas, including ambassadors, high commissioners and attaches, are hereby relieved of their duty effective April 30, 2018'.

As someone who had not risen through the ranks of the Ministry of Foreign Affairs, I was considered a political appointee and this announcement was concerning to me.

The April 25th was a Wednesday. Friday, the 27th, was our Independence Anniversary, and according to this order, we were dismissed on Monday, the 30th. This meant that we could not even reach the Ministry of Foreign Affairs before that date. It was in moments like this that I missed my beloved son Boris, who had passed away in December 2016, and who had been my most treasured confidant throughout my life. I forwarded the WhatsApp message to my sister Yamide and my children, as they were my only source of strength that I could turn to in such situations. As usual, their responses were most reassuring.

'Are you sure the message is genuine?' asked Rebecca.

'This is most unfair', was the message from Yvonne.

'Don't worry, Mum, When God closes the door, He opens a window'. Yvette comforted me.

'Neta and the ancestors will guide and protect you', affirmed Alex.

While I understood that the new government was eager to give jobs to those who had worked for their election and that the diplomatic positions were the most attractive ones, because of the access to foreign currency, I found this action irresponsible. Firstly, ambassadors were appointed and allowed to stay in the country because of their status. Removing that status overnight meant they did not have the legal right to retain their residence status. Also, they had to be repatriated back to Freetown, and with no budgetary provision for this, they could not return. Finally, diplomatic procedures are such that an ambassador who was leaving has to send *notes verbales* to the government, international organizations and embassies announcing that that he or she was relinquishing his or her post.

I decided to ignore the WhatsApp message, which was, only forwarded to me by a third party.

'I was not recruited via a WhatsApp message, so I cannot act on one that managed to get to me', I thought.

At the office on Monday, tensions were high, as the Head of Chancery, who had done absolutely nothing over the three years he was assigned to the office, took it upon himself to send a badly written *note verbale* to all the Missions in Geneva to say he was in charge, sending me a copy. I immediately had to send a follow-up *note verbale* to withdraw it.

The Ministry of Foreign Affairs must have intervened because, on May 8th, I received my recall letter, which asked me to send a budget for my relocation and indicated that I could remain in Geneva until my relocation funds were sent. I got three removal companies to provide me with a budget for the transport of a forty-foot container and a car, which were my entitlements as ambassador, and sent this to Freetown. Switzerland is a landlocked country, and the lowest quotation that I got for the shipment of a forty-foot container with my personal effects was US$17,000. Also, as per my entitlement, I needed to be provided with a business-class ticket to Freetown. The total cost of my recall was thus about US$20,000. As requested by the Ministry, this requirement was sent to Freetown on May 30, 2018.

I got no response until June 14th. In the letter I received, I was only to be given US$7,350 for my shipment and travel to Freetown, just more than one-third of the requirement. I was flabbergasted and sought to find out the basis on which only this sum was sent. I wrote, but when I got no response, I called and was told in "no uncertain terms" that this was the amount that was recommended by the evaluation department and I would not receive any more money.

For all the hard work that I had done without human resources and a paltry budget, this was the thanks I was getting from my government. What was most disturbing in all this was that I was not even asked to debrief the Minister or my successor before leaving.

'After all, I was told, ambassadors do no work'. I, however, took it upon myself to prepare a 27-page End of Assignment/ Handover Report, which I sent to my successor once he was named. He acknowledged receipt and thanked me for it, and promised to keep in touch. He never did.

While I did not get any recognition of my work by the new government, the messages that I received from colleagues, ambassadors, international organizations, NGOs and individuals in Geneva were heart-warming.

PART FOUR
Raising a One in a Million Family

Chapter 15
Unfathomable Tragedy

On 18 Oct 2016, as I prepared to leave my apartment to head to work, I received a WhatsApp message from my daughter-in-law, Agnes; 'Boris collapsed in his bath this morning and has been admitted at the Cantonal Hospital'.

My initial reaction was that I was not particularly worried and thought, 'It must be something trivial, maybe something he ate?'

But it was not, it was so much worse. He was diagnosed with pulmonary embolism — blood clots in his lungs and all attempts to dissolve the clots using medication had failed. The specialist had deemed that the only remaining viable option to remove the clots would be surgically. The evening before the surgery, as the family stood around his bedside, he said, 'Thank you very much for all the support and love you have shown to me these past few days. *We are a one-in-a- million family'.*

In the days following his surgery, I sat by his bedside at the Intensive Care Unit and watched my son be quiet for the first time in the 48 years of his life. This was not the Boris I knew, the bustling, and caring Boris, with a keen sense of humour, always commenting on my clothes, my hairdo, my makeup and everything else. The person lying down and in an induced coma, after a major operation to remove the blood clots from his lungs could not have been more removed than the son I knew.

It was incredulous that this was happening. Boris, the child who was never sick, even as a baby; Boris, who, true to his Zodiac sign "Leo" epitomized the strength and resilience of our family; a PhD graduate and a black-belt judo champion. It did not make sense to me and I felt I was caught up in a nightmare and pleading to just wake up.

I looked at all the equipment, to which various parts of his body were connected, the monitors that beeped incessantly with graphs keeping track of every heartbeat, every respiration. Their patterns were regular and I tried to find comfort in that, but being in this space reminded me of films I had watched with Boris, such as "Flatliners", and for a moment, I was gripped with fear. What if the graphs suddenly flattened out?

A nurse came in to check on the ECMO machine. He looked up at me, and seeing the anxiety in my eyes tried to comfort me. 'He is strong and should do well. We are doing our best'.

'God bless you', I replied

The Extra Corporeal Membrane Oxygenation equipment (ECMO) is the machine that supports the body for a period of time to allow the heart and/or lungs time to rest. It was frightening to look at, as the tubes which take the blood to and from the heart were passed through an external machine that performs the functions of the heart and lungs. I observed this as I noted the distinct blue colour of the blood from the veins in vast contrast to the red colour of the blood from the arteries. 'A review lesson in Biology', I thought.

As I looked around, I observed that the sombre walls of the ward had been decorated by Agnes, with family photos and homemade "get well soon" cards from his two children K'Tusha and Taio. There was also the rosary I had bought from the Monastery in Basel, hanging on the bed-stand, together with a medal of St Bernadette of Lourdes, which my sister Yamide had brought from London.

We had a staunch religious upbringing and my mother who played a strong role in bringing up my children, after my marriage broke up, always taught us that "God answers prayers". And now I needed God more than ever. A number of Evangelists and prayer leaders had been recommended to us and I called them one by one to offer prayers. I held the phone close to him and touched him as we prayed. I reassured myself after each prayer that Boris would recover.

"The Lord who raised Lazarus from the dead will heal your son", one of the prayer leaders assured me and hope flooded me. I was taken back in time to Boris, at the age of six, reassuring me when my marriage broke down that he would take care of me. I could still hear his voice: 'Mum, don't worry, we will make it. I will take care of you'. True to his word, he spent all his life caring for me, responding to my every need.

As I left the hospital, I thought: 'I am still alive. He made a promise to me, so how could anything bad happen to him?' But something did happen to him. He passed away a week later.

At the funeral, I listened to a bible reading from 1 Corinthians 15. 'O death, where is thy sting?'

'What a question?' I thought. 'Yes, death does sting'.

Chapter 16
My Family Story

A romance begins

My third dream as a child was to have an exemplary family, with children who would have all the amenities that I could not have, as a child growing up in colonial Sierra Leone; children, whom I would motivate to reach their highest potential. I did not realize that I would start a family sooner than I ever expected.

It all started when I arrived in Moscow on 1 October 1965. At the Cheremetova Airport, we were met by the Soviet authorities and a delegation of the Sierra Leonean students in Moscow led by Alex Stevens. My then boyfriend Flavius had told me about Alex.

'You must meet with Alex', he had said to me. 'He is a childhood friend of mine, and we grew up together in Brookfield, in the then suburbs of Freetown. He has been in Moscow for two years and really enjoyed the experience. He has me convinced that life in the USSR has a lot to offer African students. He should be able to help you to settle down in Moscow, until I join you next year'. Flavius was to take his final school exams the next year and was planning to study medicine in the USSR.

took a ferry from Freetown, to Lungi, at the other side of the peninsula. Lungi is a small coastal town in the Northern Province of Sierra Leone. Its history can be traced to 1806 when Momodu Dumbuya a Susu trader settled there. Under him, Lungi became a commercial hub for communities that have limited access to the capital Freetown.

As the ferry left the shores of Freetown, I looked back in awe at the fading scenery, of the town where I had spent all my life; the town that held so many memories for me. I watched the mountains grow smaller and smaller in the distance and vowed to myself that I would use this opportunity I had been given to make my country (Mama Salone) proud. I remembered a line in the Sierra Leone National Anthem which read, *'Ours is the labour, thine, the fame'.*

'World, here I come'. I thought.

On the ferry, we were joined by traders returning to Lungi after selling their wares in Freetown. Although they had sold their goods the smell of smoked fish was prevalent. It reminded me of my favourite dishes, especially the cassava leaves stew that I loved so much. How I would miss it. Some of the women were arguing over space for their empty baskets. The scene was most typical of everyday life in Sierra Leone. I wondered how different my new life would be.

I was accompanied by a small entourage, comprising Mama, my siblings Hannah and Jide and a couple of friends. At the airport, I met the nine other students, who were beneficiaries of the Soviet Government scholarship award. Among the ten of us, there were two girls, myself and Isatu. Isatu, who was also accompanied by her family, had tears streaming down her face.

'OK', I thought to myself, 'I will have plenty of time to get acquainted with Isatu'. We had to spend one night together in Las Palmas and another in London, before arriving in Moscow.

In a sense, I felt a bit guilty that I was so happy, even though I was leaving my family. There were three reasons for this. First, I was excited to enter this world outside Sierra Leone that I had dreamt about since my early childhood. Second, I was going to study science and maybe, one day even go to space. Third, when Flavius joined me in a year's time, we would get married and eventually start a family.

At the airport in Freetown, Flavius handed me a note to give to Alex, which I tucked away in my luggage. I did not think that I would need it. Why would I bother to meet someone, when all indications were that the Soviet Government would take care of me?

At the Cheremetova Airport in Moscow, I met Alex. The moment I saw him, my heart missed a beat. This Adonis of a man was every young girl's dream. He was tall, handsome, stately and charismatic, with eyes which lit up like stars. He acted as an interpreter between us and the Soviet officials. And when he opened his mouth to speak, I was entranced. His voice was like a melody. He translated the welcome remarks of the officials into English. I was so hypnotized by his personality, that I could hardly hear what he was saying. He spoke Russian with such fluency and with such ease, and even though I did not understand the language, it was clear to me that he had an excellent command of it. It sounded like poetry to my ears. I was immediately filled with admiration for him. How I wished that I would one day master the language like he did.

As we left the airport, I thought to myself, that my infatuation would soon pass, a year would soon go by, and Flavius would join me. We left the airport on a bus that had been organized for us. It was to take us to the hostel of the preparatory faculty of the Moscow State University, from where we were supposed to receive news about our placements into various universities, all over the country.

En route, I was fascinated by the view of Moscow. The sights, which I had only seen in books or on postcards, were wonderful to behold. We drove along a twelve-lane street and passed many monuments, the majority of which were Vladimir Illich Lenin, the founder of the Soviet State. He was everywhere.

I had been trying to learn some Russian from a book I took from the library in Freetown, and as we passed a sign, I wanted to show off what I had learnt. The sign read "MOCKBA", which is the Russian for Moscow. I was so eager to impress that I said out loud, 'We are at last in Mockba'. There was some laughter, and it was then that I realized that I had forgotten that the "C" in Russian was an "S" in English and the "B" in Russian was a "V" in English. I should have read it as "Moskva".

We arrived at the hostel late in the evening, and to our dismay, realized that every one of the staff spoke Russian. After being assigned to our rooms, we went to the cafeteria, where we were first served with a red soup, with a sprinkling of white cream on top of it. I was a bit suspicious of the look of it but was so hungry that I dove right in. I loved it. This was my first introduction to *bortsch* soup.

Back in my dorm room, I unpacked my luggage, took out my nightwear and placed a photo of Flavius on top of the bedside cabinet. As I looked at the picture, I felt a little guilty about how I had felt about Alex earlier that day. As I went to unpack my next luggage, I realized with dread, that I had inadvertently taken the wrong bag from the airport. By then, I was alone and did not know what to do. I remembered that Alex had given us his phone number if we needed any assistance, so I called him. He was very kind and reassured me that he would resolve the issue and locate my bag. True to his word, the next day he was back with my bag and I was most grateful; my knight in shining armour. It was then that I delivered the letter from Flavius. He read it, smiled and put it in his pocket.

'Why don't we have dinner together on Saturday evening?' he suggested. 'I need to give you some hints on how to cope in Moscow'.

I accepted with some hesitation, knowing that I was attracted to him. A part of me hoped that he was only trying to fulfil Flavius' request to assist me, and the other part looked forward to spending time with this handsome, charismatic man. On Friday, it snowed. I looked through the window and saw this beautiful white carpet all across the lawn. I could not wait to go outside and feel the touch of this snow that I had seen only in postcards and in films. I tentatively took a few steps, slipped, and unceremoniously landed on my backside. I had always admired snow from the postcards I saw but never imagined that it posed a danger to those who were not used to it. I was to look back on this incident as one of the warning signs that as with snow, in relationships, even when it looks perfect, there are hidden dangers. "All that glitters is not gold".

Alex picked me up at 7:00 in the evening. The snow was melting, but it was still slippery outside so I clung to his arm as we walked to the Sokolov metro station to take the train to Okhotny Ryad station. We were early for our reservation at the restaurant in the Metropole Hotel, so we stopped to admire the decorations in the metro station. Like all the metro stations in Moscow, it was a museum in its own right. Okhotny Ryad is situated in the very centre of Moscow in the Tverskoy District, near the Kremlin, Manezhnaya Square and State Duma. It is named after a nearby street, whose name literally means "hunters' row". I admired the silvery marble finishing of the pylons, and the walls faced with ceramic tiles. But what impressed me most was the cleanliness, with not a speck of dust in sight. At the exit of the station, there was a large mosaic photo of Karl Marx on the wall.

Outside the station, there was a *babushka* an old Russian woman, with a huge insulated basket, from which the hot smoke was exuding. She was selling her wares of *pirozhki* a Russian pastry filled with meat or cabbage. '*Pirozhkikapustoi* (with cabbage filling) and *pirozhki cmiasom* (pirozhki with meat)', she called out to the passing pedestrians. People stopped by to buy and immediately devoured it with relish. Judging from the appetising aroma, this was no surprise. 'I will have to try this one day', I thought.

We arrived at the Metropole Hotel Restaurant after a ten minutes' walk from the metro station, along a very busy route. As we entered, I was stunned by the restaurant's Art Nouveau stained-glass dome, glittering chandeliers and marble fountain.

'I would like to introduce you to Russian food and this restaurant offers the best'. He ordered bortsch for starters, beef stroganov for the main course and a dessert of assorted Russian pancakes, *blinis* with jam and sour cream. The food was tasty and I particularly loved the bortsch, which tasted much better than the one I had at the hostel. The ambience was romantic and as the live band played the tune *Podmoscovskivechera,* Russian Evenings, I was in heaven. At the end of the dinner, Alex brought me back to the hostel and we said goodbye.

When I started my studies of the Russian language, I was rather frustrated with the course, as the teacher and other classmates did not speak a word of English and I turned to Alex for comfort at the end of my days. He volunteered to come and help me with my lessons, and he would read me long poems by Russian authors, of which his favourite was Alexander Sergeyevich Pushkin, to convince me that Russian was a beautiful language worth learning. I particularly recall *Tatiana's Letter* which passionately illustrated the frustration of unreturned love. As a student of philology, he had mastered the language and, even though I could not understand the language, I felt his emotions as he read it.

"Когда я впервые увидел тебя, я захотел

Молчать: мой позор (это правда)

Никогда бы не было раскрыто тебе

Which translates into,

'When first I saw you, I desired

To hold my peace: my shame ('tis true)

Would ne'er have been revealed to you'.

He took me to the Bolshoi Theatre to watch ballet performances of *Swan Lake and Nutcracker.* I admired the dancing but was struck by how synchronized and regulated the movements were and that the dancers did not smile. This was in sharp contrast to dancing back home in Sierra Leone, where the *joie de vivre* was evident on the faces of the dancers and the beauty that arose from the lack of synchronicity.

But it was the operas that baffled me. How could large groups of soldiers find time to spend hours singing at the theatre? This was inconceivable back home, where adults were only motivated to sing in the church choir.

He brought fresh fruits from the diplomatic store for me, as they could not be found in the local stores. I convinced myself that, he was just being "the nice guy" fulfilling his friend's Flavius request and that the large framed photograph of Flavius on the mantelpiece was a reminder to him that I was already spoken for.

Then, the inevitable happened. One day, as he was reciting a poem by Pushkin to me, our faces came closer together, he kissed me. It was then I realized that I had fallen in love with him and could not resist any further. Without realizing it, I was on the verge of being "signed, sealed and delivered" to Alex.

I shared a room with a Tanzanian student Zakia, who was going through a rough time integrating in Moscow and would have tons of friends visiting to cheer her up. Alex was a student at the Moscow State University, where he had been allocated a studio by himself. So, he invited me to spend weekends with him, which I hesitatingly accepted.

While I appreciated the attention of Alex, I was a bit reluctant to let that relationship develop. Firstly, I had left Flavius, and he would join me in a year. In addition, Alex came from a political family, and we Krios grew up believing that we, as a minority group, should steer clear of politics. His father, Siaka Stevens was then the Mayor of Freetown and was the founder of the opposition party in Sierra Leone. But the circumstances in Moscow brought us close together.

I later learned that the male Sierra Leonean students, who knew about my performance at school, were competing for my attention and Alex, as the leader of the Sierra Leone students in the USSR, was pleased to play his "alpha" role and claim me as the trophy.

My relationship with Alex developed and he became the most trusted friend and confidant I had. I began to count on him to go through the gloomy winter days in Moscow. I recall particularly our train trips to West Berlin, where we had to cross the Polish and German borders. We bought tickets to East Berlin, instead of to West Berlin, because they were twice cheaper, even if it was the same train, and all we had to do was to cross the German checkpoints at the East Berlin train stop and cross on to West Berlin. It was quite an experience seeing the armed guards poised on platforms at the station, waiting for any German dissident trying to cross the border from East Berlin to West Berlin. In West Berlin, we put our bags in the station locker and sought refuge for the night in the shelters for the homeless, run by nuns, as we could not afford the hotels.

In the summer of 1966, Alex suggested that I travel to London to spend time with my sister Yamide and her family, which I readily accepted. But something very strange happened the day before I was to travel. The train ticket I had bought got lost, and I would not be able to travel without it. I was sad until Alex offered to buy me a one-way ticket to London, promising, that he would send the return ticket when he received his next stipend.

I later learnt that this was a ploy to make sure that I would not be in Moscow when Flavius arrived. As fate would have it, most of the new students, including Flavius were posted to institutions outside Moscow. I later found out that the "grapevine" had been active and that Flavius had been well-informed of my relationship with Alex, before he was posted to Kharkov.

I wrote to Flavius, at the Kharkov Medical School but got no response. In December of that same year, I discovered that I was pregnant with Alex's baby, just before Flavius came to Moscow from Kharkov to attend the Sierra Leone Students Union annual meeting. Alex promised to give us space to talk and on his first evening, we ate dinner at my hostel. He assured me that all was forgiven and I promised him that I would break up my relationship with Alex, although at the time, given my condition, I did not know how this would happen.

After some thought, I decided that I would write to Flavius to inform him of my decision to stay with Alex. He was livid and wrote me a nasty letter to say that I was a "gold digger" and only preferred Alex, because I wanted a high political status in Sierra Leone. Nothing could have been further from the truth. It turned out that my pregnancy, which was of twins, was an ectopic pregnancy occurring in a fallopian tube, which carries eggs from the ovaries to the uterus.

The gynaecologist was clear, 'this pregnancy cannot proceed normally. The fertilized egg cannot survive, and the growing tissue may cause life-threatening bleeding. I will therefore need to abort the pregnancy'.

I wondered whether this was an "act of God". I had abandoned Flavius because of the pregnancy, which was now to be terminated after I broke up with him. Besides, there had been a recent history of infertility in my family, as both my Aunt Modu and Hannah did not have children, and I was concerned that I might have missed the only chance I had.

Betrothal and wedding

In Moscow, at the time, there was no birth control pill in use, and the gynaecologist recommended that we use the rhythm method of birth control. So, I bought my calendar and religiously observed the dates. Everything worked fine, until December of 1967 when I missed my period. The tests showed that I was pregnant again. I was only in the second year of my studies but did not want a second abortion, as I was as scared that I might be exhausting my chances of reproducing.

The moment we left the clinic, Alex proposed to me. We were on the train going home.

'Why don't we just get married', he suggested.

I was not sure if my family would approve of me getting married in the second year of my course, to a non- Krio, so I only wrote to them two weeks before the date we fixed for our wedding, knowing that by the time they got the letter sent by mail, it would be too late to change our plans.

In the USSR at the time, officially recognized weddings needed to take place at a wedding palace, but we wanted to have our marriage blessed in a church, so we had to arrange for two events. In Soviet Russia, some of the post-prestigious royal palaces were transformed to wedding palaces, where couples could experience the pomp and grandeur that were enjoyed by the rich in pre-soviet times, if only for the day of their wedding.

We chose the Griboyedovsky registry office or Wedding Palace No. 1, which was located in the building of an old mansion in the centre of Moscow. On entering the building, I was struck by the sheer magnificence of the palace. The wooden staircase leading to the halls split into two at the first level, and came together again at the level of the ceremonial halls, symbolizing the coming together of two individuals in matrimony. Each room was decorated with paintings, large mirrors, stucco and crystal chandeliers. Luxury and beauty were felt in every detail.

Alex and I were led to a separate lovers' room reserved for the couple to have a few moments together before the ceremony. The ambience in this room was so romantic that when I looked into Alex's eyes, I felt so much love and thanked God for having blessed me with this opportunity to wed the love of my life. The guests were ushered into another room reserved for them, until it was time for our wedding ceremony.

We emerged from our lovers' den at the appointed hour to enter the ceremonial hall where the guests were already seated. The room was decorated with light beige shades and had large windows which were beautifully draped with beige curtains. In all, the atmosphere was perfect for a wedding. We processed up the aisle of the ceremonial room to the desk, to the tune of Tchaikovsky's famous waltz from *Sleeping Beauty*. We made our vows and were legally married on 26 January 1968. The Deputy of the Moscow Soviet then solemnly declared,

"In full accordance with law and marriage of the Russian Federative Socialist Republic, in the presence of the witnesses and friends, and by mutual consent, the marriage is registered of the citizens of Sierra Leone and the Commonwealth of Nations, Alex Hindolo Stevens and Yvette Elizabeth Paul-Short".

After the ceremony, we retired to yet another room of the palace for toast, champagne and cake.

Before our wedding, we had agreed that, as devout Christians, even if we were in the USSR, we would seek the possibility of sanctifying our wedding in a church. So, just one week before the wedding, we went to visit the priest in charge of the Roman Catholic Church of St. Louis. In those days, it was not usual for young people to go anywhere near a church, and he was so pleased that we were seeking marriage in the church, that he immediately agreed to marry us the day after our formal wedding at the registry. The ceremony was performed at a "high" mass, characterized by Latin chants sung by the church choir. It reminded me of the masses I attended as a child growing up in Freetown and we left the church feeling truly blessed. We were set for a happy married life together.

Our wedding was filmed by the Russian authorities, who used the film to showcase the lives of African students in the Soviet Union, and was even shown in Freetown. Alex's father, Siaka Stevens, who was in exile in Guinea, following a coup d'état in Sierra Leone, after he had won the 1967 general elections in April of that year, sent us a congratulatory cable on the occasion.

Apart from morning sickness during the first three months, the pregnancy went on smoothly. Neither of us had any experience with pregnancy or taking care of a newborn and feared that we would be found lacking, in the absence of the traditional African extended family to give us support. We were alone. On a trip to London, we purchased Dr. Benjamin Spock's *Baby and Child Care,* which was to serve as our bible for the next few months. Our anticipation for my first child was unparalleled. We perused every page of Dr Spock's book but were still nervous that we could fail.

Because of this fear, we were victims of three false alerts. Each time, I had some cramps, which I interpreted as going into labour and Alex was scared to death of the prospect of a child being born in the absence of anyone but himself. So, each time I said I believed I was going into labour, he panicked, called a taxi and urged the driver to speed to the maternity home. In the USSR, at the time, when you got pregnant, you were assigned a particular maternity home closest to you. Mine was the 19th Maternity Home, but if a woman was in labour, no maternity home could refuse to admit her. For the second false alert, due to traffic, we went to the 18th Maternity Home. The difference between both maternity homes was like night and day. The 18th was cleaner more modern and had a pleasant atmosphere, so I decided I would opt for it when the time came. On the evening of the 28th July, I had more severe recurrent pains, and since I was already overdue by two days, we checked in at the 18th Maternity Home in Moscow.

Birth of my first child

On 1 August 1968, I gave birth to my son, who was named after my father-in-law, Siaka, after almost three days of labour. At four kilograms and fifty-four centimetres, he was a bouncy baby, who was a joy to behold. Visitors were not allowed to visit at the maternity homes, and I knew that Alex would not see the baby until we were discharged five days later. I was put in the general ward, but suddenly a woman who appeared to be the matron came to me and said, 'We have to transfer you to another ward'. I was worried. Was there something wrong with my baby? I did not get a response, but I liked the new venue. It was a private ward, with a nice view of the garden. I thought this was good and that I could chat more freely with Alex, from my window to the lawn.

Then the door opened and in front of me were my mother-in-law and my sister-in-law, Nemahun, accompanied by Alex. My father-in-law had been reinstated as Prime Minister in April 1968, and they had travelled all the way from Freetown to welcome Siaka. As the family of a Prime Minister, they were exceptionally allowed to visit the maternity home. I was happy to see them, as at least I could benefit from their visit to Moscow for the coaching by my mother-in-law in these first days of parenting.

The Soviet authorities impressed us even further by putting us in a suite at the prestigious Leningradsky Hotel, one of the finest luxury hotels in Moscow, with the compliments of the Soviet government. We spent a pleasant three weeks together there, when we were well pampered, as we were provided everything we desired. My first lessons in taking care of a baby were quite intense, but over the three weeks we spent at the hotel, I developed the confidence that I was now equipped to take care of a baby. I had learned the essentials of breastfeeding, bathing a baby and changing the nappies.

It was quite an anticlimax, when my mother-in-law left, and we moved back to the university hostel. We were very proud of our firstborn but were so afraid that we would inadvertently hurt him. Giving him a bath had seemed very easy when my mother-in-law, who had nursed seven children, did it in the hotel, but now I had to do it myself, it did not seem so easy. We took out our Dr. Spock bible, and carefully followed the instructions, with Alex reading them out loud and me trying to follow them.

'First set the water temperature at 38 degrees', he read out. I was following the instructions, until my hand slipped and before I knew what was happening, my baby's head was under the water and he was gasping for air. 'Oh, dear', I thought, 'I have killed my baby'. I yelled, but Alex who was quite calm, took the baby out of the water and cuddled him gently.

As students, the summer months after Siaka's birth, August and September were summer vacation and we dedicated all our time to our baby, our joy and pride. We were so much in love and taking care of our baby brought us very close together. But it was soon time to go back to school and we needed to find a solution for his care. We put an advertisement on the notice board of the University and although I was sceptical, we waited patiently. One morning, we had a knock at the door of our studio. I opened the door and was shocked to find a woman who looked like she was over seventy. She, in turn, was shocked to discover that we were black.

'*Chocolatnimalchik* (chocolate boy)', she cried and proceeded to pick Siaka up. She was so tender that I thought we should give her a try. In any case, we only had a week to return to school, and no one else had responded to our advertisement. Now that I lived with Alex at his university, I had to travel for about an hour to get to my institute, but Alex studied within the campus and could keep an eye on babushka and the baby during the day.

Babushka turned out to be a 60-year-old Ukrainian woman, who lived with her daughter who worked for the university administration, on the campus. She looked much older than her age and had a slight hump. She turned out to be a blessing to us. In fact, she became a *de facto* part of our family. She called me *dochka* (daughter) and cooked for us the most delicious bortsch.

'Ukrainian bortsch is the best', she used to boast.

Alex finished his studies in 1969 in philology and international law from the Moscow State University and was assigned as third secretary in the Sierra Leone Embassy in Moscow, as the only Russian-speaking staff at the Embassy. Our status improved considerably, as we moved to diplomatic accommodation in Moscow. Unfortunately, when Alex became a diplomat, and we moved into diplomatic quarters, Babushka could not continue to work for us. The diplomatic complex was closely monitored and only staff employed through the Ministry of Foreign Affairs was allowed to work for diplomats. Babushka could not be allowed to pass through the government checkpoints daily, as an employee. We were devastated, as our attempt to secure exemption for her failed. She still tried to visit us and she would plead with the security guards saying, 'I have to visit my daughter'. They were so touched by her expression of love that they let her in every time she came. But she was not officially allowed to, and I was afraid that she might be arrested, although she did not seem to care.

'What will they do to an old woman like me?' she would ask. 'I have nothing to hide'.

As a diplomat, Alex could not go against the diplomatic code in the USSR, so we reluctantly told her not to keep coming, although she would show up from time to time in the evenings, having negotiated her way in with the guards.

'I know you must be tired, so I came so you can take a break. Go to the cinema. There is a new film being advertised'.

Luckily for us, there were possibilities for placing Siaka in a crèche, which offered care for up to five days a week. The flexibility offered at the crèche allowed me to adjust perfectly. I could pick him up every day when I had less pressure on my studies and let him stay there for up to five days during peak study periods, such as preparing for exams. This enabled me to pursue my studies. It was encouraging that the facilities at the crèche were first-class and Siaka loved it. In fact, every time we took him back to the crèche, he could not wait to rush off and join the other children as soon as we arrived at the gate.

I knew that Alex always wanted to study law in England. His dream was to be called to the bar and become a practising lawyer in Sierra Leone. I saw that as something he would pursue later in life, but he surprised me when he suddenly announced in July 1970, that he had been accepted to study law at Gray's Inn in London. I still had two years to finish my studies, so I was rather perplexed at this decision. I could not abandon my studies to go with him, and, as it turned out, I was pregnant with my second child. After the birth of Siaka, the gynaecologist recommended that I use a female condom as a contraceptive, to avoid another pregnancy.

'This device is 78 per cent effective, but if you follow all the instructions, you should have 99 per cent protection', she assured me. I followed the instructions meticulously, so, it was a big surprise, when I found myself pregnant again, just at the time when Alex was leaving for London to pursue his law studies.

My sister Hannah came to the rescue. She was then working in the Ministry of Foreign Affairs in Freetown, and was due for assignment, after spending a year at the prestigious *Centre d'Etudes Diplomatiques* et Stratégiques in Paris. She was interested in being assigned to Paris, but when she realized my plight, she sought and got an assignment as first secretary in Moscow. I was relieved, as I knew that I would have the support I needed to finish my studies.

Birth of my second child

My second child was conveniently due to arrive on January 13, 1971, 2 days after my last examination for the winter semester on January 11. On the night of July 10, I finished studying and went to bed. I was woken up by sharp stomach pains and although I prayed that they would subside so I could take my exams the next day, they did not. Eventually, as the contractions became stronger and more regular, I had to accept the obvious, I was in labour. I woke my sister, Hannah up, but since Alex was in London and two-year-old Siaka was asleep, the only option available to get me to the hospital was an ambulance. I was taken to the maternity clinic of the Second Medical Institute.

As a teaching establishment, there were a lot of students running around, doing experiments, or collecting data for their research. Although I had heard glowing reviews for this hospital, once there, I felt like a guinea pig. The students started by wiring me up with all sorts of electrodes and making measurements, until eventually, my contractions stopped and labour had to be induced. As if to confirm my doubts about being a study subject, after my baby was born, an argument ensued among the students about who should get the placenta for their research. I named the baby Hannah Rebecca.

Hannah, my sister, as a diplomat in the USSR, was allowed to visit us at the clinic, and Alex's best friend Samuel Perry was to join her, posing as my husband and the father of the child as he would not be allowed to visit otherwise. We were able to hire a young nanny Louba, through the diplomatic office to look after the baby. Unlike Babushka, she lacked experience caring for babies and was merely seeking a lucrative job in the diplomatic sector, where she could get hold of foreign currency to shop in the foreign shops in Moscow.

Alex fell in love with his daughter the moment he first set eyes on her when he came for the baptism, in March. He spent hours just looking at her and admiring her, and even nursed her and changed her nappies. He left shortly after the baptism and I was once again left with the task of raising my children, not with their father, but with my sister. I wanted to support Alex in his academic endeavours, but it left me trying to balance caring for young children while also trying to complete my degree. We spent the summer in London with Alex, and he came to Moscow in December to spend Christmas with us. We had a delightful time together as a young family during the holiday season. We had agreed earlier in our marriage to have three children and since I was coming to an end with my studies, we felt that this was the ideal time to try to complete our family.

I was most anxious to join Alex in London, and so, when I finished my Master's degree, I left Moscow for London in February 1972, when Siaka was just three years old and Rebecca was thirteen months old. Just before leaving, I found out that I was nine weeks pregnant.

Having been advised by the then Sierra Leone High Commissioner in London, that pursuing a Master's degree in Power Systems at the Imperial College would be a great career move, I had applied and been accepted to the course which was slated to start in September that year. This meant that I would need childcare. Unfortunately, unlike in Moscow, the options were very limited.

After a number of failed attempts in London, one of my sister-in-laws, Francess, who lived in Oxford, recommended to us a caregiver, Mrs Moore. Mrs Moore had agreed to take my children during the week and we would be with them during weekends and holidays. The plan would be that we would either travel to Oxford to spend time with them or bring them down to London. It was a hard decision for me to make, as, even though I wanted to continue my studies, I hated the thought of being separated from the children during the week. However, Alex was having difficulties with his studies and the demands of pursuing a Master's degree at Imperial College were overwhelming. As painful as the decision was, and through the many sleepless nights, I had to remind myself, that there was not a better option available to us.

Birth of my twins

As we sat in the waiting room at the pre-natal wing of the maternity home, I waited patiently for my turn. The posters on the wall provided a relief to my anxiety. They were pictures of proud mothers with their newborns and their smiles were reassuring.

As I approached the reception desk, the young and sprightly receptionist smiled.

'Are you Mrs. Stevens?' she asked excitedly.

'Yes', I replied nervously.

'The woman with the twins!' She was ecstatic.

'No, you must be mistaken', I said.

'No, look at the X-rays you took yesterday – two healthy-looking babies!'

I was speechless. My husband, who secretly wished we had a houseful of children, even though we had agreed on having only three, could not hide his joy at hearing the news.

I had always wished I had twins, as my best friend at school, was called Yvonne, the twin equivalent of Yvette and we were always referred to as "twins" by our classmates.

The day before, I had gone for my "36-week" check-up with the gynaecologist.

'I am afraid that we will need to induce labour', she had told me. 'This baby is too big and for reasons of your health, we cannot wait another four weeks to deliver an oversized baby. But I will send you for an X-ray today and you should call at the Maternity Home tomorrow morning for admission to induce labour'.

My first visit to the gynaecologist in London, had been rather puzzling. After the examination, she said, 'You are 13 weeks pregnant'.

'I … don't think so', I retorted surprisingly. 'This just cannot be true'. I stated with confidence. I knew that I had gotten pregnant during the two weeks Alex had visited Moscow in December 1967, so could not be more than nine weeks along.

'Come on', she said in a patronizing voice, 'We are both women. With my 20 years of experience, you cannot fool me'.

I was so puzzled that I could not say anything else. My husband was out in the waiting room, and knowing how jealous he was, the last thing I wanted to do was to let him hear this conversation. I felt like an innocent person who had just been convicted and sentenced in a court. There was no way this pregnancy could have started four weeks earlier, but I thought it was unwise to argue with the gynaecologist, so I avoided my husband's presence in consultations with the gynaecologist throughout the pregnancy. Now that it was at last established that I was expecting twins my records were shifted back four weeks. I was vindicated.

I was diagnosed with severe anaemia and spent the last four weeks of my pregnancy at the hospital, until I went into labour on the morning of 26 September 1972. Labour progressed well initially and I was taken to the labour room for the last stages at around 2p.m. It was then that progress stopped, even though I was still having severe contractions. I had noticed from the x-rays that the two babies were lying horizontally across my stomach and had asked the doctors about it.

'Don't worry', they had told me. 'We will have a bridge delivery for the first twin and would then be able to turn the second one around for a normal delivery'.

Now I realized that there was reason to worry, as the twin's positioning was causing complications that were impeding labour. Upon further examination, they discovered that the twin in the upper part of my stomach had turned to a vertical position and got her head wrapped by the legs of the other twin, in what was called "obstructed labour". At 6:30 p.m., after hours without much progress on delivering the babies, I began to lose consciousness.

'Mrs Stevens, can you hear me?' I heard the distant voice of the Doctor.

'Yes', I struggled to respond in my dazed state.

As I tried to look around, all I could see was a roomful of objects in white uniforms.

'We are afraid we need to do a Caesarean section, but we need a signature. Your husband has refused to sign. Can you manage to sign? Otherwise, we would need to request a signature by a judge, as your life is in danger'.

I could understand why my husband had refused to sign. In the past, I had delivered two above-average-sized babies naturally, and he was in the labour room when one of the doctors accused another of unduly opting for a Caesarean section to display her skills at making a "seamless" scar. But there I was, in a semi-trance and dying slowly, a fact that was later communicated to me by the Chief Midwife at the hospital.

'Where do I sign?'

I cannot imagine what my signature must have looked like because I could hardly move my hands. Still, it was enough for them and immediately the anaesthetist put yet another IV drip into my tired veins, and I closed my eyes. Gone were the excruciating labour pains, worsened by increasingly strong doses of injections and drips of hormones to intensify contractions in order to unblock the "obstructed" labour.

I regained consciousness at around 8:30 p.m. when the nurse came to my bedside with a pleasant smile. 'Congratulations, you have two beautiful girls', she beamed. The Chief midwife also came to see me. She confessed that she had never seen anyone suffer so much during labour, in all her years of experience. The babies had been transferred to the main hospital, as they too were exhausted by the hard labour. I was only able to see them after five days.

My twins, Miata Yvette and Yanor Yvonne were born on 26 September 1972, literally two minutes from each other as they were removed in one piece, with the legs of one still wrapped around the neck of the other.

The course at Imperial College started on that same day and I needed to get back quickly on my feet in order not to miss my classes. Thankfully Mrs Moore had agreed to also take the twins, so after two weeks, still healing and fatigued from sleepless nights with two newborns, we took them to Oxford to join their siblings.

I soon discovered the true character of Mrs Moore. She was bossy and self-opinionated and treated us with an air of superiority. We had to accept everything she did, and as parents, we could not have a say. For instance, she would insist on sending Siaka, aged four, alone by bus to church service, in spite of our concerns. She also drank a lot. I was miserable, especially because I saw that Siaka, who used to be happy to get back to the crèche after the weekend in Moscow, now became very sad when we brought him back. He was not happy and the other three children were too young to react. I felt that I was stuck between a rock and a hard place. I knew that I would be unable to complete my studies with all four children in my care. At that point in time, Alex was also very immersed in his schooling and having not lived with the children for their short lives, did not have the patience or fortitude to handle the demands, both physically and emotionally.

Things came to a head when Siaka got lost on one of the trips Mrs Moore had sent him for. When we got to her place that Friday evening to pick up the children, I noticed with dismay that Siaka was not there with his siblings. When I asked her about his whereabouts, she mentioned that he had gone to the store to pick up tomato paste. As we waited, I got progressively more agitated and concerned. A half hour went by, and then an hour with no sign of him. At that point, I was frantic but Mrs. Moore appeared to be unconcerned, as if an unaccompanied four-year-old, away for an hour was a normal occurrence.

'Oh', she said. 'He probably got distracted and is playing in the park'.

I rapidly threw on my coat and shoes and leaving her and Alex with the other children ran as fast as I could to the park. He was not there. The thoughts started to fly in my head. 'What if he had been kidnapped?' I know that sounded over the top, but during the time that I had moved from the USSR to London, Alex's father,

Siaka Stevens had become President of Sierra Leone and thus, it was not entirely inconceivable that someone would seek to make a little money, especially with an easy target like a grandson heading off on an errand unaccompanied. As the grandson of the President of Sierra Leone, this was not inconceivable.

I returned to Mrs Moore and immediately placed a call to the police. Due to the circumstances, they were there within minutes. They asked me to describe his clothing and, in that moment, I realized that I as his mother did not know what he had on that day. I managed to provide a general description of my son, his large probing eyes, his full lip and his dark skin. They decided that the easiest approach would be for me to get into their cruiser and drive around looking for my son. I was shivering and petrified, racked with concern and guilt. How would I ever manage without my boy?

Suddenly, at a distance, I saw a walk I recognized. It was Siaka confidently strolling on the road. He was clutching the change in his hand and had a tube of tomato paste in his shirt pocket. I burst into tears of joy. It turned out that the poor child had walked some five kilometres to the centre of town, crossing the motorway twice. I rushed to him and smothered him with kisses and hugs while thanking God that he was safe and sound. Mrs Moore was unapologetic and unfazed. I realized in that moment, that in her mind, Siaka going to the store and coming back late was a scene that had played over multiple times in the home and was an unremarkable event.

I had hoped that with the tomato paste incident, Mrs Moore would be more attentive, but she continued to send Siaka to church alone. It was becoming very apparent, that leaving the children with Mrs Moore was tempting fate and while I had been lucky with Siaka's trek to the grocery store, the same thing might not happen the next time.

This continued unabated over the next year and as a last-ditch effort, I wrote to her to reiterate that it was not appropriate for a five-year-old to be wandering the street on his own and that I did not want Siaka to do so. She took offence to the letter and haughtily packed all four children and got on a train to London. As I opened the door, my mouth hung open in shock. I was excited to see the children but puzzled as to what they were doing in London. 'I am afraid that if you mistrust me, I cannot continue to look after your children', she said, and without entering the house, she walked away. While it caught me completely off guard, it also validated the nagging knowledge I had that she was not trustworthy and that I needed to get them away from her as fast as I could manage.

Fortuitously, I was in my last months of study and soon after, I submitted my dissertation and took my final exams. Seeking out knowledge has always been a huge draw for me so when I heard from the Sierra Leone High Commission that there was an opportunity to extend my scholarship to allow me to pursue PhD studies, my interest was piqued and the temptation was great. As I contemplated how I could balance caring for four children under the age of six, with studying and a hands-off partner, I realized that it was not feasible. The conflict within me was great but ultimately, my conscience boiled over. I had to make sacrifices, and this time around, I would give priority to my children. I wanted to just give up my studies and stay at home to look after them. I had thought that once I moved from the USSR to London, Alex and I would have more opportunities to co-parent, but I was wrong. Here I was again preparing to raise the kids alone, and this time without the support of my sister. But Alex, who was struggling with his last chance for a repeat of his bar exams, having failed the initial exam for that year, felt that he could not concentrate on his studies with the children around.

The thought of caring for the children alone challenged me to the core, so I made the decision to go to the place where I would receive help and support for my children. I was going to return to Sierra Leone even if it meant leaving my husband behind. My reality was not what I had hoped for; I was alone, stressed out, and in a marriage with an unsupportive and unhelpful partner. I felt the tug to be with my family where childcare would be more available to me, and I would be loved and supported. So, much like the proverbial "prodigal son" who asked himself, 'How many of my father's servants have much and enough to eat', I planned to pack up the children and head across the ocean back home. I thought this would be a temporary move until Alex passed his exams and had more time to devote to the family, so I only packed what we would need to get by for a few months.

I sent a cable to my father-in-law to ask him for financial assistance to purchase tickets for the trip which he graciously provided. On February 26, 1974, we left for Freetown. Alex did not protest but suggested we take a six-month break in Freetown and identify someone to bring with us to London to take care of the children. He saw us off at the airport and we kissed goodbye. Little did I know that Alex had other plans and that I would never be returning to our home. This turned out to be the beginning of the end of our relationship.

On my first night back in Freetown, I slept soundly, my heart was at ease. I was looking after my children. As the days rolled by, I knew I had made the right decision to come home. There were so many people around vying to take care of the children. The twins were carried on the backs of the many aunts and I finally felt I could take a breath. With the support I was getting to raise my children, I was starting to debate whether I wanted to return to London. The children were happy as there was a plethora of family and friends eager to help me take care of them. I was happy to have my children with me and the extra support was a bonus. I missed Alex, but mentally I was happier. I was not walking on eggshells, trying to manage his temper and keeping the kids from making noise while he attempted once again to pass his law exam. I was taking care of my children and being the mother that I had dreamt of being.

After I arrived in Freetown, I found out that I was pregnant again. I had missed one day on the pill but did not think much of it. My periods were usually irregular and with the stress of the last few months and the move, I had not made much of it when I missed my period. After repeatedly waking up with nausea and feeling fatigued beyond the usual, I decided to see a well-renowned gynaecologist, Dr Bernard Frazer.

'You are very pregnant'. He quipped after examination.

I was shocked. I had had the caesarean section for my twins less than two years earlier and was still traumatized from the experience. I finally had a good balance in my life and it was becoming more obvious from the shrinking communication with Alex that he was checking out of the relationship. After I expressed some of my concerns, the doctor said,

'Well, it is still early days of the pregnancy and you could have an abortion, but you need to make a decision within the next week'.

'Let me think about it, and get back to you next week', I responded.

A week later, I had still not made a decision. As I sat there in the waiting room, conflicting thoughts raced through my head. There is a traditional belief in the Yoruba culture, adopted by the Krios, that a woman who fails to give birth to a child an *Idowu* after having twins, could go mad. I was not typically superstitious but once again, I did not want to tempt fate. There was also the risk of my caesarean scar opening, since it was less than two years after my operation.

'So, what is your decision?' he asked, and at that moment, I made my decision and replied.

'I will keep my pregnancy'.

Although I had my hesitation in returning to the UK, the decision was taken out of my hands when I found out that another woman had moved in with Alex. All the long hours away under the guise of studying had been spent having an affair with a Swiss physiotherapist, who had treated his father in Freetown. To my utmost dismay, I found out that she had bore him two children and that they were similar in age to Rebecca and the twins. I was in shock. 'How could he move another woman into this house I had furnished and which held within its walls, all our memories, our family pictures and my children's toys?'

I had left to give him the space to study and in doing so I had made it even more convenient for him to move this woman into my home.

I found out about the affair from my father-in-law.

'Yvette', he said, 'Why did you leave your husband behind to come home?'

'Well, we were having serious problems combining studies and raising four children and even though I had managed to finish my Master's course, Alex had failed twice in his Bar Exams and had been given a last chance'.

He sighed and pulled out a picture from his drawer and showed it to me.

'Do you know who these are? They are the children of your husband, whom he had with the Swiss physiotherapist who came to treat me when I was sick two years ago'.

I was incredulous. Instead of acknowledging the betrayal and hurt I was dealing with, I was being blamed for the terrible behaviour of his son.

Alex had decided to sever all links with me. He did not answer or return my phone calls nor reply to my letters. I needed answers, I needed to know why he had chosen her, how could he hurt me in this way, but above all, I needed to know what this meant for our future and for the future of our children. I hoped that with time he would come to his senses and realize all he stood to lose, including meeting his unborn child. But this did not happen. When Alex eventually wrote to me, it was to tell me that he was through with me and I could 'parade the children in the streets of Freetown to curry sympathy'.

I had returned home as the first Sierra Leonean woman Engineer, and the press was quick to interview me. I still remember the headlines, *Sierra Leone's First Female Engineer Graduates from Imperial College*. My father-in-law was ecstatic. Despite all the pomp and show, I was deeply unhappy. How could Alex abandon me?

I slipped into a depression. I was a twenty-eight year old single mom with four children, under the age of six and one more on the way. I was going mad. When I started soliloquizing, my mother grew very concerned. One night, she came to my room and said:

'I know what you're going through, but if you let that ruin you, who will take care of your children? Brace yourself up; you have the credentials to get a good job. Concentrate on raising your children, because no one else will'. To this day I remember her words as they came to me when I needed them most. She was reminding me that she had raised me to be a fighter and not a quitter. I decided that I would not let Alex win by hurting me and our children and that I would need to pick myself up by the bootstraps and reach for my goals.

After he kept asking, when we would go back to London because he missed his toys, I had to tell Siaka, who was the only child at an age to understand, that Daddy had abandoned us. He wrapped his little arms around me and said, 'Don't worry,

Mummy, I will take care of you'. That softened my heart and strengthened my resolve. He was only six years old and wanting to do for me what his father had not. Mama also offered to leave her house and come to live with us to help me on a more permanent basis with the children.

Mama was of great help providing me with physical and mental support as I awaited the birth of my fifth child. My father-in-law provided me with a modest living allowance and paid rent for me for an apartment at Liverpool Street in the centre of Freetown. I was thankful that in spite of his son's behaviour, he was looking out for us.

My landlord, who was quite well-to-do, lived upstairs in the same building and had three wives. For the first time, I had the opportunity to observe a polygamous family at close range. The wives were quite close and took turns to cook or to run a shop. The children, about ten in all played happily in the compound and were a joy to watch. I would hear the wives singing together or just gossiping in the evenings. Secretly, the thought arose in my head. 'Would I have been happier in a polygamous marriage than losing my husband completely?'

Birth of my fifth child, my "Lastina"

I had been appointed by the Fourah Bay College, University of Sierra Leone, to be a temporary lecturer in July 1974. I did not divulge my pregnancy for fear of not being hired and I decided that I would not apply for maternity leave. As it was the period of the university vacations, I did not have to start lectures but had to mark some exam papers. One week before my due date I announced to my stunned boss that I was pregnant, but assured him that I would start with my lectures when classes resumed at the end of September

On the night of 15 September 1974, I went into labour. I had wanted to give birth in one of the modern clinics that had been set up in Freetown, but Dr. Fraser advised against this because my delivery was considered high risk as it had only been two short years almost to the day, of my c-section. The government hospital the Princess Christian Maternity Home was the only venue that could provide the minimum facility in case of an emergency. He got me registered there, with a specific request that he should be called immediately once I was admitted.

Mama and I came out in the street to hail a taxi to take us to the maternity home, all the while worried about what would happen. Mama continued to pray out loud, as the taxi sped to get us there. Having dropped me off, Mama had to return home, as the children were in bed sleeping. The midwife examined me and assured me that I was only at the initial stage of labour and that she would call the doctor when she felt it was necessary. I was concerned, but she assured me that the baby would not be making an appearance for a while yet even as my contractions got more frequent and more intense. Suddenly I reached down and felt the head of the baby emerging. I screamed, at which point she started making her way back to my bedside. Before she got to my bed, the baby had slipped out. The doctor came in later and reprimanded the midwife for ignoring his instructions,

'You know that you put this woman's life in danger', he reprimanded her, but I was just relieved that the delivery had been quick and that my baby was a healthy-looking little boy with a strong set of lungs.

My last child was named Alex Konibagbe. The second name translated from Yoruba meant, 'I shall never forget', a most appropriate name considering the circumstances of his birth.

Looking after five children

I started teaching in less than two weeks after Alex's birth and thankfully, my mother had come and lived with me on the university campus. Combining my first year as a lecturer with having a newborn baby and four other children was immensely challenging. I would prepare my lectures until the middle of the night, be woken up by the baby crying a few times during the night, and then go in to teach after an almost sleepless night. This became my reality for many months. It was one of the hardest things I had done in my life at that time, but also incredibly rewarding. I was using my degree and I got to spend every night with my children.

'Either the best or nothing'.

Four of my children attended the nursery and school at the university campus and my mother, took care of the baby, Alex. During this time, a few memorable events occurred, that I remember vividly to this day.

Our house FBC10 was one of the old colonial wooden houses perched on a hill, with a huge veranda all around it. This enabled us to have a beautiful panorama of the whole of Freetown. The lush green vegetation descended into the city and onto the shores of the Atlantic Ocean. We could see before us all 40 kilometres of unspoilt beach surrounding Freetown. It was a beauty to behold.

However, it was this wonderful site that exposed us to the elements when a hurricane hit on 27 June 1975. The previous day, I had called workmen to repair the roof of the children's bedroom, where four of my children slept. The baby Alex was in my bedroom. When I realized it was raining, I decided to go and check if indeed there was no leaking from the roof. As I opened the door, I was hit by a strong wind that had forced the windows open. Part of the twins' bed was wet, but they had just moved to the dry side of their bed. After a short struggle, I managed to close the window and then wake them up.

'Your bed is wet, so you can come to sleep on my bed', I told them.

Siaka and Rebecca woke up. 'Can we come too?' Siaka asked.

I knew I was not going to sleep anyway. 'Well, you might as well'.

We settled down on my bed, as we heard the sound of wind get louder and louder. The children were in a good mood. Spending the night on Mum's bed was a treat, but I was worried, as I had never experienced a storm of this magnitude in Freetown. Then we felt the whole house vibrating. The whole roof structure was moving up and down like a yoyo, as we watched it. The movements intensified and suddenly there was a large bang from the children's bedroom, so I ran to see what had happened. The sight was horrific. That side of the roof had collapsed into the house and the huge wooden beams had hit and broken the beds of the children.

'Mummy, I can see the sky', Rebecca said excitedly.

I burst into tears when I imagined what would have happened, had I not moved the children. My mother woke up and we moved to an annexe to the house, which was not covered by the collapsing roof. I looked at the clock. It was 3a.m. and there were three more hours ahead of us before morning when we could get help. The view from the window was frightening as every single tree we had in the compound and the outlying hillside and fallen. My mother, who was a very religious person said,

'We need to pray'.

And so, we embarked on a very long praying session that lasted until the morning when the winds had calmed down. As dawn broke, we looked out to see the devastation left in the wake of the hurricane. It was horrific.

The next morning, the principal of the college, Professor Eldred Jones, went around assessing the damage to the buildings. Of all the houses around the college, ours had suffered the worst damage. The only highlight of that day was when he recognized my mother.

'Teacher Paul', he said.

My mother was pleased and so proud as she had always told me that she taught our principal at infant school and that he was a bright student. He was so thankful for the influence my mother had made in his life and arranged for us to be immediately moved to an apartment in the university guest house.

In 1977, another event occurred that has also stuck with me. Siaka had begged to go with friends, to watch the University Convocation ceremony. He ran home panting, as according to him, something "terrible" had happened. The students had humiliated his grand-dad, Siaka Stevens, by chanting insults against him and the whole ceremony had degenerated into chaos. The next day a group of his party supporters had launched a revenge attack on the students and a number of angry supporters came to the campus. It was believed that they blamed the lecturers for instigating the students. On the other side, the students were also gearing up to respond. We were caught between the devil and the deep blue sea as we could be targeted by any one of the two groups, either as a lecturer by the group from Freetown or as a Stevens, a relative of the President, by the students.

I sat there, petrified and unsure as to what I could do to protect myself, the children and my mother, when my neighbour, Mr Tunde Ibrahim, seeing the danger, came to my rescue. He helped me transfer my household equipment to the office, to lock up the house and advised us to get into the car and use the mountain route which was then very isolated, to seek refuge at my sister's house in Hill Station, as the mob was approaching the campus. We thus escaped the clashes that took place on that day.

In the summer of 1977, I used my home leave entitlement from Fourah Bay College, to take Siaka and Alex (Jnr) to go to London. Alex had never seen Alex (Jnr), our youngest child, and I was sure he would be happy to see us, and I carried the hope that just maybe he would realize the error of his ways and beg me to return with all the children.

The visit was a nightmare and not the dream I had hoped for. My sister-in-law Mabel's husband met us at the airport and explained that I could not go to our house, as Alex was now living with yet another woman, the third since my departure for Freetown three years before and that the woman was pregnant with his child.

I went to stay at my sister-in-law's place and on the third day Alex showed up. The moment he entered the house, he was showering insults on me and my mother. We were witches and tried to ruin him and I had now come with the "juju" to finish him off. I was so devastated and distracted that the next day, I inadvertently left the frying pan with oil on the stove and started a fire. I recall how Siaka valiantly tried to put the fire out before the fire brigade showed up. By the time they came, the fire was out, but the ceiling was completely destroyed and the electricity had to be switched off. My sister-in-law, who knew the predicament I was facing, was most understanding.

As the kitchen was not useable, my sister-in-law asked Siaka to go to the nearby grocery store to buy some bottled food for her baby. He had been gone a while, so I decided to go look for him. It was then that the doorbell rang. It was the police. The poor child, who was still traumatized from the fire, and unfamiliar with the direction of traffic in London, had been hit by a car. I rushed to the scene, but the ambulance had already left for the hospital. I was given directions as to how to get to the hospital, so in tears, I jumped on a bus there. Fortunately, his injuries were not serious, but he was kept at the hospital for observation for three days. I was relieved when he was finally released to return to the safety and familiarity of Freetown. At this point, I also had a feeling that my marriage was beyond being salvaged.

Alex returned to Freetown in 1978 and I went to see him. In

desperation, I bent down and held his feet to plead with him. He raised his feet and kicked me off. This was the final blow. He was done with me and our children.

In 1979, there were wide-scale protests and unrest in Freetown, which coincided with the Common Entrance Examinations, for entry to secondary school, which Siaka was due to take. It was under this atmosphere of unrest that he was to take the exams at the Albert Academy School, down the hill from the university campus. The other children's fathers had decided to go with them and wait outside during the whole exams, in case any problems occurred. I decided to accompany him. As he finished the exam, he looked at me with gratitude. 'Mum', he observed, 'You are the only mother here'. Tears ran down my cheeks.

Now that things were clear, I accepted the reality and dedicated myself to raising my children while pursuing my career. Once I accepted that, the stage was set and I was happy with my station in life and looked forward to advancing my career as an engineer. The world was out there but I had work to do at home.

In July 1980, I was recruited by the International Labor Office (ILO) to fill a post in Geneva, Switzerland. This was an once-in-a-lifetime opportunity for me and I knew it would set the stage for all the opportunities I wanted for my children. I was nervous, but once again, my mother encouraged me to pursue my aspirations. In August, I travelled to Geneva, to take up my appointment as Village Technology Expert at the ILO. After a month, I went back to Freetown to pick up my mother and five children, Siaka now aged 12, Rebecca 9, the twins Yvonne and Yvette aged 8 and Alex aged 6. The night before the trip, the children were most excited and had not slept all night. Travelling with tired children was not easy. When we transited in Paris, I remember Rebecca dragging along her favourite walking doll Tanya, which I had bought for her when I visited Moscow in 1978. She was exhausted and looked as if she would collapse any minute. I ended up carrying most of their toys, in addition to my hand luggage.

To make things worse, we missed our connecting flight in Paris, because we did not know that we needed a French visa, as flights to Geneva were considered internal flights. We were able to obtain the French visa on the spot but missed our flight, and were put on a flight three hours later. At last, we were on our last lap to our destination – Geneva. I had left the children to pack their own suitcases and was not aware that they had stuffed them, so they were bursting at the seams. It was only when we got to the carousel to recover our luggage that I got quite a shock. As our luggage tumbled out, I realized that most of our clothes had fallen out of one of the suitcases. Everything from sweaters to underwear was strewn across the carousel. Onlookers laughed discreetly at the sight, it must have been hilarious to observe: five African children, their mother, and grandmother staring at clothes being churned out of the baggage carousel like an industrial washing machine.

As we stood watching the disarray, Siaka jumped onto the carousel, pulled out the empty suitcase, and started stuffing our belongings into them. In a matter of minutes, the closed suitcase stood like a well-disciplined soldier called to attention at our feet. 'It's all taken care of Mummy', he declared reassuringly. 'Let us go get our taxi'.

I was relieved. Siaka had fixed yet another problem, resolved yet another challenge. He had taken control of yet another stressful situation and had fixed it — and he was only twelve years old.

From the airport, we took a taxi to the hotel Mon Repos, where I had booked a hotel apartment to stay until we could find an apartment. Settling down in Geneva with five children and a seventy-year-old mother became my first challenge. I was starting a new job, and at the same time, I had to resolve the problems of accommodation and schooling. My mother wanted to help as much as possible, but she was hampered by her ill health and the fact that she found herself in a strange environment and could not speak French. In any case, taking care of five excited children in a hotel setting occupied her full-time.

I could not afford to stay in the hotel for much longer than the two weeks I had paid for, so the search for accommodation was urgent. We applied for a number of apartments advertised in the *Tribune de Geneve,* only to be told that we had not been selected. Time was running out, and we needed to leave the hotel.

'You would need to find a furnished apartment for maybe three months while looking for a long-term rental', a colleague at the office suggested. 'In any case, that would be cheaper than the hotel'.

I settled for the rental of a three-bedroom furnished apartment at Avenue Wendt, in the Servette district of Geneva. While cheaper than a hotel, it was quite expensive and I realized I would need to intensify my search for an unfurnished apartment.

I had been almost completely ignored by Alex and his family, even while in Freetown, so I decided that we should live incognito in Geneva. The only blatant tell-tale of our links with the presidential family was the name of my first son Siaka Stevens, who bore the name of the President, my father-in-law. I discussed this with Mama and Siaka and we agreed that he would go by a new name "Boris". And so, Siaka left Freetown and Boris reached Switzerland. Apart from the Sierra Leoneans, no one suspected that we were related to President Stevens and I believed that that was also good from the security point of view.

Schooling for my children was another major preoccupation. Even with the education grant from the United Nations, I could not afford to send them all to the private international school, which had English streams. With a contract of only two years, I did not want their education to be disrupted by the language change. On the other hand, I saw our stay in Geneva as a good opportunity to make them bi-lingual. I decided to enrol the two eldest children Boris and Rebecca at the international school, College du Leman, and the three young ones, Yvette, Yvonne and Alex, to the free public Swiss school in Servette. I provided opportunities for Boris and Rebecca to learn French by signing them up for activities in local social clubs. Academically, the kids had been provided for. Next on the agenda, was to find us a place to live. I felt that I would not be ready to start my job in earnest until we had secured a home.

We had sought the help of the social counsellor at ILO, to advocate for us to rent a flat that was soon going to be vacant in Versoix, a small village on the outskirts of Geneva. With five children and my mother in tow, I was hopeful that the odds would be in our favour. They were, and on 26 February 1981, we moved into our new home in Versoix.

Being the only one in the household who understood some French, I found myself becoming a running interpreter for TV programmes. There were in all, only six TV channels, of which four were in French. I had to keep awake to perform this function and I can recall the frustration that the children, especially Boris felt, having to wake me up repeatedly to translate, as I fell asleep.

Unfortunately, in 1983, my mother, who had been a great source of help, had to go back home due to ill health. She had been ill multiple times since we had arrived and with my heavy travelling schedule it was an additional source of concern, worsened by the fact that the children were at school all day. So here I was, with no job to go back to in Freetown, as I had lost my job at the University for failing to return within the period of the leave of absence and raising five children single-handedly in Geneva. I spent sleepless nights thinking about what my next steps would be. Despite this, I did not write back to appeal the decision of the University. I knew that the opportunities would be better for me and my five children if we could stay in Geneva. They were doing so well, growing up in an international atmosphere with friends from around the world.

After a nail-biting few weeks, I was given a nine-month contract at the United Nations High Commissioner for Refugees (UNHCR). With my mother gone and Boris being only fourteen, taking up a demanding job at UNHCR posed challenges for me as it would require a significant of travel. I needed to figure out how to thrive in my day job and also at my "home" job. I could not afford to hire home help, as in Geneva, this would have meant handing over more than half of my salary each month. As a family, we initiated "Project Survival". I could not have asked for better kids, they understood our predicament, they knew that in order to make this work we would all have to chip in.

We agreed to split the chores among us. We drew up a roster of activities and responsibilities. On school days, I made breakfast in the morning and packed lunch for the kids and the girls aged 12 and 11 at the time, prepared dinner on a rotation basis when they got home from school at 4 p.m. I cooked on weekends and would tackle exotic dishes from all over the world. I purchased a whole library of cookbooks and would incorporate my own twists and ingredients which the children loved.

The example I set by making cooking so much fun was useful. Everyone wanted to impress when their turn came to cook, and the girls even invented secret recipes. They would lock themselves up in the kitchen and only open the door when they had finished cooking. To this day, some of the recipes remain secret and are still a topic of discussion at family reunions over 40 years later. Even Boris got interested in cooking and developed his own recipe, but Alex was too young to be entrusted with cooking. We did have some mishaps, like the time Yvonne emerged from the kitchen with shocking pink mashed potatoes. Everyone burst out laughing and she was reduced to tears.

As my field trips got longer and longer, extending to as long as four weeks, I thought that it would be too big a task to leave the cooking with the girls. I bought a huge freezer, big enough to hold a full-size human, where I could put food to last during the period I was away. Prior to my trip, I would spend the whole weekend cooking then loading the labelled plastic bowls into the freezer. All that my children had to do was to heat up the food every night for dinner.

In order to facilitate transportation to and from school when I was away, I had moved all the children to College du Leman which was conveniently located within walking distance from the house. I also relied on the small close-knit Sierra Leone community who would check on the children daily. As another security blanket and source of comfort for me, the children had the phone numbers of friends and colleagues that they could call in time of need.

While not ideal, I knew that from a standpoint of safety outside of the home, the kids should be safe as Switzerland was very low risk. What really concerned me was safety at home. We used gas for cooking and I was concerned that the kids might leave the gas on or lock themselves out of the apartment. I found a solution. I would put bold notices at the appropriate places in the apartment. For instance, on the door, the notice would read, 'Before going out, have you taken the keys?' Another on the door to the kitchen would read 'Before leaving the kitchen, have you turned off the gas?'

Boris also came up with the idea of a reward board, in which he attributed stars to each of his four siblings and which I used to give rewards for behaviour when I returned home. And so, we continued, trip by trip, year by year. At one point, I asked the children if they would like an au pair, but by then, they had gotten so used to taking care of themselves that they replied in unison, "No". My children were most understanding and this gave me the impetus to work hard. In fact, I always maintain that it was thanks to my children and not despite them that I was able to succeed in my career at the United Nations.

Over the years, through looking after each other and spending a lot of time together, the children developed a close bond and I knew that they could rely and be there for each other even if I was not there. Boris grew up to become a well-built boy, who excelled in Judo and displayed such maturity, that it was difficult to believe he was so young. He took it upon himself, from an early age, to assume the role of father in the family.

Rebecca, a pretty girl with big eyes, attracted the attention of all around but was a bit of a dreamer. The twins since infanthood were so confident in each other's company, that from birth they were content being by themselves, as they would stay for long periods in a cot without craving attention. I always remarked that I had fewer problems raising the twins than I did with any of their single siblings. Alex, the "lastina", as we call the last child in Sierra Leone, was in every way a last child – spoilt by everyone, a situation that was only worsened by his poor health when he was a baby.

In all, there were six years between Boris and Alex, a fact which I was not always willing to disclose to strangers, after an unpleasant experience with a Brazilian colleague.

'How could you be so irresponsible, reproducing like rabbits?' she had said to me. I felt judged and embarrassed. I did not feel comfortable sharing with her that, apart from the twins, each conception was because of a failed contraceptive.

Once, we were attending a conference and having dinner with a delegate from Sri Lanka. 'How many children do you have?' she asked me.

In an attempt to prevent any criticism, I replied, 'Too many'.

She immediately burst into tears and jolted out of the

restaurant leaving me sitting there in bewilderment.

I later learned that she had failed to have children and was now being threatened with divorce by her in-laws for being barren. I learned to be cautious and refrain from talking too much about my children to strangers, especially when they did not know the context. I refused to be judged for having my children and doing my utmost to provide and care for them. I was doing this on my own, and I had nothing to be ashamed of.

During my missions, I used up my allowance calling home regularly, sometimes twice a day. In those days, the only option we had was to use the phones at the hotel, which were very expensive. Usually, this worked out well, but one day, I got a scare when I was on a mission to Costa Rica.

Before leaving Geneva, a colleague at the office, Daniel Mora-Castro, a Costa Rican, had informed me that his family would like to meet with me while I was in Costa Rica. I never imagined that his whole family— mother, father, brother and sister-in-law would show up at the airport, holding up a sign with the name "Yvette Stevens" written boldly on it. In all my years of travel, that was the warmest and most memorable reception I have ever received from complete strangers. I went to the hotel in their vehicle, but refused their invitation for lunch that day, as I was anxious to call my children.

Once in my room, I called home immediately. The phone at the other end was ringing, but there was no reply. This was unusual as I always got a response after two or three rings. 'Maybe some problem with the line', I thought. 'I will just have a quick lunch and try again'. It was on the 17 March 1985 and the time was noon in San Jose (8 p.m.) in Geneva. I knew that my children would be waiting anxiously to hear from me. I had so much to tell them about my trip to Costa Rica, which had lasted 26 hours.

On our way to the hotel, I observed the scenery, which reminded me of my country Sierra Leone. The whole atmosphere, the greenery, the hedges shaped in the form of animals and even the smell of the warm, humid air was reminiscent of my home country. The fruits on sale at the roadside stalls were identical to those in Sierra Leone and I gasped as I had never seen them anywhere else. It made total sense when I later found out that Costa Rica and Sierra Leone, shared the same latitude. Although I could not understand the language, I felt very much at home.

After lunch, I rushed back to my room. It was getting late in Geneva, but I knew that my children would not go to bed without hearing from me. The phone rang again — still no reply. I started to worry.

I checked to make sure that there was no dialling error. I looked at the hotel manual and verified the access to the international line from the hotel and country code for Switzerland — it was all right. So, why was there no response?

Then it struck me that something terrible might have happened. What if my five children had gone to bed with the gas on and they had suffocated to death? What if they had been kidnapped? How could I ever forgive myself? How could anyone forgive a woman and more specifically, an African woman for leaving her children alone while she travelled? I was mortified and desperate with worry.

I thought about the reassurances I had gotten from my children before the trip, as always. 'Mum, we know you have to undertake this trip. Don't worry about us. We will be ok. We have all the telephone numbers of the Aunties and Uncles and even of your boss. They all call every day to find out how we are doing'.

But how could I explain this to anyone? How could I avoid being labelled an irresponsible mother? Of course, I could not go back to sleep. I knew it was getting late in Geneva, but I called every hour — still no reply. Something had to be wrong. By 4 p.m. in Costa Rica (midnight in Geneva) I realized it was too late to call my friends, so I thought I would have to wait until 11p.m. when it was 7 a.m. in Geneva to do so.

I called my long-time friend with trembling fingers. I had been up all night imagining the worst. 'Ayo', I said, 'something terrible must have happened, I have been trying to call home for the past eleven hours but the children are not picking up the phone', I said shivering and in tears.

'Oh', he said, 'there has been a massive snowstorm in Geneva and we are snowed in. I will try to call them too'.

When I did not hear back from them by 1a.m. in Costa Rica (9a.m. in Geneva), I decided to call the school, which was down the road from our apartment building. 'Could you please excuse me, I wanted to ask if the Stevens children came to school this morning?'

'No', came the reply. My heart missed a beat. So, I started calling all my friends one by one but got the same response. I had one last friend on the list, the Liberian ambassador and figured that if she had not heard from the children, I would have to call the police. I held my breath as I dialled her number.

She answered the phone promptly. 'Oh', she said, 'I have your children here with me'. I breathed a giant sigh of relief; my children were safe.

'I had invited them for dinner on Saturday, but by the time we finished eating, there was this huge snowstorm, so we could not drive them back and they had to stay the night. They kept worrying about you, but without the telephone number of your hotel, we could not reach you. Things only got worse and even though the snow stopped at 9p.m. on Sunday we have been completely snowed in. As soon as the road is cleared, we will take them back home'.

It was by then 2 a.m. in Costa Rica and I was exhausted. My eyes closed before my head could hit the pillow and I fell into a deep sleep.

Family life

I tried to compensate for my absences by spending time with the children while in Geneva. They were all registered in sports, church and other social activities within our village. All five of them took up competitive judo and I would drive them all over Switzerland to attend tournaments. They did very well in the sport and made me incredibly proud. In one memorable tournament, five of the six medals obtained by Versoix in a tournament were won by the five Stevens'.

As part of my employment with the UN, I had been granted home leave every two years. These were an amazing opportunity for the children to learn more about Sierra Leone and spend time with extended family. Most enjoyable for them, was hanging with their cousins who knew all the right places to be, including the beaches and nightclubs. It also gave me time to relax, take a breath and feel that comfort that solely comes from being around your family. We went on one-month home leaves together in 1984, 1986, 1988 and 1990 and made beautiful memories. I would smile as I sat with my mother and watched the children sitting on the veranda storytelling with their cousins. During these trips, electricity was sparse and there certainly were not all the amenities, such as hot showers that the kids were accustomed to, but they did not miss a beat and thrived. To this day, I am thankful for those opportunities as they helped the children and myself stay connected to Sierra Leone. We loved going to the beaches encircling Freetown. Freetown is a peninsula surrounded by over forty miles of unspoiled, palm-tree fringed sandy beaches, each with different characteristics – ranging from the powdery white sands of No. 2 Beach, to the grainy golden sands of Kent Beach. Before leaving the beaches, we would observe the setting of the sun. The whole sky would be lit up in shades of yellow, orange and red, like an inferno, encircling the floating sun, as it disappeared into the horizon.

University education of my children

I became the head of a substantive section at the UNHCR headquarters in 1990, and my functions shifted to that of a middle-level manager, rather than a "foot soldier". This meant that I would need to undertake fewer missions to the field. As fate would have it, this happened at a time when my children were grown up and had started leaving for university. I was immensely proud to have managed to raise them on my own and that now they were venturing into the world with the foundation I had built in them. Unlike some of your typical university students, they had been cooking and doing their own laundry for years.

In 1989, I had the pleasure to take Boris to begin his studies in Electrical Engineering at Hull University in the United Kingdom. I remember arriving in Hull with Boris, and at the registration desk, after registering him, the lady turned to me and asked, 'And you, what faculty are you enrolling for?'

It suddenly struck me that I did not look much older than him, or indeed the other new students. I found this flattering.

With the other children approaching college age, I worried about how I would meet the cost of their university education, especially since they would all be at university close to, or at the same time. I was having lunch one day with a colleague and I expressed my concern.

'Why don't you send them to Canada?' he suggested.

'Canada?' I asked. 'Why Canada?'

'Well, in terms of quality/price, Canada offers the best opportunities for students'.

I got the details from him and wrote to the agency in Ontario responsible for university admissions. He was right; Canada was an affordable option to pursue. It was far, but the cost-savings outweighed the disadvantage of the distance and at least if the children could be close together, they would have each other for support. In September1990, I accompanied Rebecca to Toronto as she had been accepted at York University to pursue a joint Bachelor's course in Sociology and Communication.

The following year, the twins graduated from College du Leman and did well in their GCE "A" levels in science. I had hoped they would be interested in attending my alma mater, Imperial College, so convinced them to send in their applications. They were readily accepted, but when I got the invoices for tuition, it was clear that I could not afford it. Meanwhile, Rebecca, who had spent a year in Canada, had convinced them that Canada was an exciting place to pursue their studies.

I prepared an application for them to the agency in Toronto, that was helping us through the application process, to study at the University of Waterloo, and left it for them to mail as I headed out on a mission. It was only when two acceptances came back from the University of Waterloo and the University of Western Ontario, that they did confess they had changed the preference for Yvette to Western University, at the advice of Rebecca.

"We have spent every day of our lives together since birth, and we thought this was a good opportunity for us to develop our separate identities".

They had always been "The Twins" and although I could not understand why they wanted to go their separate ways, I had to accept it, even though I knew that would increase the cost of their education. In September 1991, I took them both to their respective universities, then the following year, I took Alex to Toronto to pursue a bilingual course in International Studies at Glendon College, York University.

In November of 1994, I was attending the African preparatory conference in Dakar, when I received a message through the

UNHCR office in Dakar to call my sister Hannah in Freetown. After finishing the session that I was chairing, I rushed to my hotel room and placed a call to Freetown. It took me some time to get through and I paced my hotel room frantic with worry. At last, I got a line and it was Hannah on the phone.

'Brace yourself up', she started. 'We have lost Mama'.

For a moment, I was tongue-tied. There are things in life that one never believes could happen. For me, this was one of them. Mama, the person who made me who I was, the person who supported me during the most difficult periods of my life was no more. How could life be so cruel? I broke down sobbing and told her I was going to travel to Freetown immediately. There was no way I could concentrate on the conference.

Thankfully, my boss was an understanding person, and I travelled to Geneva the next day to leave for Freetown immediately. My children were very sad to hear the news and Rebecca who had just finished her studies in Canada, accompanied me to the funeral.

My children were settling down in their lives. Boris had completed his Bachelor's degree at Hull University in 1993 and wanted to be close to me, so he started studying for his PhD. in robotics at the Ecole Polytechnique Fédérale de Lausanne (EPFL). Rebecca had finished her Bachelor's degree in Communications and Sociology from York University, Canada in 1994, and was also back in Geneva and working as a journalist/communication specialist.

Yvette had obtained her Bachelor of Science in Biochemistry, from Western University in 1995 and was doing her Masters in Science at the University of Toronto. In the same year, Yvonne had also completed her Bachelor of Science in Biochemistry from the University of Waterloo and was doing her Masters in Science at the same institution. Alex was in his final year studying

International Relations at the bilingual Glendon College of York University in Canada.

I felt satisfied that I had met my objective of giving my children the best opportunity for education and was proud that they had taken advantage of this and taken their studies seriously. My task was now completed.

My assignment outside Geneva

In 1995, I was assigned to Ethiopia as UNHCR Deputy Representative. Leaving Geneva after fifteen years was not easy, and for the first time, I actually shed tears at the airport. Strangely enough, I was somehow concerned about leaving Boris and Rebecca behind in Geneva, even though they were now adults. Going off on my own, was not attractive to me. How would I cope without their continued day-to-day support? In those days, when international communications were problematic, this was not going to be easy.

My stay in Ethiopia was characterised by a number of personal events that further shaped my life trajectory in ways I could not have anticipated. I celebrated my 50th birthday and also experienced the loss of both my brothers in Freetown, within two weeks. Being away from family, I was lucky to be in such a congenial setting for these events. The staff celebrated my birthday with me but also joined me in mourning the deaths of my two brothers.

The death of my two brothers meant I only had two surviving siblings, my sisters Hannah and Yamide. We had always been close, but the death of our brothers brought us even closer. Both of my brothers had each left three children behind and I decided, as a support to their families, to adopt one child, the youngest from each of their families. The only way that I could provide them the benefits allocated by my job and the hopes for more opportunities in the future, was to pursue legal adoption. I travelled to Freetown, to conclude the legal process for their adoption in 1995 and 1996. Thus, we had two new additions to my immediate family, Josephine born on September 24, 1983 and Ambrose born on April 6, 1994.

One highlight of my stay in Ethiopia was the visits of my children. Alex and Yvette visited early in my stay. Alex, came soon after I arrived to help me settle in and Yvette, who had just finished her Bachelor's degree came later that year before taking up her Master's course at the University of Toronto. The most memorable of these visits was in December of 1996, when Boris, Rebecca, and her then fiancé, Emmanuel, visited me. We travelled to the renowned Lalibela and visited the breathtaking archaeological monuments. Lalibela is a town in the Amhara Region of Ethiopia, renowned for its famous rock-cut monolithic churches. The rock-hewn churches were declared a World Heritage Site in 1978. Lalibela is one of Ethiopia's holiest cities and a centre of pilgrimage. We also visited several wonderful sites, including the Blue Nile Falls a beautiful and unspoilt attraction.

Soon after the visit, in 1997, I got the good news that Rebecca was getting married to Emmanuel. It was the first marriage in the family and we all travelled to Geneva to celebrate it in style. The wedding was celebrated in a quaint little church in Nyon followed by an animated reception in which all our friends celebrated with us.

In July of 1997, I was assigned as UNHCR Representative in Kenya. While in Kenya, the civil war was raging in Sierra Leone. My newly adopted children, Josephine and Ambrose were staying with my sister Hannah in Freetown. As the terrors of the war were revealed, I worried for their safety and decided to bring them to Kenya to join me. After all, I was living in this massive house. I made arrangements for their trip to Kenya. They had to travel by road, through a war zone, to arrive in Guinea, where my UNHCR colleagues were kind enough to assist them on their onward travel to Nairobi in September of 1997.

In October 1998, my daughter Yvonne who had finished her M.Sc. announced that she was getting married to her boyfriend, Pete whom she had met at the University of Waterloo. Pete was Canadian, a quiet and pleasant young man, whom I had met during my first visit to the University after Yvonne started her studies. I was most impressed with his comportment and immediately approved of him as a prospective son-in-law. It was thus good news to me when they announced their wedding. He had been offered a job in Seattle by Microsoft and she wanted to join him. They had arranged to have a registry wedding, followed by a pot-luck reception, because, as students, they could not afford anything else.

'Maybe, one day in the future, when we can afford it, we will have a church wedding', she wrote in a letter to me.

I reflected on this and thought that I would make them an offer they could not refuse. 'How about you have a church wedding in Nairobi, at my expense', I offered. After all, I thought, my residence offered an ideal place for celebrating a wedding.

They agreed, and so on 21 December 1997, we celebrated their wedding in Nairobi, with a mass at the Consolata Catholic Church, in Westlands and the reception at my residence in Muthaiga. It turned out to be a social event of the season, with almost 150 attendees. All the family, including my sister Yamide, travelled to Nairobi and were accommodated in my six-bedroom residence. Yvette came with her fiancé Toke and his mother Ellinor. After celebrating the wedding, the children and their guests went on a safari in Ngorongoro Safari Park in Tanzania, before returning to their respective homes.

The twins always did things together and it was no wonder that Yvette announced her marriage shortly after Yvonne's. Her wedding to Toke, a Dane, took place in Copenhagen in April 1999. The two had met their partners while at university and I believed that happened because of their decision to attend different universities. They were so used to having soul mates that in the absence of each other, they quickly became romantically attached to the men, who were to become their life partners. Interestingly but not surprisingly, as they were identical twins after all, both their partners shared physical and personality traits, from their tallness to their gentle dispositions and their devotion to their wives.

In 1999, I took up an appointment at the United Nations Headquarters in New York. My interaction with my family during my stay in New York was a great inspiration for my work. I arrived in New York just before the start of the new millennium, with my sister Hannah and my adopted children. My children and their partners, all decided to join us in New York to witness the turn of the millennium. I was living in a small studio in Manhattan, but I wanted so much to spend this auspicious event with them. To cater for them, I moved into a bigger apartment and rented yet another apartment to accommodate the "crowd".

There had been all types of predictions as to what would happen at the turn of the clock, and we waited with anticipation. Boris had insisted on going to Times Square, but could not make it there due to the staggering crowds, so here we all were gathered in my apartment to watch the year roll. We watched the ball drop at Times Square on TV and rejoiced that in spite of all the anxiety and anticipation, nothing spectacular had happened and the clock just kept right on ticking into the new year. We had reached the new millennium in one piece and united as a family.

Living in Manhattan was not sustainable and since I knew we would likely be there for a few years, I decided to invest in a house. After I bought my house in Norwood, New Jersey, some twenty-two miles from the United Nations in New York, I received many visits from the children. The first was Boris, who, as usual, came to help me to move and to furnish our new home. He visited often, once with his new girlfriend Agnes, whom he later married.

In the summer of 2000, Rebecca announced she was expecting my first grandchild in February 2001 and I was incredibly excited. Not long after, the news came, that both the twins were pregnant, and were expecting their babies in September. Nathan was born on 1 February and Bryanna and Kristoffer, the children of the twins, were born on 21 and 22 September respectively, just one day apart from each other. One more thing that the twins were again doing together.

The house boasted of a swimming pool which was a great attraction during the family visits. For me, it turned out to be a nightmare, as even though I could not swim and never used it, I had to keep it in good shape for the family visits. This occupied much more time than I expected.

Hannah had been away from Freetown since 1997 and was eager to go back home. She did not have many friends in New Jersey and getting around was not as easy as it had been back home. She missed her independence. To compound this, we had been having a lot of behavioural problems with Ambrose at the Norwood school. After some discussion, we felt that it would be best for her to return to Freetown with him in 2002. She had always been very connected to him, and I felt that being with her and the different environment might help him settle.

In March 2003, Yvette gave birth to her second child, and my fourth grandchild Olivia.

Return to Geneva

I was approaching the mandatory retirement age of sixty for the UN and wanted to spend my last years working in Geneva in order to qualify for seeking naturalization in Switzerland. The requirements for naturalization were that I should have spent a total of 12 years in Geneva, of which the last three years before the application, should have been spent in the country. It was a stroke of luck that a vacancy occurred in Geneva to fill a post as Director of the United Nations Office for the Coordination of Humanitarian Affairs. I applied for it and was selected.

My return to Geneva reunited me with my family living there. Rebecca was well established with her family and Boris was living with his fiancée Agnes. In November 2004, I travelled to Freetown with, Boris, Agnes, Rebecca, Manu and Nathan to commemorate the 10th anniversary of my mother's death. Alex travelled from Cameroon, where he was working as a volunteer for the Canadian University Service Overseas (CUSO), to join us. A huge traditional ceremony was held in Freetown, with all the *awujor* foods and rituals in place.

To my surprise, my husband Alex showed up, dishevelled, and looking physically and mentally ill. I could not believe this was the man I had loved for his charisma and strength. He was a mere shell of the person he had once been, and it was sad to see him try to talk to his children whom he did not know. I could not help but wonder how he felt that day. Did he feel regret for how he had treated me and our children?

Rebecca's second daughter and my fifth grandchild was born in August 2005 and in December of the same year, Boris got married to Agnes who was expecting their first child. Once again, we were blessed with a warm family event and everyone came with their families, for the occasion. Boris, who had taken his three sisters up the aisle, was getting married and it was a grand celebration. Their first daughter K'Tusha, my sixth grandchild was born in January of 2006. Yvonne's second child, my seventh grandchild, Sebastian was born in February of that same year.

In May 2006, I celebrated my 60th birthday in Geneva. It was an occasion to bring together my family and friends. The Stevens "clan" was present in force. Yvonne and Pete came with their two children, Yvette came with Toke and their two children, while Alex showed up with a new girlfriend Mk'Tehuti, whom we got to meet for the first time. It was a great celebration of my life, and after the many tributes, I sang my favourite song *My Way* by Frank Sinatra- a song which adequately spoke to my life story.

Yvette gave birth to twins Theodor and Majken on 11 December 2009 and Boris' second child Taio was born on 7 May 2012. This brought the number of my grandchildren to 10.

EPILOGUE

The email from Imperial College read:

Dear Yvette,

You were nominated for the 2021 Imperial Alumni Awards. On behalf of the Judging Panel, it gives me great pleasure to inform you that you have been chosen as the winner of the 2021 Distinguished Alumni Award. Congratulations! We hope that this acknowledgement by Imperial of your achievements is very exciting. Please confirm if you are happy to accept this award by replying to this email by Friday, November 27.

Strangely enough, this all-important email was discovered in my Spam folder three days after the deadline and I was ecstatic. Over my forty plus years' career I have been honoured to receive a number of prestigious recognitions, but from an emotional standpoint, this surpassed them all. Imperial College is known for its highly competitive engineering program so, to be recognized for my achievements within the field of engineering and beyond was something that really struck a chord. While at Imperial, I had been faced with so many challenges while balancing my education with caring for four young children. There were so many days when I wondered how I would make it through, and now here I was, being recognized by this institution that had played such a pivotal role in my life. The citation read:

As Sierra Leone's first female engineer, Yvette Stevens broke the mould early in her career. Her talent and ambition saw her rise to Director at the UN, take the lead in developing her country's first

energy policy and be chosen by Sierra Leone's president as the
country's first Permanent Representative to the UN in Geneva.

I had wanted to be a space scientist, but life had other plans for me. Instead, I became an electrical engineer and was able to help provide access to electricity, a privilege reserved for the rich in the developing world, to the poor. By setting up a dedicated energy unit at the Ministry of Energy, I lay the framework for electrification in my homeland of Sierra Leone,

This little girl from an impoverished nation, with a head full of dreams, who had gone to school barefoot, had made a name for herself. I have now retired twice, from the UN and from my government. The desire for continuous growth and learning in is in my DNA. I am currently an Executive in Residence at the Geneva Center for Security Policy, where I have been active in providing training and promoting actions for policymakers concerned with international affairs and security in today's world. I am also active in helping teach and coach young, curious minds who will be the leaders of tomorrow. My message is always clear-Challenge Yourself, Dream Big, Reach Higher than You Ever Thought Possible, but most importantly, it is through adversity that you grow,

As I reflect on the last 77 years, I am so proud that in spite of the challenges I faced, most notably, the collapse of my marriage and being a single mum, I am so incredibly proud of the exceptional human beings, both personally and professionally my children are. My late son Boris, who unfortunately passed away in 2016, achieved a PhD in Robotics; Rebecca who obtained a BSc in Sociology and a Diploma in Communications, until recently headed the outreach program for a very large pharmaceutical company; Yvette has her PhD in Molecular Biology and is a Vice President at another well-known pharmaceutical company; Yvonne obtained her MSc in Molecular Biology and is a Director in the immunotherapy space, and my "lastina", Alex works for the government of Canada, having qualified with a Master's degree in

Economics. I am also a proud grandmother to 10 grandchildren, 5 girls and 5 boys ranging from 13 to 23 years old, three of whom are currently attending university.

I would like to be remembered as someone who worked hard in every aspect of her life. My school motto became also my life guiding credo,

'Either the best or nothing'.

My advice to young girls is,

"Persevere and make the most of all the opportunities that come your way to improve yourself and your future. Nowadays, there is nothing a woman cannot do. But not even that, nothing they cannot beat men at. You should never believe that because you are a woman, you cannot cope. You need to believe in yourself".

Made in the USA
Las Vegas, NV
29 August 2024

94576089R00184